# From Violence to Speaking Out

# Incitements

**Series editors:** Peg Birmingham, DePaul University and Dimitris Vardoulakis, University of Western Sydney

An incitement is a thought that leads to a further thought or an action that solicits a response, while also testing the limits of what is acceptable or lawful. The books in this series, by prominent, world class scholars, will highlight the political import of philosophy, showing how concepts can be translated into political praxis, and how praxis is inextricably linked to thinking.

## *Editorial Advisory Board*

Étienne Balibar, Andrew Benjamin, Jay M. Bernstein, Rosi Braidotti, Wendy Brown, Judith Butler, Adriana Cavarero, Howard Caygill, Rebecca Comay, Joan Copjec, Simon Critchley, Costas Douzinas, Peter Fenves, Christopher Fynsk, Moira Gatens, Gregg Lambert, Leonard Lawlor, Genevieve Lloyd, Catherine Malabou, James Martel, Christoph Menke, Warren Montag, Michael Naas, Antonio Negri, Kelly Oliver, Paul Patton, Anson Rabinbach, Gerhard Richter, Martin Saar, Miguel Vatter, Gianni Vattimo, Santiago Zabala

## *Available*

*Return Statements: The Return of Religion in Contemporary Philosophy*
By Gregg Lambert

*The Refusal of Politics*
By Laurent Dubreuil, translated by Cory Browning

*Plastic Sovereignties: Agamben and the Politics of Aesthetics*
By Arne De Boever

*From Violence to Speaking Out: Apocalypse and Expression in Foucault, Derrida and Deleuze*
By Leonard Lawlor

## *Forthcoming*

*Agonistic Mourning: Political Dissidence and the Women in Black*
By Athena Athanasiou

# From Violence to Speaking Out

## Apocalypse and Expression in Foucault, Derrida and Deleuze

*Leonard Lawlor*

EDINBURGH
University Press

In Memory of Hugh J. Silverman

Edinburgh University Press is one of the leading university presses in the UK. We publish academic books and journals in our selected subject areas across the humanities and social sciences, combining cutting-edge scholarship with high editorial and production values to produce academic works of lasting importance. For more information visit our website: www.edinburghuniversitypress.com

© Leonard Lawlor, 2016

Edinburgh University Press Ltd
The Tun – Holyrood Road, 12(2f) Jackson's Entry, Edinburgh EH8 8PJ

Typeset in Bembo
by R. J. Footring Ltd, Derby, UK

A CIP record for this book is available from the British Library

ISBN 978 1 4744 1824 9 (hardback)
ISBN 978 1 4744 1826 3 (webready PDF)
ISBN 978 1 4744 1825 6 (paperback)
ISBN 978 1 4744 1827 0 (epub)

The right of Leonard Lawlor to be identified as the author of this work has been asserted in accordance with the Copyright, Designs and Patents Act 1988, and the Copyright and Related Rights Regulations 2003 (SI No. 2498).

# Contents

Acknowledgements — vii
Preface — ix

Introduction: From Violence to Speaking Out — 1

**Part I: On Transcendental Violence**
[1] A New Possibility of Life: The Experience of Powerlessness as a Solution to the Problem of the Worst Violence — 15
[2] What Happened? What Is Going to Happen? An Essay on the Experience of the Event — 44
[3] Is it Happening? Or, the Implications of Immanence — 68
[4] The Flipside of Violence, or Beyond the Thought of Good Enough — 87

**Part II: Three Ways of Speaking**
[5] Auto-Affection and Becoming: Following the Rats — 115
[6] The Origin of *Parrēsia* in Foucault's Thinking: Truth and Freedom in *The History of Madness* — 143
[7] Speaking Out for Others: Philosophy's Activity in Deleuze and Foucault (and Heidegger) — 174

## CONTENTS

[8] "The Dream of an Unusable Friendship": The Temptation of Evil and the Chance for Love in Derrida's *Politics of Friendship* — 206

[9] Three Ways of Speaking, or "Let Others be Free": On Foucault's "Speaking-Freely"; Derrida's "Speaking-Distantly"; and Deleuze's "Speaking in Tongues" — 241

Conclusion: Speaking Out Against Violence — 277

*Bibliography* — 292
*Index* — 303

# Acknowledgements

I would like to thank Daniel J. Smith, who provided invaluable insights on a draft of this book. I would also like to thank Janae Sholtz and Daniel J. Palumbo for their contributions to Chapters 7 and 6 respectively; Claire Griffin provided essential research for Chapter 8. My longtime friend, and interlocutor, Fred Evans, read most of the chapters in draft form. I cannot thank him enough for his feedback, guidance, and inspiration. Finally, as always, I must thank my family for enduring my almost-obsessive work habits. No one has shown more patience with me than my wife, Jennifer Wagner-Lawlor.

The following journals and presses have granted me permission to reproduce material for this book.

Lawlor, Leonard. "The Flipside of Violence, Beyond the Thought of Good Enough," in *A Blackwell Companion to Derrida*, eds., Zeynep Direk and Leonard Lawlor (London: Wiley Blackwell, 2014). 565–81.

Lawlor, Leonard. "Is it Happening? Or the Implications of Immanence," in *Research in Phenomenology* (Brill Publishing), volume 44, issue 3 (2014). 347–61.

Lawlor, Leonard. "What Happened? What is Going to Happen?

## ACKNOWLEDGEMENTS

An Essay on the Experience of the Event," in *The Ends of History: Questioning the Stakes of Historical Reason*, edited by Amy Swiffen and Joshua Nichols (Abingdon, Oxon: Routledge, 2013). 179–95.

Lawlor, Leonard. "Following the Rats: An Essay on the Concept of Becoming-Animal in Deleuze and Guattari." *Sub-Stance* 37.3 (2008). 169–87. © by the Board of Regents of the University of Wisconsin System. Reproduced courtesy of the University of Wisconsin Press.

Lawlor, Leonard. "Speaking out for Others: Philosophical Activity in Deleuze and Foucault (and Heidegger)," co-authored with Andrea Janae Sholtz, for *Between Deleuze and Foucault*, edited by Daniel W. Smith, Thomas Nail, and Nicolae Morar (Edinburgh: Edinburgh University Press, 2016).

# Preface

Like most prefaces, this one is being written from the completion of this book and it is written with a view to future projects. I anticipate writing another book to be called *Violence against Violence* (which will appear with Edinburgh University Press). In it, I hope to develop more thoroughly the ideas presented in *From Violence to Speaking Out*. In particular, *Violence against Violence* will develop the *ethical* position that is only hinted at here. Although it does not appear so, *From Violence to Speaking Out* is a work in ethics, taking the word "ethics" in its broadest sense. The position I am advocating here and in my next book is opposed to any ethical (or political) position that advocates the repression of potentiality or that aims to control potentiality by imposing *relative ends* on what's possible. The opposition to relative ends is why *From Violence to Speaking Out* starts with globalization and ends with poverty.

Being opposed to the imposition of relative ends, *From Violence to Speaking Out* takes its inspiration from Kant. Yet, the argumentation and position advocated here do not resemble any of the contemporary Kantian discourses. The lack of Kantian argumentation, however, does not mean that the argumentation resembles utilitarianism. In fact, it is exactly the opposite.

## PREFACE

What *From Violence to Speaking Out* advocates is a non-utilitarian relation to others, even a *hyperbolic* non-utilitarian relation to others. In addition, the argumentation and position advocated here do not resemble those of care ethics – although I am sympathetic to care ethics. Because the position advocated here is opposed to all possession of others, in other words, because the position advocates the releasement of others, it seems to resemble a non-caring relation. The idea would seem to be: don't possess others; just let them alone; don't care about what others are doing. However, in order to achieve the releasement of others, one must confront the question of how one can know whether one has *truly* released another from possession. Doesn't another person or animal need protection and therefore care so that it is able to develop and be free? Doesn't protection, however, amount to imprisonment? Isn't care a kind of possession? These are hard questions to answer. If one wants to truly release others from their pain, suffering and bondage, these questions require the greatest effort of thinking. Although Kantian inspired, opposed to utilitarianism, and sympathetic to care ethics, the argumentation and the position advocated do not emerge from any ongoing debate in contemporary ethics. My research in phenomenology – Husserl, Heidegger, Merleau-Ponty – and in what we used to call "post-structuralism" – Derrida, Deleuze, and Foucault – gave birth to this book. However, if I were to attach the ideas presented here to any previous philosopher it would be *Nietzsche*. The primary issue in *From Violence to Speaking Out* is *the problem of nihilism*.

The problem of nihilism lies behind what I call here, following Derrida, "the problem of the worst violence." While reading *From Violence to Speaking Out*, one must not confuse the worst violence with what I call "transcendental violence." By speaking of both the worst violence and transcendental or pre-ethical violence, I am borrowing from Derrida's 1964 text on Levinas, "Violence and Metaphysics." In many of the chapters in Part I (frequently mentioning "Violence and Metaphysics" explicitly), I explain transcendental violence at length. To simplify the idea, we can refer to linguistic performativity and the violence it can do. Judith Butler of course has described this kind of violence very well. Hate speech is the occasion of a performative that categories the person (or the people) mentioned in the statement under a general concept (and its presuppositions or prejudices) that effectuates a change in their social status and thereby violates what the person is as a singular individual. Transcendental violence resembles this sort of performative violence. However, transcendental violence is so because it appears in the fundamental structure of experience. As fundamental, this violence cannot be eliminated. The violence irreducible in the fundamental structure of experience motivates reactions, one of which is more and more violence to repress and control what is fundamental in experience. This more violent reaction to repress the fundamental violence is what I call "the problem of the worst violence."

In the Conclusion to this book, I try to elaborate the idea of the worst violence. To simplify the idea, we must recognize that the worst violence is a reaction. As a *reaction* to the violence irreducible in the structure of experience, it wills the end full stop; it wills the end *as such*. I think there are phenomenological reasons to believe that the end as such is not possible. The phenomenological reasons imply that the end is always the end *as* something other than the end. The end is always related to something that remains. Even when we approach the end of something, there is always something heterogeneous to the end.

# PREFACE

There is always a remainder. Even if the end as such, a complete and final vanishing without remainder, even if this hyperbolic exaggeration of the end is impossible, or even "the impossible," as Derrida would say, this book is concerned with the *tendency* toward complete devastation. Deleuze and Guattari have described this tendency in *A Thousand Plateaus* when they speak of fascism and its slogan of "Long live death." As Nietzsche knew, this tendency to stamp out life and its possibilities is nihilism. I think there is no greater problem that we confront (and perhaps have always confronted) than the problem of a desire to end life because the pain of living cannot be reduced. Every effort must be made *not* to have our slogan be "Long live death." The nihilistic idea of complete devastation without remainder has to be criticized. The remainder always happens, even in the end of the world. We must reveal the falsehood of the idea of the end without remainder. We must stop thinking that we can get rid of violence once and for all. To desire to get rid of violence once and for all implies wanting to get rid of potentiality once and for all. Therefore, although this book amounts to a plea for no good conscience – there is never enough said or done; what we say or do is never sufficient – it is also a plea, as in Nietzsche, for more activity, more potentiality, and more life.

# Introduction:
# From Violence to Speaking Out

Like Merleau-Ponty, we can speak of signs. There is one contemporary sign that we must consider: globalization. The expansion of globalization is limitless. The sign "globalization" signifies a will to establish control over the whole world and apparently other planets ("interplanetary tourism"). In other words, globalization wants to place the earth within a sphere with a determinate shape, within an enclosure called "the globe." As it pursues its conquest of other cultures and lands, globalization acts in the name of peace. If globalization could speak and it would speak in English, it would say that "Capitalism has brought more people out of poverty than any other economic system."[1] Yet in order to speak this way, capitalist economy must have become hegemonic. As Lyotard would say, globalization is "the hegemony of the economic genre" (Lyotard 1988: 178).[2] Globalization or global capitalism wants to, and seems to be able to, measure everything and assign it a value. It wants to treat everything and everyone, the whole world, as means to an end. How could this value-assignation and hegemony be anything other than violence? Nevertheless, the expansion of globalization appears as world peace and is able to because the violence of the so-called "peace" is usually quiet and disguised.

Therefore, the sign of globalization indicates a formula for our times: "peace without peace." Of course, globalization represses local ways of life in favor of making commodities available on the global market. And yet, often in the last twenty year or so, local groups and individuals have reacted violently against this "peace," making globalization's own violence noisy and naked.

To continue with our signs, we can descend to a less global, less anonymous, and more individualistic level. At the level of the individual, we see more and more instances of hate crimes, in which one shooter kills many people and then he kills himself. And for the last two decades, we have seen suicide bombers, whose formula for killing seems to reverse the hate criminal's formula for killing. Instead of "kill others in order to kill oneself," the suicide bomber thinks: "kill oneself in order to kill others." At the limit, like globalization, hate criminals and suicide bombers leave no one out and no one behind. These three signs indicate a movement that aims to be limitless and total, a limitless and total effort or will. Globalization, hate criminals, and suicide bombers, these three signs – which are limited neither to the West nor to the East (and neither to the global North nor to the global South), neither to Christianity nor to Islam (nor to Judaism, Hinduism, or Buddhism) – indicate, through the meaning of limitless and total, that the problem we confront today is a superlative problem, a problem I call here, following Derrida in "Violence and Metaphysics," the problem of "the worst violence" (Derrida 1978: 149). In its simplest terms, the problem of the worst violence is total suicide, in a word, apocalypse.[3]

To be immediately clear, *the hyperbolic way of reacting to violence*, in which no one is left out and no one is left behind, is itself the worst violence. The hyperbolic reaction wants to eliminate

INTRODUCTION

any and all activities, any and all speech acts that violate the immanent value of capital or the transcendent values of religion or homeland. However, these examples are not only reacting to these ordinary and seemingly eliminable violations of values, but to a kind of violence that cannot be eliminated. They are reacting against a kind of violence that is fundamental; it is so deeply rooted in experience that one cannot eliminate the violence without eliminating every possibility of experience. The worst violence is a total violence that aims to eliminate the ineliminable violence of experience, and therefore it aims to eliminate experience itself, which is, to say this again, total apocalypse without remainder.

If we want to resist this worst violence, then we need a reverse hyperbolic reaction. We need something like a reaction of "the least violence." If we want to reduce the impulses that drive the hate criminal, the suicide bombers, and the hegemony of the economic genre, we need a new way of thinking, or, more precisely, a new way of writing and speaking. In *From Violence to Speaking Out*, I aim to outline this new way of speaking, a friendlier way of speaking that does not insult friendship. *From Violence to Speaking Out* is the dream of friendship. It is "the dream," as Derrida says "of an unusable friendship" (Derrida 1997: 217).

*From Violence to Speaking Out* develops the problem of the worst violence through the idea of the reversal of Platonism (or the overcoming of metaphysics). I know that my pursuing the problem of the reversal of Platonism looks like me remaining attached (perhaps stubbornly so) to an outdated idea. Even Derrida seems to think so (Derrida 1997: 163). While my appropriation of the idea of the reversal of Platonism might seem outdated in relation to contemporary European philosophy (materialism) and contemporary analytic philosophy (naturalism),[4] as well as outdated in relation to political issues (like animal rights) and contemporary political philosophy (like autonomy studies), *it is not.* I try to show that what defines Platonism (or the "old metaphysics") is violence. I am not saying that the entire Western metaphysical tradition is corrupt. However, its general tendency, as Deleuze has shown in *Difference and Repetition*, lies in suppressing difference itself (Deleuze 1995: 29). The general tendency consists in hierarchizing differences in the name of a unity. Like any hierarchy, the "metaphysical" hierarchy must be enforced and it must be violent. Providing us with a vivid image, Deleuze speaks of the "old metaphysics" "shackling" difference to identity. We must see the violence definition of the "old metaphysics" as a definition of synonymy. If "the old metaphysics" equals the form of thought that wills the worst violence, then any form of thought that wills the worst violence equals "the old metaphysics." All forms of unconditional hatred like racism equal "metaphysics." This equivalency holds, even if these forms of discourse never use the word "metaphysics," even if these forms of thinking believe that they are anti-metaphysical. Therefore, we need the reversal of Platonism because Platonism belongs to the problem of the worst violence. If Platonism is violence, then the reversal of Platonism necessarily means the liberation of difference and differences (multiplicity), and, more importantly, the overcoming of violence, all sorts of violence and injustices, and especially the worst violence. Indeed, only the attempt to reverse Platonism allows us to see the heart of the worst violence, which beats with an extreme fear that makes us build up, as Freud would say, a massive substitute formation. This fear is insane and it should make us feel ashamed. The reversal of Platonism shows us that the fear needs to be overcome, as Foucault would say, with "courage." The revelation that the fear of others (and of losing purity) is the heart of the worst violence is why we must pursue, again, the problem of the reversal of Platonism.

As a work in the reversal of Platonism, *From Violence to Speaking Out* extends the phenomenological tradition, even though classical phenomenological figures like Husserl and Heidegger, or Merleau-Ponty and Sartre do not play an important role here. If I were inclined to speak of a methodology for the work I am doing here and will continue to do for some time, I would start with the phenomenological method. It seems to me that there is no way to philosophize without something like the *epoché* taking place, that is, without the moment of suspension or even of criticism – the negative experience of crisis – of the natural belief in a world in itself or in a transcendent world.[5] What happens with the *epoché*? Minimally, when we suspend belief in a world in itself, the suspension makes us "transcend" the world understood as a world in itself, independent of experience. No longer being attached to a world in itself, the phenomenologist finds himself in a "field of experience" that is neither strictly subjective nor strictly objective. In other words, the *epoché* takes us to immanence. At the level of transcendental immanence, phenomenology has given us a remarkable insight. I have found this insight to be not only compelling, but also unavoidable. It is the foundation of the problem of the worst violence.[6]

The phenomenological insight is this: in order for any other – defined as a strict singularity: different, unique, unrecognizable, a first time, unlike any other time, an event – to be understood or experienced as other, the other must appear; it must be a phenomenon, and therefore it must be meaningful in a broad sense as other. How would I be able to speak to another unless the living being (perhaps an animal) appeared to me? For me to care about the other, any other, that other must appear to me. The idea of another that somehow affected me without appearing is nonsense. Yet, if we accept the essential necessity of appearing, then we must equally acknowledge that, when the other appears as other, that is, when the other appears as having the general meaning of alterity so that one is able to *speak of* the other, the singularity of the other is forced to be iterable. The irreducible fact that all experience is temporal necessarily implies iterability. The iterability therefore opens up the possibility of generalizing, and the essential possibility of generalization necessarily violates the singularity of the other. The essential possibility of generalization is not willed violence. Instead, it is "transcendental violence," and as transcendental, it is a "pre-ethical violence," as Derrida would say (Derrida 1978: 128). The pre-ethical violence, because it is fundamental, transcendental, and essential, cannot be eliminated. We are powerless in the face of this violence. Yet from this powerlessness or weakness, an extreme kind of power emerges. It is the power of letting iterability happen – so that the other in its singularity becomes free. The question for me in *From Violence to Speaking Out* is the following: is it possible to imagine an iteration, that is, an expression, or a statement, or a mark, based in the experience of powerlessness, that not only functions and has an effect on the one to whom it is expressed, uttered, or given (*speaking to*) – but also that at the same time minimizes the irreducible violence of repetition found in all experience, expressions, utterances, and marks? In other words, is it possible to produce a speech act that at once is an act (that is actual or that actualizes) and a potentiality? Is it possible to imagine, as in a dream, a speaking that says: "Let the others, all of them, be ends in themselves!"

INTRODUCTION

This way of speaking is perhaps philosophy's genuine activity. Its most general title is *speaking out*. The question of how to speak in the least violent way (or how not to speak in the most violent way) led me over the last eight years to investigate Derrida's idea of "teleiopoetics" (or speaking-distantly) in *Politics of Friendship*. The question has also led me to investigate Foucault's final lecture courses at the Collège de France on *parrēsia* (or speaking-freely, *libertas*). And finally, I investigated Deleuze (and Guattari's) *A Thousand Plateaus*, where they speak of *glossolalia* (or speaking-in-tongues). Through these investigations, I came to the conclusion that there is a convergence among their thinking. These three ways of speaking share one conceptual feature, which is the *dissymmetry* of the relation between the one speaking and the one to whom the speaking is addressed. However, in Foucault, Derrida, and Deleuze, the dissymmetry is presented in different ways. In Foucault, it is presented through the idea that speaking-freely (as opposed to flattery) aims at making the listener to whom the speaking-freely is addressed be sovereign and independent of the speaker. In Derrida, the dissymmetry is presented through the literal meaning of the word "teleiopoetics": a teleiopoetic statement makes something happen in proximity and soon (*telos*) and at a distance and in the future (*tele*). In Deleuze (and Guattari), speaking-in-tongues, which is at the center of their idea of a minor language, makes something happen that is so extreme that the whole world goes into becoming. Dissymmetry means placing others in a non-economic, non-relative, and unmeasurable relation. Therefore, speaking-freely (*parrēsia*), speaking-distantly (*teleiopoesis*), and speaking-in-tongues (*glossolalia*) – all three ways of speaking aim at *liberating* the addressee. However, I claim that the root of this convergence between

Foucault's *parrēsia*, Derrida's *teleiopoesis*, and Deleuze's *glossolalia* is Kant's categorical imperative.[7]

I know my placing Kantian moral philosophy in the background of the thought of Derrida, Deleuze, and Foucault is controversial.[8] What happened to Foucault's idea of self-formation? What happened to Derrida's idea of justice? What happened to Deleuze's nomadism? Although I will not argue this point here, it seems to me that the treatment of others in a non-economic or non-useful way is at the heart of their thinking. In any case, even if I am wrong about the ends-in-itself form of the categorical imperative playing a crucial role in their thinking, I am really interested in the philosophical resources found in Foucault, Derrida, and Deleuze. Instead of a correct interpretation, I am more interested in a creative appropriation of their thinking. Certainly my own thinking is based on what is usually called "the second formula" for the categorical imperative: never treat others as means to an end. The end-in-itself formula for the categorical imperative requires of us never to think of others in terms of economy, prices, and values.[9] The way of speaking that defines philosophical thinking, I think, must be one that is non-economic, non-relative, and unmeasurable. It must be a way of addressing others that outstrips or even overpowers the speaking of others that turns them into objects represented under a general concept. Speaking to others must treat them as wholly or absolutely other. Such speaking is responsibility itself.

Although I will not provide an account here, I think that the ends-in-itself formula of the categorical imperative requires phenomenological grounding. If we pursued this grounding, we would see that the idea of an end-in-itself is generated from the experience of alterity. It is generated in particular from the fact that the experience of alterity is always a mediated experience.

## INTRODUCTION

In the experience of another, any other, I never have direct or immediate access to his or her interior life. The inaccessibility (based on an inability of experience: again, powerlessness) implies that any other whose interior life I cannot access is more than what he or she appears. The "beyond" of the experience of alterity means that the other is "beyond," as Kant would say, any "market price" (Kant 1996: 84). Whatever value we assign to others, this value is not enough. When he formulates the end-in-itself version of the categorical imperative, Kant, of course, says that we should never treat others *"merely"* as means to an end. But, if our outline of a phenomenological grounding is correct, we can see now that Kant did not understand the nature of his own insight. The experience of alterity requires that we exaggerate, hyperbolize, and even intensify the idea that all the others are *only and never merely* ends in themselves. Again, we must say: "Let others, all the others, be ends in themselves!"

In 2007, I published a book that analyzed and extended Derrida's final thinking about animal life.[10] *This is Not Sufficient* opened up for me the investigation of violence and possible reactions to violence. *From Violence to Speaking Out* is the fruit of this almost ten-year investigation. As the book's title suggests, *From Violence to Speaking Out* follows a specific trajectory, which is based in two impulses (Part I and Part II): one negative and critical; the other positive and creative. The negative impulse moves towards a criticism of violence. In particular, it moves toward the criticism of the reactions to violence that are based in transcendent or absolute values. These reactions – including and especially the reaction based in the valorization of peace – I think, are actually worse than the violence against which they are reacting. At the end, these reactions approximate suicide and apocalypse (without the possibility of truth being revealed).

These reactions end up in a great will to nothingness; they are nihilism in person. Therefore, the other and positive impulse moves toward the creation of a different, smaller, and less violent reaction. There can be no question that today there is violence in the world. As we just tried to show, experience itself is violence, and life is nothing other than violence, constantly struggling against illness and death. If life is nothing more than struggle, then there can be no more important question than that of a reaction that is not reactive and nihilistic. Perhaps, the less violent reaction amounts first to understanding (and not explaining) the causes of the violence. However, the reaction must go further. Can we really understand those others who intrude, those others who escape? Can we really know what happened? No, the reaction must go beyond understanding: it must let the violence be. Opening oneself to the violence, affirming life, this reaction would be an event. Then we would become other than what we were so that those others whose violence we really don't understand would become other than what they were. Is this reaction mercy, friendship, love? It would be anything but tranquil. It would speak out for those others. Taken together, the two impulses steer us "from violence to speaking out."

## Notes

1   This quotation comes from David Brooks of *The New York Times*, made on the NPR radio program, "All Things Considered" on 19 June 2015. He was discussing Pope Francis' encyclical on climate change. For the transcript of the discussion, see http://www.npr.org/2015/06/19/415809452/week-in-politics-charleston-s-c-shooting-papal-encyclical. Current facts do not support what Brooks said. As of 2011, only 13 per cent of the global population is living at a middle income level. See The Pew Research Center's "A Global Middle Class is more Promise than Reality":

http://www.pewglobal.org/2015/07/08/a-global-middle-class-is-more-promise-than-reality. Accessed on 9 July 2015.

2 See Leonard Lawlor, "The Postmodern Self: An Essay on Anachronism and Powerlessness," for *The Oxford Handbook to the Self*, ed. Shaun Gallagher (Oxford: Oxford University Press, 2011), pp. 696–714.

3 Ted Toadvine is doing ground-breaking work on the discourse of Apocalypse. Ted Toadvine, "Thinking after the World: Deconstruction and Last Things," in *Eco-Deconstruction: Derrida and Environmental Ethics*, ed. Matthias Fritsche, Philippe Lynes, and David Wood (Bronx: Fordham University Press, 2016).

4 See Hilary Putnam, "Naturalism, Realism, and Normativity," in *Journal of the American Philosophical Society*, vol. 1, issue 2 (summer 2015): 312–28. While situating his own thinking, Putnam summarizes the contemporary analytic debates around naturalism (and normativity). Putnam says that he is "a realist in [his] metaphysics," while he is not a "metaphysical realist." Although Putnam goes on the record that he "totally rejects 'the end of philosophy' story," his "realism" is still a form of anti-Platonism.

5 See Leonard Lawlor, "Becoming and Auto-Affection (Part II): Who are We?" in *Graduate Faculty Philosophy Journal*, vol. 30, no. 2 (2010): 219–37.

6 Leonard Lawlor, *The Implications of Immanence* (Bronx: Fordham University Press, 2006).

7 It is important that, in *The Order of Things*, Foucault places Kant between ancient ethics, in particular, Stoicism and Epicureanism, and modern ethics. The movement Foucault charts in Chapter 9, Section called "The 'Cogito' and the Unthought," places Kant in the middle as the "hinge" between the two (Foucault 1997: 279–80). The Stoics and the Epicureans based ethical action on natural laws; Kant moved the law to the interiority of the subject; and apparently "modern thought" moves the law to the unthought (like the unconscious) (Foucault 1970: 328n2). It is also worth noting that despite the immense influence of Levinas on Derrida, Derrida resorts to the feeling of respect in "Violence and Metaphysics" (Derrida 1978: 96). And Deleuze wrote a study of Kant in 1963, *Kant's Critical Philosophy* (Deleuze 1984).

8 Although I invoke here Kant's moral philosophy, the relation to others, in particular, the letting others be free, refers more directly to care ethics or relational ethics, as I suggest in the Preface to this book. Sarah Clark Miller has written an excellent summary of relational ethics. Sarah Clark Miller, "Relational Ethics," in *The International Encyclopedia of Ethics*, ed. Hugh LaFollette (Malden, MA: Wiley-Blackwell, 2016).

9 Derrida has discussed this very imperative in *Negotiations* (Derrida 2002a: 324–6). But in a roundtable discussion, Derrida says, "So I am ultra-Kantian. I am Kantian, but I am more than Kantian" (Derrida 2001: 66). On Derrida's relation to Kant, see Eddis N. Miller, *Kantian Transpositions: Derrida and the Philosophy of Religion* (Evanston: Northwestern University Press, 2014).

10 Leonard Lawlor, *This is Not Sufficient: An Essay on Animality and Human Nature in Derrida* (New York: Columbia University Press, 2007). *This is Not Sufficient* was based on lectures I presented at the 2006 Collegium Phaenomenologicum in Umbria, Italy, invited by Michael Naas. I am truly indebted to Michael for this invitation because writing those lectures and then *This is Not Sufficient*, based on them, opened up a new investigation for me, an investigation of violence and possible reactions to violence.

# Part I: On Transcendental Violence

# 1

# A New Possibility of Life: The Experience of Powerlessness as a Solution to the Problem of the Worst Violence

As we announced in the Introduction, the problem of the worst violence is a limitless reaction to fundamental violence. However, as a limitless reaction, the worst violence arises from the essential nature of a limit. The essence of all limits is divisibility, which means, to say this immediately, that any attempt to reach a haven unscathed by violence, any attempt to reach a place behind an impervious wall, is impossible. Now, by means of the essential divisibility of any limit, we shall be able to present the formal structure of the problem. As we shall see in a moment, the problem can be presented in two reversible versions. What is important to see is that the problem of the worst, being a superlative, is a hyperbolic problem. But the essential divisibility of the limit leads to an obvious question. What is the foundation for essential divisibility? The chapter's second section will attempt to answer this question. It will explain why the limit is fundamentally divisible. Here we shall rely on phenomenology and Bergsonism, both of which have discovered, in their own ways, a fundamental or transcendental experience. The basic experience each philosophical movement has discovered is the experience of powerlessness, or, even more precisely, the experience of blindness. The abyss of blindness grounds the essential divisibility of the limit, and therefore it grounds both the problem of the worst and, as we shall see, its solution. The third section will attempt to construct a solution to the problem of the worst. It will return to current time, which, as we pointed out in the Introduction, is the time of globalization. If our times are defined by "war without war," then the solution would lie in the direction of "peace without peace." The mechanism of the solution lies in reversal. And if the problem is hyperbolic, then the solution must also be hyperbolic. But there is more, and this is where we shall conclude. If the hate criminal and the suicide bomber are the personae essentially connected to the problem of the worst, then we must look for another persona connected to the solution. We must look for a new mode of existence, *a new possibility of life* (Deleuze and Guattari 1994: 72–3). If the persona of the problem of the worst is someone who treats everyone, the whole world, including himself, as the enemy, then the solution of peace without peace must imply a mode of existence that treats the whole world as the friend. This friendship would not be the friendship among brothers (it would not be fraternity), it would not be the friendship of philosophy (it would not be the philosopher–king as the friend of the idea); it would not even be the universal love of all humanity.[1] No, the persona envisioned here – as in a prophetical dream – is a friend of the outside.

## I. The Formalization of the Problem of the Worst Violence

While the worst alludes to the old problem of the theodicy (the best possible world as in Leibniz), we must say that the problem of the worst does *not* consist in the worst possible world. It consists rather in the *loss* of the world itself. This loss alludes to the event, in Western metaphysics, of Platonism being overcome. The world, the second world, the world in itself or essential world is gone, lost, leaving only *this* world. Before losing the essential world, we would have called this world the "world of appearance." Yet, without an essential world behind it or above it, we see that *this* world is no longer unified; it is cracked, fragmented, with borders everywhere. The problem of the worst arises then because what defines a crack, a fragment, a border, or a limit is *essential divisibility*.[2] Divisibility means that the limit is porous, allowing things to mix that should not mix. The mixing together of things that are incompossible cannot be stopped. The divisibility of the limit therefore exceeds everyone's *power*. I am *unable* to hold the limit closed and stop *entrance* and I am *unable* to hold the border closed and stop *exiting*. This formula gives us two reversible versions of the powerlessness in the face of the essential divisibility of the limit. The two versions arise respectively from the thought of Derrida and from the thought of Deleuze and Guattari. If we follow Derrida, we see the inability to stop entrance (the door opens and intrusion occurs); if we follow Deleuze and Guattari, we see the inability to stop exiting (the door opens and escape occurs).

The worst is a problem insofar as it is a reaction to the powerlessness that comes with the porous limit. In order to see how the problem of the worst comes about, let us look at the inability to stop entrance *first*. The worst occurs when I cannot keep all the others from entering *in*, when I am too weak to protect myself from all of those who might *contaminate* me, and then I react – this immediate reaction is precisely the worst one – by sending all of them *outside* to such a degree that I kill them and myself, all of us. The worst is the suicide of all, of everyone and everything, the whole world ("tout le monde," to use the common French idiom). Here we can provide a second meaning to the loss of the world: pure self-destruction (Deleuze and Guattari 1987: 162). As in Derrida whose terms ("contamination," for instance) we were just using to formulate the problem, the worst in Deleuze and Guattari arises from the essential divisibility of the limit. But here in Deleuze and Guattari, in contrast to Derrida, but *not* in opposition to him, the worst occurs when I cannot keep all the others from getting *out*. Now, with Deleuze and Guattari we turn to the other version of the formula of the powerlessness in the face of the essential divisibility of the limit: the inability to stop escape. The worst, in this case, occurs when I cannot keep all the others from getting out, when I am too weak to protect myself from all those who might *flee*, and then I react – this immediate reaction is precisely the worst one – by pushing all the others toward the *inside* to such a degree that I kill them and myself. The worst occurs when there is total capture or no way out (Deleuze and Guattari 1986: 10). But in either case – Derrida or Deleuze – the problem of the worst consists in the reaction to the experience of powerlessness; it is a *super-reaction* that unconditionally arrests passage: don't let them in; don't let them out – with no elsewhere and no future. Simply the problem of the worst is *unconditional im-passage*.

Before we turn to the fundamental experience that grounds the problem, let us anticipate the *solution* to the problem of the worst, which would be either the least bad (Derrida) or the best (Deleuze), and would also arise from the essential divisibility of the limit. The worst and the best are inseparable (Deleuze and Guattari 1987: 7). The best is not transcendent; the worst is not a fall from some sort of perfect state. Therefore, whenever we approach the best, we are also very close to the worst. So, given this essential inseparability, let us start with a *reversal* of the worst in order to understand the least bad or the best. And indeed let us start with Derrida's terminology. If the worst consists in the reaction of not letting all the others *in*, if we can define it, in other words, as unconditional inhospitality, then the least bad would be the reaction of letting all the others in unconditionally, that is, the least bad as *unconditional hospitality*. In contrast to Derrida, but *not* opposed to him, Deleuze and Guattari would say that the best consists in "following a line of flight." But here too we would have to be hyperbolic in our reversal. We would have to up the ante on flight and make the line unconditional. So, if the worst consists in the reaction of not letting all the others *out*, in other words, as unconditional capture, then the best would be the reaction of letting all the others out unconditionally, that is, the best as *unconditional flight*.

But it does not matter whether we adopt Derrida's conception or that of Deleuze, whether we speak of unconditional hospitality or unconditional flight. What is at issue is to let everyone no matter what or whom *in*; what is at issue is to let everyone no matter what or whom *out*. What must be thought, what must be experienced – and experienced as a kind of imperative ("un mot d'ordre," as either Derrida or Deleuze would say, or better, as a kind of password) – is "an inside that would be deeper than any interior world and an outside that would be more distant than every external world" (Deleuze 1988: 96). We have already spoken of what Deleuze and Guattari call "conceptual persona" (Deleuze and Guattari 1994: 61–84). Associated with this deep inside and this distant outside is the nomad or the monad for Deleuze, and the guest or the ghost for Derrida. Yet, there is a third persona that we can invoke. It comes from Foucault's *History of Madness* (and Deleuze has pointed to this persona): the madman at sea, in passage, as a "prisoner of the outside" (Deleuze 1988: 97; Foucault 2006: 11). We can modify this Foucaultian figure in a way that indicates the direction in which we are going. Instead of the prisoner of the outside, we are able to speak of a "friend of the outside." The friend of the outside loves nothing but passage. Above all else therefore, what must be thought today is *unconditional passage*.[3]

Connected as it is to the word "past," passage refers however to time. If the worst is unconditional non-passage, then the worst is also unconditional non-future, a way out that is not a way in, *the end*. We must not believe in such a *final event*. Instead, the thought of unconditional passage must involve a belief in the future. In French of course the word for "future" is "avenir." We must then find a way to believe, not in some other world (like heaven), but in *this* world of other possibilities still *to come*, future possibilities. We must find a way to wait and to know how to wait for a land to come and a people to come (*à venir*), whose coming (*venir*) or becoming (*devenir*) would make the event of an other world. Not only must our thought today be one of immanence and life, not only must our thought be a thought of the outside, it must also be a thought of the messianic. What we must wait for is not the Apocalypse and certainly not for a new celestial Jerusalem (Deleuze 1997: 45–6); we must wait for an "elsewhere," a land (*une terre*) whose name is still lacking. And if this thought of the messianic does not sound like Deleuze – or like Deleuze and Guattari – we should recall not only how often they call for a land (*une terre*: an earth) to come, for a people to come (an *à venir* that belongs to the consistency of the *devenir*), but also this statement from *A Thousand Plateaus*: "The Body without organs, we do not get to it [*on n'y arrive pas*], we cannot get to it [*on ne peut pas y arriver*], we have never finished with gaining access to it, it is a limit ... *it awaits you*" (Deleuze and Guattari 1987: 149–50, my emphasis).

Before we turn to a greater specification of the problem of the worst in Deleuze and Guattari, let me summarize this first general movement. It consists in two tracks that overlap and reinforce one another. On the one hand – *first track* – we have constructed a general formula for the problem of the worst and an outline of a solution. On the other – *second track* – we have constructed a series of titles for, to use Deleuze's phrase, "the image of thought" that the problem of the worst calls forth from us today. So, let us start with the first track, that of the problem of the worst violence. Once more, the problem of the worst violence is a problem of the limit. Essentially, the limit, any limit or border, is divisible, that is, *porous*. It is porous in the sense of being unable to stop entrance and it is porous in the sense of being unable to stop exit. All of us are powerless to keep the others out; all of us are powerless to keep the others in. The problem of the worst violence consists in the reaction to the powerlessness, the super-reaction that unconditionally arrests passage: don't let them in; don't let them out – with no elsewhere and no future. Simply the problem of the worst violence is *unconditional impassage*. Then, also simply, by means of a reversal – reversal is the very mechanism of the solution – we can see that the solution lies in the direction of *unconditional passage*. But it is obvious that unconditional passage is impossible; it is perhaps even the impossible itself. It is not possible to let everyone in; the door is not wide enough. It is not possible to let everyone out; again the door is not wide enough. This inability means that even the solution we are constructing here – unconditional passage – is *never enough*. We must always do more, speak out more, write more, *and think more*.

Now we pass to the *second* track, which is that of what thought must be today. Most generally, the thought required by the problem of the worst violence is a thought of the absolute as passage (or the absolute as duration) (cf. Deleuze and Guattari 1987: 494). More specifically, we can call this thought of the absolute "the thought of the outside." The outside however is life, but not life alone, in separation from death; the outside is life in its resistance to death ("Bichat's zone" [Foucault 1994: 154; Deleuze 1988: 129]).[4] We require a new thought of life because the problem of the worst is a problem of death. The thought required today then must be a thought of life, and not a thought of being. As a thought of life, it must be a thought of immanence, and not a thought of transcendence. And even though what is required is a thought of immanence, it must still be a thought of the event, the "to come." One thought of the "to come" is indeed the thought of the worst, the complete loss of the world, the complete devastation of the earth apocalypse. But there must be another thought of the "to come." There must be another concept, which opens up for us a new mode of existence, a new way to live, elsewhere. If we are to be friends of the outside, we must let passage be our immediate reaction when the others knock on the door!

## II. The Fundamental Experience of Powerlessness

As we can now see, both the formalization of the problem of the worst and its solution depend on the idea of passage. A limit is essentially divisible because it lets pass. As the word "passage" suggests, with its connection to the word "past," the divisibility of the limit is grounded on the experience of time. Here we must return to philosophical discoveries made at the beginning of the twentieth century; these discoveries are irreversible. We must return to phenomenology and Bergsonism. We know that Husserl had placed time at the very foundation of consciousness; he had given it a transcendental status, a status that, we know, Heidegger would take up and radicalize. But like Husserl and Heidegger, Bergson had placed time, through his concept of the duration, at a foundational level. What we are seeking is the fundamental experience, even the intuition, which grounds the essential divisibility of the limit. Let us turn first to Husserl.

In his 1913 *Ideas I*, Husserl had presented a basic description of time consciousness (Husserl 2002: 155–8, §81). There, Husserl had alluded to a level of consciousness that is more fundamental than what the reduction had transcendentally opened up: "the primal source that is ultimately and truly absolute." This small paragraph in *Ideas I* (§81) was based on lectures Husserl had given at Göttingen from 1905. In these lectures, we find a short description of absolute time consciousness (Husserl 1964: 98–100, §34–6). In these two paragraphs, Husserl describes the flux of absolute time consciousness in terms of continuity and alteration; this combination of continuity or sameness, *and* alteration or otherness, for Husserl, makes absolute consciousness "enigmatical." But the enigma of the temporal flow of absolute consciousness refers back to earlier discussions in the lectures, to paragraphs 16 and 17 (Husserl 1964: 60–4). After having described time-consciousness in terms of three phases – the now phase, the phase of retention or primary memory, and the phase of protention or anticipation – Husserl focuses on the relation between the retentional phase and the now phase. Throughout the lectures, Husserl had described time-consciousness in terms of the present perception, the living present, in a word, in terms of presence; the now-phase is, so to speak, the "center" of the living present, its "eye." When he turns to retention, Husserl reinforces the demand of presence. In paragraph 17, he says that "primary memory is perception." *But*, just previously in paragraph 16, he had described primary memory in terms of the "contradiction of perception." This contradiction of perception, in which primary memory consists, implies that the eye of present perception closes; this non-presence, so to speak, gouges out the eye, leaving behind a hole, a kind of blindness. And, it is precisely this contradictory relation between past and present, memory and perception, and correlatively, between future and present, expectation and perception, that results in the enigma of absolute consciousness, an enigma for which Husserl himself says "all names are lacking" (Husserl 1964: 100, §36).[5]

Here of course we are following Derrida's analysis of phenomenological time consciousness found in his 1967 *Voice and Phenomenon* (Derrida 2011). But we can simplify the analysis and description in the following way in order to see what is at stake in it. If we reflect on experience in general, what we cannot deny is that experience is conditioned by time. Every experience, necessarily, takes place in the present. In the present experience, there is the kernel or point of the now; Husserl had alerted us to this kernel, the "eye" of present perception. What is happening right now, however, must be described as an event, different from every other now ever experienced; there is alteration. Yet, also in the present, the recent past is remembered and what is about to happen is anticipated. The memory and the anticipation consist in repeatability, which results in continuity. Because the present being experienced right now can be immediately recalled, it is repeatable and it therefore motivates the anticipation that the same thing will happen again. Therefore, what is happening right now is also *not* different from every other now ever experienced. *At the same time*, the present experience is an event and it is not an event because it is repeatable; *at the same time*, the present experience is alteration and it is not alteration because there is continuity. This "at the same time," this simultaneity is the crux of the matter. The conclusion that we must draw is that we can have no experience that does not essentially contain these two forces of event and repeatability in a relation of disunity *and* inseparability. They necessarily pass into one another with the result that we can say that the absolute is passage (Derrida 1989: 149).

Clearly when we engage in a description like this, we are being, as Derrida says in his 2004 *Rogues*, "responsible guardians of the heritage of transcendental idealism" (Derrida 2005a: 134). Yet, we can also be like Deleuze and be responsible guardians of the heritage of Bergsonism. In his 1896 *Matter and Memory* – the book that most inspires Deleuze – Bergson had defined the philosophical endeavor as seeking the source of experience up above the turn where experience becomes human. Instead of investigating experience as it is relative to human life, Bergson is seeking an absolute experience (Bergson 1994: 184). Then in his 1903 *Introduction to Metaphysics*, Bergson laid out his absolute in the idea of the duration (*la durée*). There, he says that the duration is "a multiplicity like no other"; the duration is a temporal multiplicity, which means that the flow of duration has no spatial separations – it is temporal – *and yet* the flow is heterogeneous (Bergson 2007: 14). Therefore, in order to understand the duration and the intuition of duration, we must push to the side any type of multiplicity that is spatial and homogeneous (that is, a multiplicity of the same sort of things, like sheep, juxtaposed to one another). Having set this standard kind of multiplicity aside, let us follow Bergson from his first book, the 1889 *Time and Free Will*, when he presents for the first time the idea of the duration. Here, Bergson describes the evolution of the feeling of sympathy (Bergson 2001: 18–19). This is a brilliant description. Bergson says that the experience of sympathy begins with us putting ourselves in the place of others, in feeling their pain. But, he continues, if sympathy consisted only in feeling the pain of others, sympathy would inspire in us abhorrence of others, and we would want to avoid them, not help them. The feeling of horror is at the root of sympathy. But then, one realizes that, if one does not help this "poor wretch," as Bergson says, it is going to turn out that, when I need help, no one will come to my aide. There is a "need" to help the suffering. Bergson claims that, so far, we have described only "the inferior forms of pity," since they are based only on horror and then need. Bergson however says that this "inferior form" becomes "true or superior pity." Superior pity is not so much fearing pain as desiring it. It is as if nature had committed a great injustice and what we want is not to be seen as complicitous with it. What Bergson is now describing in this desire to experience pain is a downward aspiration. But, this downward aspiration into pain develops upward into a sense of being superior. One realizes that one can do without certain sensuous goods. In the end, one feels humility, since one is now stripped of these sensuous goods. This emotion consists in a qualitative progress: a transition from repugnance to fear, from fear to sympathy, and from sympathy itself to humility.

This is the conclusion we must draw from the description. On the one hand, there is a heterogeneity of feelings in sympathy, and yet, on the other hand, no one would be able to juxtapose them. The feelings are continuous with one another and heterogeneous with one another to the point of making an opposition between inferior and superior. Importing some of the wording from the phenomenological argument, we could say that *at the same time*, the present experience is an event (it is the experience of heterogeneous feelings) and it is not an event because it is repeatable (it is the experience of a continuous feeling). This "at the same time" is a point of indiscernibility (or undecidability). This occurs when the multiplicity passes over into duality. In the description of sympathy, this point would be that at which repugnance passes over into humility. This remarkable point would not be able to have, necessarily, the form of either side of the duality, the form neither of repugnance nor of humility, neither of superiority nor of inferiority, neither of memory nor of matter; sympathy would never appear as such. Lacking a form, the remarkable point could not be seen or remembered or anticipated. The fundamental experience being described both here in Bergsonism and in phenomenology is the experience of blindness, the intuition of a blind spot. Lacking a form, the blind spot would make passage possible for things that are contradictory or incompossible. The spot would constitute a limit that is essentially divisible between repugnance and humility, between past and present. Through this blind spot, what is outside would be able to force its way in, and through this point, what is inside would be able to force its way out. No one would have the power to stop this passage.

## III. War Without War

The secret of the descriptions that we have just seen lies in the idea that any medium of sameness heterogenizes. Earlier we had seen that the problem of the worst consisted in a reaction to the inability to stop others from entering and in a reaction to the inability to stop others from exiting. Now we are able to explain why these two inabilities exist. No one is able to stop entrance because the medium between self and others is temporal (or spatial in a strange sense). The medium is temporal because experience is fundamentally or transcendentally temporal, and that means that experience always consists in a potentially universal and repeatable trait, which can be distributed to all the others. The repeatability or iterability of the trait allows for continuity (or sameness) between me and others, and it forbids the separation that would protect me from others getting in. *And*, no one is able to stop exit because, once again, the medium between self and others is temporal. The medium is temporal because experience is fundamentally or transcendentally temporal, and that means that experience always consists in a potentially singular and non-repeatable trait, the event. The singularity or event-character of the trait allows for variation (or differentiation) between me and others, and forbids the homogenization that would protect me from the others getting out. The limit or threshold or border or crack or hiatus between me and others divides in order to include (hospitality) and it divides in order to exclude (flight). There is an inseparable doubleness in which the event or heterogeneity *violates* repetition or continuity *and* the repetition or continuity violates event or heterogeneity. This radical violence takes place in a zone of imperceptibility. When I intuit this zone, my eyes are too weak to discern and separate. We are so weak therefore that we cannot stop continuity from turning into heterogeneity and we cannot stop heterogeneity from turning into continuity. We are so weak that we cannot stop others from entering and we cannot stop others from fleeing.

With this violence at the root, this fundamental violence, we have not however encountered the worst. The worst, we recall, is a hyperbolic reaction, a super-reaction to this inability. To the point of total suicide, it unconditionally excludes and it unconditionally includes. The worst is not radical violence; the worst is total violence. The hate criminal says, "Don't let the others, none of them, not even me, enter in; don't let the others, none of them, not even me, exit out!"

For Deleuze and Guattari, the problem of the worst violence is equivalent to the problem of fascism. Fascism is based on a kind of desire for one's own death and the death of all the others (*tout le monde*); it is destructive. In *A Thousand Plateaus*, Deleuze and Guattari determine more precisely the desire found in fascism (Deleuze and Guattari 1987: 227–31). They do this when, near the end of the Ninth Plateau, which is called "1933: Micropolitics and Segmentarity," they speak of the dangers associated with "lines"; desire moves on lines.[6] So, let me briefly summarize this difficult concept of the drawing of lines (see also Deleuze and Parnet 2007: 124–47). The different ways in which lines are drawn result in kinds of differences. Deleuze and Guattari list three lines: rigid, supple, and flight (Deleuze and Guattari 1987: 222). Rigid lines divide groups of individuals or "flows" of individuals into large statistical or "molar," binary oppositions (the sexes for example, man versus woman). In contrast to the molar rigid lines, supple lines move towards the "molecular" and allow what Deleuze and Guattari call "conjugations" between the flows of individuals (not two sexes but a multiplicity of sexes [for a similar comment about the multiplicity of sexes, see Derrida 1987: 198]). But, with supple lines, one of the flows ends up dominating and therefore plugging up all the flows, closing all ways out (male traits end up dominating female traits).

FROM VIOLENCE TO SPEAKING OUT

Because a supple line allows one flow to dominate, it consists in what Deleuze and Guattari call a "relative de-territorialization." A *line of flight* in contrast is an "absolute de-territorialization"; instead of conjugating, it "connects" flows and makes the flows increase or augment (Deleuze and Guattari 1987: 220). We can see now that the line of flight is a movement without stoppage; it is a movement towards infinity. But, importantly, wherever there is a line of flight, there is "at the same time and inseparably overcodings and re-territorializations": stoppage (Deleuze and Guattari 1987: 220). For Deleuze and Guattari, it is impossible to separate the dangers of stoppage from the lines of flight.

When Deleuze and Guattari introduce the dangers associated with the lines, they in fact say that "there are three and even four dangers" (Deleuze and Guattari 1987: 227). While this wording may appear to be imprecise ("il y a trois et même quatre dangers"), it is not. The wording indicates that the four dangers constitute a complicated structure.[7] The structure consists in this: the first three dangers are grouped together, while the fourth stands alone and has a different status. This grouping is possible because the rigid line and the supple line are related to one another by means of a reversal, which has the consequence of the first three dangers being reducible to one. They are reducible to the danger of power (*pouvoir*). But power is always directed at the problem of holding in, which is conservative, and getting out, which is destructive. Therefore power organizes all four dangers. And, in fact, the dangers do not really arise from power itself, but from the lack of power, from impotence. Grouping the first three dangers around the problem of holding in and conservation, we can see that they concern *totalitarianism*. The supple line however, as we have stated, is very close to the line of flight, and therefore the danger associated with the supple line anticipates the danger of the line of flight: totalitarianism can become fascism. The fourth danger then is worse. The essential distinction between the first three dangers and the fourth is the distinction (but also the alliance) between totalitarianism and fascism. While the first three are primarily dangers that result in conservation, the fourth is destructive. But, to say this again, all four of the dangers arise from problem of impotence. Now let us turn to the four dangers, one by one.

So, correlated with the rigid line, there is the *first* danger, which is "fear." Deleuze and Guattari provide a simple definition of fear: "we are always afraid of losing" (Deleuze and Guattari 1987: 227). "Losing" means the loss of things such as values, morals, fatherlands, religions, and private certitudes, things that support our "vanity." In other words, loss means losing molar qualities. But on the basis of this loss, we are afraid that we do not have the strength to continue the mutation and then, lacking strength, being fatigued or impotent, we retreat all the more into the molar rigid lines.

Correlated with the supple line, the *second* danger lies in what Deleuze and Guattari call "clarity" (Deleuze and Guattari 1987: 227). By means of drug experiences, for example, one can reach the clarity of "micro-perceptions," through which "spaces and voids, like holes in the molar structure" are revealed (Deleuze and Guattari 1987: 227–8). The clarity of perception makes everything appear supple.[8] The second danger consists *first of all* precisely in the clarity and suppleness themselves. Supple segmentarity runs the risk of reproducing in miniature the rigid. The reproduction takes place by replacing; one replaces a community with a family. But then, with such replacements, the rigid is able to affect "directly," that is, systematically reproduce, the molecular, resulting in fascisms of the couple (the Oedipus complex in which the father and the son are rigidly divided), in fascisms of the family, school or office, in "micro-fascisms." We should notice that, while Deleuze and Guattari speak of micro-fascisms here, what they have described so far is only totalitarianism (cf. Deleuze and Guattari 1987: 228). This molecular reproduction of the molar divisions is still conservative. But, there is a *second aspect* to the danger of suppleness and clarity. So, *on the other hand*, it is possible that the dangers of the supple segmentarities "are not content with reproducing in miniature the dangers of molar segmentarity" (Deleuze and Guattari 1987: 228); they are *not* content with compensating for the molar and allowing it to act directly on the molecular. The "micro-fascisms" then – this is their term – *may* "float along the supple line on their own and suffuse every cell." Then they function like a "virus," producing individuals who have the mission of judging, policing, dispensing justice, "the neighborhood SS man." But notice these individuals functioning on the local or micrological level still have a positive mission; they are not destructive, they are not yet cancerous, not yet. Deleuze and Guattari conclude the discussion of the second danger by saying that, "Instead of great paranoid fear, we find ourselves *taken* into *a thousand little monomanias, taken* into things that are obvious and into clarities that surge forth from each [soul: they use their technical term here, "black hole"], and which do *not form a system*" (Deleuze and Guattari 1987: 228, my emphasis). One can see how close the danger is to the saving: "a thousand monomanias" versus "a thousand little sexes" and of course versus "a thousand plateaus." But here too we must see that the monomanias that take us in result from the powerlessness to resist being taken in, in a powerlessness not to continue to augment and mutate. This powerlessness is precisely what is at issue in the third danger, which is power itself (*pouvoir*).

According to Deleuze and Guattari, power is on both lines, rigid and supple, at once. Power is able to move in this way because the rigid lines and the supple lines are entangled (Deleuze and Guattari 1987: 224). This entanglement means that power is not transcendent, as in a king; this system of power is not sovereign power.[9] Although this is not sovereign power, power nevertheless is still centralized. There is what they call "a center of resonance" for all the other points of power: "the state," Deleuze and Guattari say, "is not a point taking all the others upon itself, but a resonance chamber for them" (Deleuze and Guattari 1987: 224). Each power center or resonance chamber then exercises its power on a "micrological fabric." In the micrological fabric, the power center exists "only as diffuse, dispersed, geared, miniaturized, perpetually displaced, acting by fine segmentations, working in detail and in the details of details" (Deleuze and Guattari 1987: 224). What we have to recognize here, according to Deleuze and Guattari, is that within something like, for example, the micrological mass of economic transactions, within the flow of money on a micrological level, there is something like a central bank; but the central bank will never be able to eliminate the possibility of perverse monetary uses, uses such as we find in the black market or in "guest workers" without documentation. This micrological mass of transactions cannot be controlled. As Deleuze and Guattari say, "we cannot dominate the growth of the 'monetary mass'" (Deleuze and Guattari 1987: 229). Always, power centers encounter their limit: "there is no Power [*pouvoir*]," Deleuze and Guattari say, "regulating the flows themselves" (Deleuze and Guattari 1987: 229, also Deleuze and Guattari 1987: 226 and 217). The impotence causes a reaction against the micrological flow, a reaction that attempts to control the flow and its augmentation, a reaction that either retreats to the molar level (a totalitarian regime tries to isolate its economy from other economies) or a reaction that encourages the "neighborhood SS man" to try to dominate the micrological flows of cash. It is this reaction to the impotence in relation to micrological fabric that makes power so dangerous. This source of danger in impotence is also true of the fourth danger.

The fourth danger concerns the lines of flight themselves, and is the one that Deleuze and Guattari say interests them the most (Deleuze and Guattari 1987: 229). The first three dangers really concern totalitarianism (when Deleuze and Guattari speak of micro-fascisms, they are really only speaking of what we could call "micro-totalitarianisms"). The fourth, in contrast, concerns fascism, it concerns precisely the effort to escape. Fascism is defined by destruction, while totalitarianism is conservative. Unlike the rigid and supple lines, which conserve, lines of flight are necessarily destructive; they undo forms and uncode what is coded. We can see the danger when Deleuze and Guattari ask (after mentioning F. Scott Fitzgerald), "Why is the line of flight a war one risks coming back from defeated, destroyed, after having destroyed *everything one could* [*tout ce qu'on pouvait*]" (Deleuze and Guattari 1987: 229, my emphasis)? One has the strength to destroy, one can do that, one can empty the space, break down the walls and striations, one can un-code significance and de-subjectivize the subject. But there is not enough power to fill in the space that has been emptied and smoothed down, not enough power to follow the flows escaping. One "has lost," Deleuze and Guattari say, "the *power* [*puissance*] for mutation" (Deleuze and Guattari 1987: 230, my emphasis).[10] It is out of powerlessness, "fatigue" or "imprudence" (Deleuze and Guattari 1986: 33), or better, out of weakness that one then "*turns* to destruction, abolition pure and simple, the passion of abolition" (Deleuze and Guattari 1987: 229, my emphasis). It is important to recognize the image of turning here. The weakness makes one "turn away" (Deleuze and Guattari 1987: 134), and now turning, one rotates around the walls that one is trying to destroy, a turning around that makes the line of flight relative. One turns away from following the positive objective of lines of flight, which is connection and creativity. The weakness makes one "repudiate" the positive objective. The word rendered in English as "repudiate" is *renier*, which means to deny (Deleuze and Guattari 1987: 133); the objective becomes negative, a mere negation of the walls being torn down. Death then becomes the supplement that fills in the emptiness left behind by the turning away from the positive objective. As I have pointed out, Deleuze and Guattari associate "persona" (or conceptual persona) with each of the dangers. So, here in the fourth danger, there is the persona, suggested by the mention of F. Scott Fitzgerald, of "the alcoholic."[11] The alcoholic persona usually reaches a limit that allows him always to start his drinking over. But it is also possible for the alcoholic to reach a threshold in which the alcoholic changes nature and becomes suicidal (Deleuze and Guattari 1987: 438): "a way out that turns the line of flight into a line of death" (Deleuze and Guattari 1987: 229). Having crossed this threshold, the alcoholic substitutes hatred and self-hatred for love and self-love, or more generally for friendship.

But the turning into a line of death can happen not only at the level of individuality (the alcoholic) but also at the level of a collectivity. Here Deleuze and Guattari use their concept of the "war-machine" (Deleuze and Guattari 1987: 396). Suffice it to say that a war-machine is a collectivity (the nomads of course) that tears down walls and cross boundaries, who are opposed to molar and rigid states. Therefore the fourth danger arises in the formation of a "war-machine that has no other objective but war, it is when it substitutes destruction for mutation, that it frees the most catastrophic attack. Mutation is in no way a transformation of war; on the contrary, war is like the fall or the failure of mutation" (Deleuze and Guattari 1987: 230). What this fall means is that a war-machine, like any line of flight, contains the same possibility of turning toward a negative objective and remaining relative to what it is attacking, relative to the state. The line of flight moves only from one stratum to another, which allows for something worse to happen. It is possible for the negative war-machine to "construct for itself a State apparatus capable only of destruction" (Deleuze and Guattari 1987: 230). Deleuze and Guattari say that people cheering in Nazi Germany (using clichés of course like "long live death!") "wanted that death through the death of others. Like a will to wager everything [*tout*] you have every hand, to stake your own death against the death of others, and measure everything [*tout*] by 'deleometers'," that is, by meters of destruction (Deleuze and Guattari 1987: 230). As with the other dangers, the fourth and final concerns everything and everyone: *tout est concerné*. The war-machine reacts to its loss of potential to mutate by forming a state apparatus that is suicidal to an extreme degree, complete suicide. Deleuze and Guattari conclude the discussion of this danger by saying that "all the dangers of the other lines are nothing besides this one" (Deleuze and Guattari 1987: 231).

Before I conclude this section, we should recognize that the fourth danger can expand in a more terrifying way (yes, still more terrifying!). The fourth danger consists in an alliance between, or better, an appropriation of, the war-machine by the state apparatus. This appropriation is a necessary possibility due to the weakness (or "hesitation" [Deleuze and Guattari 1987:

418]) of the war-machine. In its appropriation, the objective of the war-machine is war and destruction (the negative objective), but the aim of the state apparatus is peace and conservation. The state appropriation of the war-machine then results in limited wars in order for the state to achieve its aims, which are *political* aims. Here war is politics by other means, to quote Clausewitz's famous saying. But the world wars of the twentieth century imply something else, something like *total war* (and we should associate this phrase "total war" with totalitarianism). We can see how the appropriation of the war-machine led to the fascism of World War II. But after the war, in our "current situation," as Deleuze and Guattari say, there is the worldwide expansion of capitalism and technology (in a word, "globalization," as we say now). The expansion results in the war-machine being worldwide; the states then become parts of this worldwide war-machine. In the "current situation," however, the objective of the worldwide war-machine is not war but peace, but it is the peace of survival or terror. In other words, the worldwide war-machine takes peace as its objective, while its aim remains negative, the aim of destruction. Here Deleuze and Guattari in 1980 seem to be prescient, and Deleuze fulfills this prescience when he speaks of "control societies" in 1990 (Deleuze 1995a: 177–82).[12] In a control society, the barriers of confinement and discipline have come down; yet one is still enclosed insofar as one's movements are always under surveillance and therefore controlled. Therefore, as we have seen with the United States' so-called "war on terror," everyone is potentially under surveillance, prone to a drone attack, and therefore everyone is being controlled. The war-machine now being worldwide no longer has qualified enemies; it aims its destruction at "the unspecified enemy," which makes the destruction, at the limit, total suicide.

In the current situation today, we can say as they do, reversing Clausewitz saying, that "politics is war by other means." Our "current situation" therefore is an epoch of unlimited war disguised as peace, which we can call "war without war."

## IV. Conclusion: The Friend of the Outside

As we anticipated above, it is possible to approach a solution. A solution to the problem of the worst violence lies only in one direction. Today, in order to eliminate the worst from happening, we must reverse the formula of "war without war" and instead let us turn our world, at the least, into one of "peace without peace." How? We have seen that we are too weak to stop those who contaminate us from entering in and we are too weak to stop those who flee from exiting out. Yet, there is strength in our weakness, and we are also strong enough, we have enough force, to let the others in, we are strong enough to let the others out. Letting passage happen changes the manner in which the others are coded. Instead of everyone being coded, indeed, super-coded, as the enemy, now let us super-code everyone as the friend. The idea of unconditional friendship brings us to the primary definition of what we call above "the friend of the outside," the mode of existence that is the reverse of the mode presented to us by the hate criminal or the suicide bomber. The friend of the outside is defined as the one who embodies the weak force.[13] A weak force is defined as a power to let happen, a power to be powerless, an ability to be unable. Like the suicide bomber, the friend of the outside has a super-reaction to powerlessness. Just as the suicide bomber is blinded, the friend of the outside is blinded. Just as the suicide bomber is not able to discern friend from enemy, the friend is not able to discern friend from enemy. Yet, in the moment of indiscernibility, the friend is not the suicide bomber. The friend of the outside says, "Open all the borders and doors! Open all the factories, all the schools, all the barns, dams, and slaughterhouses! Let everyone without exception exit and go out!" We can see who this friend really is. Everybody will say that this unconditional passage is not possible; no one could deny that! Yet, the friend of the outside is the one who denies what everybody knows. The friend of the outside is an idiot (Deleuze 1995: 130; Deleuze and Guattari 1994: 62–3). Simply, she is the friend of everyone and the whole world. This friend of everyone, however, is not the philosopher-king, not the friend of the idea, by means of which all the friends are hierarchically ranked and ordered. Nor is this friend of everyone the one who embodies the universal love of humanity (Deleuze and Guattari 1987: 199). That love is no better than the anonymous enmity of the worst. This friend is no friend of anonymity. Indeed, it is impossible to conceive friendship without the name; friendship is inseparable from naming (Derrida 1997: 251). The friend of the outside then *is* not the friend of everyone. Rather, she *becomes* everyone by seeking to find or write or speak the name that properly defines every single thing, the name that is proper to every singularity. Earlier we spoke of the secret of the medium that heterogenizes. The secret in fact lies in the name that is at once event and repetition, in the address that remains singular in its universalization. Unlike the general name which gives the death sentence, the proper name – the singular name that never compromises with its universalization – is the password of friendship. But this is not all we can say about the friend who becomes the whole world. Although she is conscious of the becoming of everyone, of the whole world, although he or she undergoes joy in the search for the right name for every single other, the friend of the outside also knows with a disturbing clarity (this is a kind of clairvoyance, "as in a dream") that the solution of unconditional passage is only the mirror image of the problem of unconditional im-passage. The friend knows that there is always and must be violence; peace can and must be without peace. Therefore, the friend of the outside suffers constantly from bad conscience or even shame. She knows that *never* will there be enough said, done, or thought in the name of what resists the worst violence. She knows that the signs must be changed, before it is too late, so that we can believe in the future, so that we can believe in something to come.

## Notes

1. For more on friendship, see Chapter 8.
2. For more on the concept of the limit with which we are working here, see Deleuze 1995: 37. Deleuze says, "Here, limit, *peras*, no longer refers to what maintains the thing under a law, nor to what sets an end to it or separates it; but, on the contrary, it is the limit that is on the basis of which the thing is unfolded and unfolds all its potency [puissance]. *Hybris* stops being simply something that can be condemned, and *the smallest becomes the equal of the greatest* as soon as it is not separated from what it is able to do" (Deleuze's emphasis, translation modified). Or one should see Derrida's *Aporias* (Derrida 1993: 20). Here Derrida says, "The non-passage, the impasse or aporia, stems from the fact that there is no limit. There is not yet or there is no longer a border to cross, no opposition between two sides: the limit is too porous, permeable, and indeterminate."
3. In *For What Tomorrow*, Derrida speaks of unconditional hospitality. But then when Roudinesco asks him about specific immigration issues, he argues for a more "generous" approach to immigration issues within the framework of conditional hospitality, saying that "no one was demanding the effacement of the borders or the elimination of visas" (Derrida 2004a:

59–61). Here too, I am prioritizing unconditional hospitality or passage, but I am trying to be even more generous. To imagine the effacement of borders and the elimination of visas could be an important thought-experiment. It should not be dismissed as sheer madness.

4 According to Deleuze, "Bichat's zone" is "an outside, an atmospheric element, a 'non-stratified substance' that would be capable of explaining how the two forms of knowledge can embrace and intertwine on each stratum, from one edge of the fissure to the other ... This informal outside is a battle, a turbulent, stormy zone where singular points and the relation of forces between these points are tossed about. Strata merely collected and solidified the visual dust and the sonic echo of the battle raging above them. But, up above, the singularities have no form and are neither visible bodies nor speaking persons. We enter into the domain of uncertain doubles and partial deaths, a domain of emergence and vanishing (Bichat's zone). This is a micro-physics" (English translation modified). According to Deleuze, for Foucault, "... Bichat broke with the classical conception of death, as a decisive moment or indivisible event, and broke with it in two ways, simultaneously presenting death as being co-extensive with life and as something made up of singular deaths. When Foucault analyses Bichat's theories, his tone demonstrates sufficiently that he is concerned with something other than an epistemological analysis: he is concerned with a conception of death" (Deleuze 1988: 95; English translation modified). Deleuze makes one other significant mention of Bichat in relation to Foucault: "... it is Bichat who breaks with the classical conception of death, as being a decisive, indivisible instant ... Bichat's three great innovations are to have posited death as being co-extensive with life, to have made it the global result of partial deaths, and above all to have taken 'violent death' rather than 'natural death' as the model ... Bichat's book [*Recherches physiologiques sur la vie et la mort*] is the first act of a modern conception of death" (Deleuze 1988: 152n12). See also my *Implications of Immanence: Towards a New Concept of Life* (Bronx: Fordham University Press, 2006), Chapter 10.

5 Does this description imply that all perception is not just memory but a kind of dreaming?

6 With Deleuze and Guattari, there is always the problem of explaining their novel terminology. At times (unfortunately) I am simply going to use their terms without explanation, but I think the general sense of the term can be discerned from the discussion and context. In order to define basic Deleuze and Guattarian terms, I have generally relied on the glossary found

in Mark Bonta and John Protevi, *Deleuze and Geophilosophy: A Guide and Glossary* (Edinburgh: Edinburgh University Press, 2004). Overall, this is an excellent book.

7   Here is an outline of the structure: The first three (1. rigid line: fear; 2. supple line: clarity and suppleness; and 3. rigid line and supple line intertwined: power [*pouvoir*]): totalitarianism and conservation. The fourth (line of flight: destruction): fascism and destruction. The fourth danger can be individual or collective (the war-machine). All four dangers arise from powerlessness (*impuissance*).

8   Deleuze and Guattari say, "We believe we understand everything [*nous croyons avoir tout compris*], we draw the consequences from it" (Deleuze and Guattari 1987: 228). We must note here Deleuze and Guattari's use of the verb "croire", which they follow with the comment concerning the mode of existence or persona that accompanies the second danger: "we are the new knights," as in Kierkegaard's "knight of faith" (cf. Deleuze and Guattari 1987: 279). If we were going to lay out in its entirety the solution to the problem of the worst violence, we have to develop a concept of faith. See Conclusion.

9   Here Foucault's analysis of power in *Discipline and Punish* explicitly influences Deleuze and Guattari (see Deleuze and Guattari 1987: 217n16). The model of power they present in *A Thousand Plateaus* is not sovereign power; it is the "modern," as Foucault would say, form of power, "the microphysics of power."

10  "Pouvoir" and "puissance" are connected etymological. However, while "pouvoir" has more of a sense of power as in the power to dominate, "puissance" has more of a sense of potency or potentiality.

11  For more on the role of the alcoholic in Deleuze and Guattari's thought, see Chapter 5 below.

12  Deleuze 1995a: 177–82.

13  I am borrowing the idea of a weak force from Derrida. In the Preface to his 2002 *Rogues* (called "Veni"), and this is the only place where he says this, as far as I know, Derrida defines a weak force as "this vulnerable force, this force without power [*sans pouvoir*] [that] opens up [*expose*] unconditionally to what or who comes and comes to affect it" (Derrida 2005a: xiv). And while Deleuze or Deleuze and Guattari never speak of a weak force, we must recognize however that, in *A Thousand Plateaus*, they attribute the creation of a new regime of signs to the Jewish prophets who were able to turn their passivity into a passion, who were able to turn God's word that orders death, they were able to turn that death sentence into a password

(Deleuze and Guattari 1987: 124–5). They were able to turn a lack of power into force. In this privation of power – the "sans pouvoir" that we saw in the Derrida quote – there is something positive. Derrida seems to appropriate here Benjamin's idea of "a weak messianic power," found in his "Theses on the Philosophy of History." See Walter Benjamin, *Illuminations: Essays and Reflections*, trans. Harry Zohn (New York: Schocken Books, 1969), p. 254.

# 2

# What Happened? What Is Going to Happen? An Essay on the Experience of the Event

Nietzsche's simple definition of the reversal of Platonism is well-known. To reverse Platonism means that we value this world in itself, immanently, and no longer value it in relation to transcendent forms such as the Platonic idea of the good. In other words, the revaluation of existence means that existence is measured neither in terms of an origin from which existence might be said to have fallen nor in terms of an end toward which existence might be said to be advancing. More precisely, we must say that the reversal of Platonism means that the duration of existence has no beginning and it has no end. It has no primary origin and no ultimate destination. In the reversal, the time of duration becomes unlimited, and time itself looks to be composed of nothing but fragments and remainders. While we started out from a well-known definition of the reversal of Platonism, we have ended up in a complicated idea. The reversal of Platonism leads us to the idea of time imagined as a line that has no terminal points, a line that never bends itself back into a circle. It leads us to the imagination of an unlimited straight line. It seems to me that, despite all the philosophical reflections on time that have taken place across the twentieth century, the implications of the idea of unlimited time remain, at the least, under-determined, and, more likely, I think, the implications remain largely unknown.

In the twentieth century, Deleuze of course is the great philosopher of the reversal of Platonism. In his 1968 *Difference and Repetition*, he assigns the reversal of Platonism as the task of contemporary philosophy (Deleuze 1995: 59). It is, however, in his 1969 *The Logic of Sense* that Deleuze gives us the most precise definition of the reversal of Platonism. There, he says, "To reverse Platonism is first and foremost to depose essences and to substitute *events* in their place" (Deleuze 1990: 53, my emphasis). Thus, if Deleuze is the great philosopher of the reversal of Platonism, he is also, by means of this definition, the great thinker of the event.[1] The question that therefore drives the investigation in which we shall engage is: what is an event? As we shall see, we arrive at an answer to the question of event only if we conceive the event in terms of the straight, unlimited line of time. That is, we know we have experienced an event when the two questions of its primary origin and its ultimate destination are and remain necessarily unanswerable. In other words, an event is happening when we cannot say, with certainty, what happened and what is going to happen. In fact, if one *can* answer these questions, then one knows that one has not *really* experienced an event. And if one thinks one can answer these questions, then one has not really broken free of Platonism.

I just alluded to the title of this chapter. The subtitle, "the *experience* of the event," indicates a second part to our question of the event. Not only are we seeking the definition of an event, but also the means to make ourselves acutely aware of the event. By calling the awareness acute, sharp, even painful, we see that the experience of the event is in fact an experience of violence. Indeed, it is the experience of fundamental violence. And, as you might expect from this characterization, the experience is deeply connected to death. More precisely, the experience is deeply connected to life in its struggle with death, which means that the experience is necessarily connected to aging.[2] More dramatically, it is necessarily connected to the suffering of an accident in which things get mixed up, to being infected with a plague, or to being wounded in a battle. It is only by means of the wound that one becomes acutely aware of the event, so acutely aware that one can finally see. The vision however does not complete the event: it only allows one to have the chance to produce a work, a work of art or a work of philosophy. The event happens only when the work is produced, only when the work attains a kind of "eternity" that transforms it into a "remainder." With the work, we know we have experienced an event – even though the unlimited becoming of the work implies that the event never really happens. The event is always still to come. We have of course returned, through the work, to the unlimited straight line of time. By stressing that no matter how far we go out into the future, there is always still another "to come", we shall finally be able to refine our understanding of the reversal of Platonism. Insofar as Platonism wills the end of time, insofar as it wills that all existence constantly approximate a *telos*, it wills, we shall argue, the very worst violence. Thus the reversal of Platonism amounts not to willing, but to letting the event continue to happen ceaselessly. Letting the event happen without end, letting all the ends of the event happen implies that the reversal of Platonism is a hyperbolic response to the hyperbolic will of Platonism. Of course, such a hyperbolic *Gelassenheit* makes us think not only of Heidegger but also of Derrida (Derrida 1995: 255–87).

Like the entire book, this chapter attempts to appropriate the thinking of Heidegger, Derrida, and Deleuze in a way that will open up new possibilities of thinking and acting, which is really what the reversal of Platonism amounts to. As I anticipated in the Introduction, what we must first appropriate is immanence since these great thinkers all belong, in their different ways, to the phenomenological tradition. Thus, we are going to start our investigation with phenomenological immanence, that is, with internal, subjective experience. After all, it is impossible to reverse Platonism without passing through, as Merleau-Ponty knew, a phase of Cartesianism. The phase of Cartesianism means that we must examine the *cogito*, or, in Greek, it means that we must examine *dianoia*. The Greek term for thinking brings us to the *first* landmark in Plato himself. Perhaps it is surprising to see us turn so quickly to Plato when all we have spoken of is the reversal of Platonism. Yet, as Deleuze has pointed out, Plato himself was the first philosopher to begin the movement of the reversal of Platonism. Our first landmark – there will be four, as we shall see – is the *Theaetetus* (Plato 2006: 179, 189e–190a). Here Plato says (through Socrates, of course) that thinking is interior monologue.[3] This means that thinking is equivalent to hearing-oneself-speak. Therefore what we shall engage in first is a phenomenology of hearing-oneself-speak, by means of which we shall be able to approach the definition of the reversal of Platonism in terms of the event.

## I. The Phenomenology of Hearing-Oneself-Speak and Some of its Implications

If this investigation is to be a genuine phenomenological investigation, we must enact the epoché. In agreement with the epoché, we turn back from the objects of our experience to the experience itself. Following the basic trajectory of the phenomenological movement, we must not stop with the epoché. We must radicalize it with the universalization of the transcendental reduction.[4] Through its strict universalization, the reduction relates all beings, that is, all constituted things, including me as a psychological subject, back to an experience that is itself extra-psychological and even pre-ontic. The universalization of the reduction takes us therefore to a level of experience that is non-existent and ultra-transcendental. Through the universalization of the reduction, what we experience resembles nothing that we grasped in the natural experience of objects or subjects. What has come into view, where have we landed due to the universal reduction? Below the functioning of the natural experience of objects, we find *pure* auto-affection. As Plato anticipated, at first glance pure auto-affection looks to be interior monologue, hearing-oneself-speak.

Now, let us pursue the investigation of the pure auto-affection of hearing-oneself-speak. Auto-affection *seems* to include two aspects. *First*, I seem to hear myself speak at the very moment that I speak; and, *second*, I seem to hear my own self speak. The question we must ask is clear: is it really the case that in hearing-oneself-speak, one hears oneself speak *at this very moment* and that one really hears *one's own* self? In other words, is auto-affection really that pure? What we are going to pay particular attention to in the investigation is these "seems." This is how auto-affection seems to take place. When I engage in interior monologue, when, in short, thinking takes place – it seems as though I hear myself speak at the very moment I speak. It seems as though my interior voice is not required to pass outside of myself, as though it is not required to traverse any space. So, my interior monologue seems to be immediately present, and not to involve anyone else, and seems therefore to be different from the experience of me speaking to another. However, are we really, truly able to distinguish and separate interior monologue from external dialogue? When I speak in general, that is, with or without the intention of communication, some moment always comes prior to the speaking. It could be silence or noise, but something like a context precedes all speaking. The prior context implies that the present speaking, whether it is internal or external, whether it has the purpose of communication or not, is in a secondary position. The present speaking is necessarily a "second." In a few moments, below, by means of an eidetic variation, I shall attempt to demonstrate this claim about the necessity of the secondary position of present speaking. For now, however, we must recognize that the necessity is this: whenever I start to speak – to myself, to others, for the sake of phonation whatsoever – I find that some other speaking has already taken place and elapsed. There is always some elapsed moment that has expired, that has been lost and reduced to silence, even as something of that elapsed moment has been retained, even as something of it remains. Necessarily, my speaking is not a pure first time, even though it takes place right now. The secondary character of all speaking means that there is a delay between one speaking and another. This delay then functions as well in between speaking and hearing. Just as the apparent initiating speaking is in truth a "second," the hearing of the speaking is not immediate. In other words, the delay in interior monologue means that interior monologue is always involved in something like a process of mediation. We must therefore conclude from this description that my interior monologue in fact resembles my experience of external speech, in which a distance separates me from my hearer. I cannot, it is impossible for me to hear myself *immediately*. Regardless of whether the action is hearing or speaking, the action is a response to the past. Similar to the first necessity of the delay in time, we encounter another necessity. This second necessity appears despite the radicalization of the reduction, despite the universal bracketing of all natural beings. Here it is. In order to hear myself speak at this very moment, I must make use of the same phonemes as I use in communication (even if this monologue is not vocalized externally through my mouth, even if it does not have the purpose of communication). It is an irreducible or essential necessity that the silent words I form contain repeatable traits. This irreducible necessity means that, when I speak to myself, I speak with the sounds of others. In other words, it means that I find in myself other voices, which come from the past: the many voices are in me. I cannot, it is impossible for me to hear myself speak *all alone*. There is always a very quiet "murmur" coming from the past.[5] Others' voices contaminate the hearing of myself speaking.[6] Just as my present moment is never immediate, my interior monologue is never simply my own.

As I said earlier, I think that the implications of this description are unclear. Here are some of the implications of the description as far as I understand them. First, I think that the description shows, fundamentally, that auto-affection is based on a structure which consists of two contradictory forces. On the one hand, there is always a present moment, a point or a singularization. Each thought I have, as I speak it, has a kind of novelty to it, giving it a singular location. It is important to realize that what makes the singular point novel is that its appearance is haphazard and determined by chance. Undoubtedly, this first force of singularization is the root of what we naturally call an event-like experience. Yet, this experience is not the experience of the event. It is only the experience of an accident, an accident due to the mixed up way in which the singular points succeed one another. As we shall see, more is required for an event than an accident.

Now, let us turn to the other force in the structure we have been examining. Beside the singularizing force of chance, there is the universalizing force of repetition. As the description showed, the singularity of a thought, my present interior speech, is always connected back to some other thoughts in the past or its location is connected back to some other places elsewhere. Because of this necessary inseparability of the present thought to past thoughts, the present thought is necessarily composed of traits already used in the past, traits standing nearby. These traits are necessarily repeatable to infinity. The structure we have discovered therefore consists of the force of singularization and the force of universalization. These two forces are irreducibly connected to one another but without unification. In other words, they are necessarily bound to one another and necessarily dis-unified. The paradoxical relation of the two forces implies that auto-affection is really, necessarily, at the same time, hetero-affection. The paradox is that the relation is heterogeneous and yet the alterity does not make a separation. The inseparability is a distribution of the unity into a duality. Or, more precisely, insofar as a new now is always, necessarily linked to repetition, the unity is distributed into a multiplicity.

The wording of this last formula for the structure implied in the description of hearing-oneself-speak (that is, "the one distributed into a multiplicity") brings us to our second landmark in Plato's dialogues: the ancient problem of the one and the many in the labyrinthine discourse of the *Parmenides*. Here, Parmenides presents astonishing arguments that support the description of the structure we have just laid out: the one is the same as the many insofar as it is different from them, and unlike the many insofar as the one is the same as the many (Plato 1939: 266–71, 147c–148c). However, also in the *Parmenides*, we find this argument. It concerns the one touching itself, and therefore it concerns auto-affection. Parmenides argues that, if the one were to touch itself, it would have to be situated next to itself (Plato 1939: 273, 148e). Yet, Parmenides counters by saying that the one does not have this "next to itself" distance since it is not two and therefore cannot touch itself. In the structure we have been outlining, however, the one of the "auto" is necessarily distanced from itself and distributed into two. So, according to Parmenides' argument, we must be able to say that, since the structure is a "two," the structure in some way touches itself or makes contact with itself. How are we to understand this self-contact of the two forces?

We said that the two forces are contradictory. The terms with which we designated them clearly indicate their contradictory character: the one is the force of singularization, while the second is the force of universalization. Their contradictory character means that the two are in competition with one another, the one overstepping the other. We might imagine the competition as a race, with the two forces going beyond one another on a straight line. But, the image of the competition does not really emphasis the back and forth of the two forces. We might think that forces are playing. Play captures the back and forth of the forces but does not really capture the idea of them as forces. Therefore we could also imagine the contradictory character as a border-crossing. If we understand the "contra" of "contradiction" in its logical sense, then we must say that the two forces are the negation of one another. Or, taking up Heidegger's discourse on the *Ereignis*, we could say that, even though the two forces are appropriate to one another, the one dis-appropriates itself into the other (*aneignen* and *enteignen*). Through the language of appropriation and disappropriation, we have retained the negative relation. But also, we see now that the relation between the two forces is one of "pain" the one dis-appropriates itself into the other, crosses a border in order to transgress the other force, it penetrates a membrane, so that the movement now resembles an infection (Heidegger 2001: 203). In short, the two forces are trying to annihilate one another. The self-contact of the two forces is a struggle, and the distance between them is not a threshold (as Heidegger would say), but a battlefield. Therefore by pursuing the implications of the description of auto-affection, we have entered into what we could call "fundamental violence."

The paradoxical relation of the two forces has taken us very far from the apparently peaceful experience of my own interior monologue. In light of how far we have come, how should we now characterize the experience? Not only did we speak of the two forces in terms of contradiction, but also we spoke of them in terms of necessities. Indeed, could we imagine a force that did not build up and demand or even command its discharge? It is as if the forces are saying to one another: "Singularize!" "No, universalize!" and "Universalize!" "No, singularize!" These two commandments must be obeyed, and yet they cannot be obeyed. In other words, the two commandments cannot be reconciled. They form, as Lyotard would say, a differend (Lyotard 1988: 13). The impossibility of reconciliation tells us how to characterize the experience we have entered into. It is the experience of injustice. It is impossible to make the relation right or just. Does the experience of the impossibility of justice imply that the two forces are *strong*, too strong not to be obeyed?

In order to find an answer to this question, we must return to the structure which the description of auto-affection implies. What defines the structure is the necessary inseparability of the two forces. The inseparability is due to the way temporalization functions. So, let us engage in an *eidetic (or imaginative) variation* concerning the experience of time.[7] Let us imagine any experience in any domain. We could imagine an experience in the domain of the everyday, in the practical, the arts, the theoretical sciences, or in mathematics. No matter what the experience and no matter what the domain, we see that, each and every time, the experience involves a before and an after. As we imagine a variety of experiences, we never find an experience in which there is a before with no other before prior to it; likewise, we never find an after that does not have another after coming later than it. In other words, it is not possible to imagine a present moment or a now-point that does not come after a previous point and that does not remember a past moment. Likewise, it is not possible to imagine a retention that does not come before and that does not anticipate another now-point. In other words, there is no repetition without the supervenience of a singularity and there is no singularity without the supervenience of universality. If this imaginative exercise has disclosed a truth about the structure, then we must say that, within the structure, it is impossible to speak of an origin in the traditional sense, a principle (or *arché*), a unitary starting point, complete in itself, an unprecedented beginning. Instead, the origin is always *origin-heterogeneous*, that is, the origin is heterogeneous from the start or what starts is itself heterogeneous to the very idea of origin (Derrida 1989a: 107–8). Likewise, if there is always another singularity beyond every repetition, then we cannot speak of an end in the traditional sense, a purpose (or *telos*), a unitary stopping point, complete in itself, with nothing left over. Instead, the end is always *end-heterogeneous*, that is, the end is in the end, finally, heterogeneous or what finishes is heterogeneous to the very idea of an end. In short, there is no original principle and there is no final purpose.

This claim provides us with an answer to our question concerning the strength of the forces. The lack of an original principle and the lack of a final purpose tell us that the forces cannot be characterized as strong. A strong force would be one that is based on a principle from which it would derive all of its functions or it would be based on a purpose toward which it would orient all of its functions. Because the two forces function *without* an *arché* and *without* a *telos*, we *cannot* describe these forces at the bottom of auto-affection as strong. They are *weak* precisely because they are neither archaeological nor teleological. Yet, despite their weakness, the forces continue to work, to function, and to struggle. And their continuing struggle implies that the auto-affection of hearing-oneself-speak is structured like a war with itself, as if the interior monologue is really saying, "I am at war with myself" (Derrida 2007). This is a war at the depth of the ultra-transcendental.

## II. The Experience of the Event

We reached the ultra-transcendental level by following the phenomenological method of the universal *epoché*. It was as if we had merely "leaped" out of the natural attitude into the depth of the experience, a leap made possible by "our complete freedom," as Husserl says in *Ideas I* (Husserl 2002: 54, §31). Yet, later in *The Crisis of European Sciences*, Husserl says that this "shorter way" of the leap into the transcendental level – this is the Cartesian way, of course – has "a great shortcoming" (Husserl 1970: 155, §43). The shortcoming, for Husserl, lies in the fact that the shorter way places us in an experience that seems to lack any content. Then, because it lacks content, it is "all too easy right at the beginning to fall back into the naïve-natural attitude" (Husserl 1970: 155, §43). Thus in the Cartesian way, it is not clear that one is not copying the transcendental level off the naïve level of natural experience. It is not clear that one has escaped a vicious circle. As we know from *The Crisis*, Husserl thinks that a "preparatory explication" of the epoché is necessary to avoid this shortcoming. In other words, we must engage in a criticism of the history of philosophy in order to show how the transcendental level differs from all other philosophical positions. Yet, it seems to me that something else is required in order to escape the vicious circle. If the epoché is taken up on the basis of "our perfect freedom," it amounts to an act of will. In an act of will, one is directed toward something one already has a sense of. One projects a series of means in order to reach a goal that one has outlined in advance. The will always seems to be about recognition. Through our "perfect freedom," through this voluntary epoché, we have not really escaped the vicious circle. We reach only that which we had projected ahead of time, something we are able to re-cognize. As Husserl says, we move from "doxa" to "proto-doxa." "Proto-doxa," however, is still "doxa." In other words, through an act of will, no change occurs in me: at the other end of the action, I find myself again; I have not become other, I am not thinking otherwise. Unlike an act of will, what is required is an experience that is *undergone*, a *negative* experience that throws all accepted opinions into question. It is only through such an *involuntary* epoché that the phenomenological attitude can become, as Husserl wanted, a vocation. In this way alone, can it become a complete, personal transformation, like a "religious conversion" (Husserl 1970: 137, §35). It must start from the violence of being struck blind, like Paul on the road to Damascus.[8]

Perhaps, however, we can start from a simpler experience. Let us take another clue (our third landmark) from Plato, from Book VII in the *Republic* (Plato 1968: 202–3, 523c–524b). Appearing after the allegory of the cave, there is a well-known illustration. The illustration is supposed to answer the question of what sensation would motivate one to ascend from the depths of the cave. In other words, Socrates is trying to tell Glaucon how certain kinds of sensations provoke "thought" (here again the word is *dianoia*). The sensation is *not*, Socrates stresses, that of things "far away"; the sensation is *not* "shadow paintings." It is simply the sensation of Socrates' hand being held up to Glaucon's vision. In particular, it is Socrates' hand composed of only three fingers, the index, the middle, and the little finger. The question is not whether the fingers held up are fingers; the question is not whether Glaucon is able to recognize these fingers as fingers (Deleuze 2000: 100–1). Instead, the question is whether the middle finger is big or small. It seems to be at once both big (in relation to the pinky finger) and small (in relation to the index finger). The sensation of the middle finger is a *mixture* of big and small. According to Plato (through Socrates' mouth), it is this simultaneously contradictory sensation that provokes thought. The type of sensation Plato is pointing toward is the paradox of mixtures. Indeed, Socrates choice of the fingers indicates something more than the mixture of big and small. It also indicates the mixture of sensing and sensed, since the hand, as Merleau-Ponty knew best of all, both touches and can be touched (Merleau-Ponty 1968: 141). There is a duplicity to the very experience of the hand that makes the sensation of touching itself paradoxical.[9] When one clasps two hands together, it is not possible to determine whether the hand touching is not also the hand being touched. Which is the actor and which is the patient, which is the beginning and which is the end? Such paradoxes – like the Sorites paradox of the large and the small, but also the paradox of auto-affection with which we started – plunge thought into unlimited becoming.[10] It is from the depth of these mixtures that thought must emerge. And, just as Plato knew, when thought emerges from these mixtures, it no longer possesses its former opinions, it no longer possesses the attitudes with which it finds itself naturally. Here with these double sensations, we have *para-doxa* against the *doxa*.

This whole experience of the hand, however, even with all of its facets, does not bring us to the experience of the event. Socrates holding his hand in front of his student Glaucon is too friendly. My clasping your hand in a handshake is not disturbing. These experiences have no danger to them. However, we know the dangers involved in the experience of alcohol and of hallucinogenic drugs. Indeed, Deleuze (both when he writes alone and when he writes with Guattari) has more than suggested that these experiences might have a philosophical function. He suggests a philosophical function for drunkenness because, for Deleuze, the event is like a plague, a wound, or a battle (Deleuze 1990: 151). In fact, Deleuze says, "the battle is not one example of an event among others … , [it is] the [event] in its essence" (Deleuze 1990: 122).

The battle is the event in its essence because, *first*, it involves mixtures, deep mixtures down in the battlefield, mixtures in this case of bodies, the soldiers clashing. The mixtures consist in accidents and chance encounters, which make the battle singular, unlike any other battle. Here we have the force of singularization that we described earlier. However, a series of chance accidents does not make an event. If the event were nothing more than a series of accidents, it would indeed be the simple equivalent to drunkenness. There is a *second* reason why the battle is the event in its essence. Due to the chance mixtures of bodies on the battlefield, a soldier comes to be mortally wounded. Being caused by the mixture, the wound is an effect. It is the effect of the soldier risking his life in the abyss of the battle; he has risked and lost. Due to the mortal wound, the soldier has become aware, painfully aware that he is going to die. The awareness of his wound blinds him to the means and the purposes of the battle. The blindness to the battle's causes, however, releases the soldier enough to able to see the battle in its unlimitedness hovering above the battlefield. What does the soldier see? It is the vision of *impersonal* death.[11] This soldier, who has a proper name, is dying, his person is dying from the wound. Yet, what he sees is other soldiers dying, whose names he does not know; he sees them dying and that they never stop dying (Deleuze 1990: 152). It is the vision of incessant dying and being lost – and not just incessant dying of unknown soldiers, but also animals perishing, and countrysides and cities being destroyed. It is the vision of intolerable suffering. It is the vision of life in its endless struggle with death. This vision is why the event is horrifying. In this intuition, chaos has risen from the depths to the surface. Because the surface that the vision sees – like a plane – never comes to an end, the vision itself cannot be grasped. It is this vision of death never ceasing, never ending, never accomplishing itself, never making itself be over once and for all, this vision cannot be thought. The inability to stop the struggle of life with death is the impotence of the event. It is, however, a powerlessness that includes a kind of power.

So far, we have seen that the experience of the event involves two features. On the one hand, it involves the depth of mixtures, chance relations of cause and effect, accidents, which make this battle a battle unlike any other. This is the force of singularization. On the other hand, however, there is the force of universalization. Through the effect of being wounded, one is forced to see, intuit, have a vision of the battle; the battle rises to the surface and is no longer limited to the accidents. Without end, incessantly singularities pass away, as if a plague is taking place. There is, however, a third feature of the experience of the event. *It is the most important feature.* The mortally wounded soldier has no choice in relation to the two forces we have just described. The effect of the battle is that he is dying and others are incessantly dying. Although the vision of the battle's incessant deaths cannot be grasped, cannot be thought, the unthinkable must be thought, the ungraspable must be grasped. Due to the force of universalization, something remains of the singularities as they pass away. In this moment of grace between life and death, the mortally wounded soldier is able to effectuate the battle differently, *against* the incessant deaths being caused in the battle. *Counter* to the accidental, *de facto* characteristics of the battle, he is able to select traits from the battle that are ideal and *de jure*. In other words, he is able to create an ideal sense of the battle. In still other words, he is able to create a philosophical concept or an artwork. Responding to the vision, the mortally wounded soldier, through the selection of traits, a selection that is like a single act of violence, includes all violence and all mortal events in one single event – a book, a speech, a picture, a song, or a concept – that denounces and deposes all violence and all death (Deleuze 1990: 152–3). The mortally wounded soldier must write the story of the battle – in order to liberate it, as Deleuze says, "always for other times" and "to make us go farther than we would have ever believed possible" (Deleuze 1990: 161).

This third feature of the experience of the event amounts to what Deleuze in *The Logic of Sense* calls "counter-effectuation." Effectuation, which is the deep, accidental mixture of bodies, takes place in the present. The counter-effectuation in the artwork, in a novel, in a concept, makes the battle "eternal." The counter-effectuation is "eternal" not in the sense of an eternal present that never changes or of a circle of time that constantly returns to the present, but in the sense of being non-present, that is, it is the experience of the openness of an unlimited past and future (Deleuze 1990: 61). The experience of the event is no longer simply the present of effectuation; instead, the battle is always to come and always already passed. That is, as an ideal sense, the battle appears to lack an origin; but also, as an ideal sense, it exceeds all actual fulfillments. In this sense, the event has never taken place and never will take place. What is the experience of the event? It is the grasping in a work of the ungraspable vision of incessant struggle: endless fundamental violence. The terrible nature of the event means that we really do not know, in the strong sense, what happened and what is going to happen.

## III. Conclusion: What Happened? What is Going to Happen?

Like the vision of the mortally wounded soldier, Nietzsche's Zarathustra has a vision of unlimited time (Nietzsche 1968:

267–72: "The Vision and the Riddle). Zarathustra's vision of the moment standing at a gateway over a road that stretches far out of sight, this is the image for eternity: a straight line without a termination point, a straight line that never bends itself back into a circle. Earlier, we had tried to provide this image of the unlimited straight line with conceptual determination by referring to the features of origin-heterogeneous and end-heterogeneous. Let us return again to these conceptual determinations. Perhaps I am mistaken, but I think it is more difficult for us to imagine the world continuing without end than to imagine the past extending indefinitely. Assuming I am correct about this difficulty, I would like to try one more eidetic variation, in particular, in relation to the idea of the end. So let us therefore try to imagine the end of the world. Let us even try to imagine the obliteration of the world. Now, let us vary the image of how the obliteration takes place. However we would think of the devastation, as an explosion, extinction, or cataclysm, etc., no matter how destructive or catastrophic, that end of the world would leave some fragment behind; there would be something residual. We cannot imagine destruction without something left over. Whatever this leftover might be, however we would think of this residual something, as energy, micro-particles, dense matter, space, gases, light, micro-organisms, it would necessarily continue. It would necessarily continue to have some sort of effects, and thus it would continue to have a future. End-heterogeneous means that it is necessarily the case that something else or something other is always still to come from or in the future. In other words, end-heterogeneous implies that there is always a *remainder*. It seems to me that a remainder necessarily includes two features. *On the one hand*, a remainder indicates that something has really been lost and gone away. And, insofar as the remainder indicates loss, it truly indicates the end of a singular world. However, *on the other hand*, insofar as the remainder remains, it indicates that something more is coming. And, insofar as the remainder indicates more, it is truly the promise of other worlds. Thus, expressing both features of the remainder – backward and forward, loss and promise we can say with Derrida, quoting Paul Celan: "The world is gone. I must carry you" (Derrida 2005: 135–63). Here, the "I must carry you" probably signifies pregnancy. Nevertheless, what the remainder indicates – it is only an indication; it does not deliver the future in pure immediacy – can never be known. I cannot know what is coming. I cannot know whether what is coming is the best or the worst.[12]

The claim of non-knowledge returns us to the question of Platonism. Platonism, or, as Derrida used to say, "the metaphysics of presence," or, as Deleuze used to say, "the old metaphysics," or, as Heidegger used to say simply, "metaphysics" – metaphysics thinks that it knows what is coming. By positing absolute and transcendent values, it thinks there is an absolute or ultimate end and an absolute or primary origin. Through this knowledge, metaphysics in fact knows nothing of the "eternity" of the event. Metaphysics, however, not only posits absolute and transcendent values, it also wills the means to achieve the fulfillment of these values. As we saw at the beginning, such a will reduces the value of this world, of existence to being nothing more than a function of this end and purpose. But the reduction of value is not the only result of the metaphysical will. When the metaphysical will wills the means to achieve the end, it thinks it is willing the good. Such a teleology implies the willing that all of existence, all of life, all remainders be brought to the end. In truth, however, this willing can have no other outcome than the absolute and hyperbolic elimination of all remainders. In short, the metaphysical will does not will the best; it wills the worst. Thus we see the stakes in the reversal of Platonism are higher and more extensive than a problem within the history of philosophy. The stakes, simply, are more violent.

If our ultra-transcendental investigation of auto-affection is correct, there can be no denying that the Apocalypse willed by metaphysics is impossible. Yet, despite its impossibility, what the metaphysical will wills is a constantly increasing approximation to this apocalypse. Perhaps we can understand globalization only in reference to this constantly increasing approximation. As it encloses the earth in a globe, it aims at the complete obliteration of remainders. How are we able to reverse the incessant obliteration of remainders? If metaphysics thinks that it knows the one value or purpose for existence, then the reversal must base itself in the *non-knowledge* of the heterogeneity of origin and end. We do not know the answer to the questions of what happened and what is going to happen. In short, the reversal amounts to a vision, an acute awareness of not knowing, of not being able to know, of not having the power to know what is coming. Yet, as we saw, from this powerlessness flows a kind of power: the power to be powerless. If we are unable, we are able to be unable. We are able to let the unknown ends happen. But then, just as the metaphysical will is hyperbolic – it wills that all remainders march toward the end – the reversal must be hyperbolic. It must let every single remainder be, without exception. Through this *Gelassenheit*, as Heidegger would say, the reversal "values" (but "value" does not seem to be the right word here) every possible remainder, every imaginable remainder and, especially, all of what they indicate is coming, every single end that they might indicate. The reversal of Platonism therefore does not aim for the worst violence, but for the *least violence*.

There is one more question. Is this hyperbolic *Gelassenheit* equivalent to what we were calling "counter-effectuation"? Is it equivalent to the experience of the event? We know already that the answer to this question is "no." The unlimited *Gelassenheit* becomes a counter-effectuation *only if* it results in a work. It remains nothing but an accident unless it produces a work of art or a work of philosophy. But what is the purpose of the work? This question brings us to the fourth and last reference to Plato's dialogue. The final reference is to Book Two of the *Republic* (Plato 1968: 45, 368c–369b). There Socrates suggests to Glaucon that they investigate the constitution of the soul by looking at the bigger image of the constitution of the *polis*. A couple of books later, of course, we land with Plato in the ideal city. As we have seen however, the reversal of Platonism in fact starts, not from the larger political image, but from the smaller psychological image. It starts with the soul, with internal subjective experience; it starts with interior monologue. An implication of our investigation of pure auto-affection, an implication we left in the dark above, is this: the heterogeneity of auto-affection – that auto-affection is always in fact hetero-affection – means that, instead of an identical or unified self, I find, inside myself, an other. The other in me turns the "I," the self, into a "we." But this "we," it also, is heterogeneous, and therefore not strictly a "we" at all. The self is a "we" and yet the "we" is absent. In other words, we can say that *the people is lacking*. Then the question becomes: how are we to call the people forth? How are we to make them come? This calling forth, we see now, is the purpose of the work. The purpose of a work of art or a work of philosophy lies in calling forth a new people. But the unlimited straight line of time implies the work can only and must necessarily call forth a new people, a *"demos,"* that always remains *to come*. In this way, we see, finally, that the reversal of Platonism does not land us in an ideal city; it does not land us in a new shining Jerusalem on the hill.[13] It places us in a land that has no borders, where the people are so aware of being at war with themselves that they never stop letting themselves become other than what they are.

## Notes

1  For more on the event in Deleuze, see my "Phenomenology and Metaphysics, and Chaos," in *The Cambridge Companion to Deleuze*, ed. Daniel W. Smith and Henry Somers-Hall (New York: Cambridge University Press, 2012), pp. 103–25.
2  For more on aging, see Chapter 5 below.
3  Aristotle reiterates this claim in the *Posterior Analytics* (Aristotle 1984: 124, Book I, 76b25).
4  The discussion of epoché and the reduction is based on Edmund Husserl, "Phenomenology" (Husserl 1997: 159–79). It is also based on the presentation of the phenomenological method in *Ideas I* (Husserl 2002). For a lucid and exhaustive treatment of the "Encyclopedia Britannica" essay, see Joseph J. Kockelmans, *Edmund Husserl's Phenomenology* (West Lafayette: Purdue University Press, 1994).
5  Maurice Blanchot, "Death of the Last Writer," in *The Book to Come*, trans. Charlotte Mandell (Stanford: Stanford University Press, 2003), pp. 222–3.
6  Fred Evans has developed an important conception of the voice in *The Multivoiced Body: Society and Communication in the Age of Diversity* (New York: Columbia University Press, 2008), see especially pp. 144–68 and 280–2.
7  Although I am using a method from classical phenomenology, I am trying to make the method have an effect not just on the objective side of the variation but also on the subjective side of the variation. In other words, when I vary to determine a structure, I am also trying to make that variation change the one engaged in act of variation. I am here following a clue provided by Foucault in his course called *Hermeneutics of the Subject*: "Meditating death (*meditari, meletan*), in the sense that the Greeks and Latins understand this … is placing oneself, in thought, in the situation

of someone who is in the process of dying, or who is about to die, who is living his last days. The meditation is not therefore a game the subject plays on his own thought, with the object or possible objects of his thought. It is not something like eidetic variation, as we would say in phenomenology. A completely different kind of game is involved: not a game the subject plays with his own thought or thoughts, but a game that thought performs on the subject himself. It is becoming, through thought, the person who is dying or whose death is imminent" (Foucault 2005: 359–60). In Husserl, an eidetic variation results in an eidetic intuition. What Foucault is implying here is that the phenomenological eidetic intuition does not transform the subject doing the variation and having the intuition. In contrast, the intuition I am trying to bring about, like meditation in this sense, is supposed to transform the subject.

8   See Acts of the Apostles, Chapter 9.
9   John Sallis, *Being and Logos: The Way of Platonic Dialogue* (Atlantic Highlands, NJ: Humanities Press International, 1986), p. 430.
10  Sorites paradoxes are what drives Deleuze's *The Logic of Sense*.
11  Deleuze cites Maurice Blanchot, *The Space of Literature*, trans. Ann Smock (Lincoln: University of Nebraska Press, 1982), p. 123.
12  The claim of non-knowledge opens the way for the development of some sort of "blind thinking" or a kind of faith.
13  The allusion is to the Book of Revelation, Chapter 21.

# 3

# Is it Happening? Or, the Implications of Immanence

Let us begin with the following proposition from *The Critique of Pure Reason*: "We assert," Kant says, "that the conditions of the *possibility of experience* in general are at the same time [*sind zugleich*] conditions of the *possibility of the objects of experience*" (Kant 1998: 283, B197/A158, Kant's italics [Heidegger 1997: 84, §24]).[1] We know that this proposition opened the way for the circular path of the Hegelian dialectic.[2] But, closer to our time, and cited so often across the twentieth century, Heidegger's Kant book taught us how to deconstruct the Kantian correlation between the possibility of experience and the possibility of the objects of experience. For Heidegger, it is not the correlates of the correlation that are important. Heidegger emphasizes the "at the same time," the "zugleich." The logic of Heidegger's deconstruction seems to work in this way: the "zugleich" refers to pure auto-affection; pure auto-affection refers to time; and finally, at the bottom of time, far below the sameness of the "zugleich," there is a difference. This fundamental, transcendental, or even absolute difference — the difference that Heidegger later in his career calls "pain" (Heidegger 2001: 201) — cannot be erased. It cannot be made coincident. It can neither be closed up nor can it be closed off. No matter how we imagine the movement of time ("temporalization," as we say in the phenomenological tradition), whether we think far back into the past or we think way out into the future, we encounter this unclose-able difference. It is the unclose-ability of the difference that unwinds the circle of time into a straight line. It is the straight line of time therefore – this straight line is one of the images Nietzsche provides for this eternal return doctrine – that disabuses us of any illusion of a primary starting point and any illusion of a final stopping point. It disabuses us of any illusion of transcendence, and thereby it opens the way for the true sense of immanence.

So, let us reflect on the idea of immanence. Immanence is required because of the primary event of Western metaphysics that Kant initiated. This event is the reversal of Platonism. In fact, the discourse of anti-Platonism or of the overcoming of metaphysics requires the use of the term "immanence." The *first* sense of the word "immanence" must be opposed to the transcendent. In the reversal of Platonism, we are no longer concerned with a second, transcendent world; our concern is not with transcendent ideas. Our gaze is now turned back to this world and to our ideas. Subjectivism is the necessary outcome of anti-Platonism. If we are overcoming metaphysics, where the "meta" of "metaphysics" means a transcendent realm of ideas "beyond" this world and our experiences, then we must reflect on our experience, on "inner experience." Yet, thanks to phenomenology and Bergsonism (which made Heidegger's work on time possible[3]), we know that the temporal conditioning of inner experience implies that inner experience can no longer be conceived as an enclosure. The fact that inner experience is fundamentally temporal opens the inside to the outside; the limit between inside and outside becomes porous; temporalization necessarily implies that passage happens. In other words, due to the structure of temporalization, that is, due to the fact that every present moment is differentiated into a recollection and an anticipation, inner experience must be conceived as becoming. We come once more upon the image of time as an unlimited straight line: time never stops becoming. Indeed, becoming is the *second* and more profound sense of "immanence," the sense of immanence that we find in Deleuze (and Guattari) (Deleuze and Guattari 1994: 48–9).[4]

It is this second and more profound sense of immanence – becoming – that produces problems. In particular, it produces "the problem of the worst violence." As we know already, the problem of the worst is the problem of the end of the world; it is based in apocalyptic thinking. Such apocalyptic thinking comes about as a reaction to the transformation that immanence produces. Because of its unclose-able difference, immanence transforms the concept of limit: all limits must be defined by essential divisibility. In other words, because all limits are porous, I cannot keep out contaminants. Then, I react to the contaminants that are violating me by attempting to destroy them. However, these contaminants, these animals, these killers are already within me. I know that they are inside me. And yet I think, and then I will that they and therefore me too, all of us must be destroyed. We see immediately that the problem of the worst amounts to a suicidal impulse. In order to stop the violence, in short, in order to stop time and becoming, this reaction attempts to bring about the most extreme and worst violence.

This kind of thinking thinks that this hyperbolically violent reaction is the only possible reaction to the irreducible violence brought about by temporalization. It is not. Through a reversal, we can see, minimally, that the worst violence becomes the least violence, and then the willful reaction becomes a kind of letting be. And since the worst and the least are superlatives, we know that the least bad reaction would also have to be a super reaction: a hyperbolic *Gelassenheit* (appropriating this word from Heidegger). Thus, what is really at issue is a reaction to this irreducible violence that is *not* the worst reaction. However, the analysis of the reactions we have produced so far opens onto a more pressing question: how are we to bring about this reversal from the worst to the least, how are we to reach this hyperbolic *Gelassenheit*? And, since we have already alluded to Nietzsche, we could rephrase the question as: How are we to bring about this extreme revaluation of all values, revaluation of a kind of thinking that makes protection from the outside and enclosure within the inside, that makes, in a word, purity be the highest and absolute value?

As we saw in Chapter 2, we reach this extreme level only through the phenomenological reduction. In the phenomenological tradition, we know that the reduction is the only method by means of which one can reach the transcendental level, the level of absolute consciousness, which is absolute temporalization. But, Husserl conceived the reduction as an act of will. If we want to escape from the will and yet reach this absolute level, then the reduction must be triggered – triggered by an experience, which I shall call "the experience of the event." Thus the question we are really asking is: is the event coming (Lyotard 1988: xvi)? This question explains the title of this third chapter: is it happening? In order to reach absolute temporalization and therefore in order to reach "the implications of immanence" – hence the chapter's subtitle – we must undergo the experience of intolerable suffering. The experience of the event is an acute awareness of intolerable suffering. In this experience, we realize that we really do not know what happened to bring about the suffering and what is going to happen with the suffering. When one no longer knows what happened and what is going to happen, then one can only feel *shame*, shame that what has happened in the past was beyond one's control and shame that what is going to happen in the future will be beyond one's power. As Spinoza knew, shame is the crucial emotion for change. In order to enter into this transformative event, let us return to the infamous presentation of the reduction found in *Ideas 1* (Husserl 2002).

## I. The Infamous Description of the Reduction in Ideas 1

I am calling this description "infamous" because scholars, phenomenologists, and many philosophers generally lament that Husserl described the epoché and the reduction in Cartesian terms, as a kind of doubting made possible, Husserl says, by "our perfect freedom" (Husserl 2002: 54, §31). Yet, what is most infamous is *not* the conception of the epoché on the basis of Cartesian doubt. What is most infamous is the description, found in §49 (Husserl 2002: 88–90), of the reduction as the "annihilation of the world." This description became infamous, for many philosophers after Husserl (and after Heidegger), because the "phenomenological residuum" appeared to exist outside the world; to put it simply, absolute consciousness looks not to be being-in-the world. However, what is striking about the description is its *violence*; after all, the title of the section is "Weltnichtung": "world-annihilation." By saying that this annihilation is "conceivable" (*denkbar*: thinkable or imaginable), Husserl beckons to us to engage in a thought experiment;

therefore, he calls us to an experience. What is this experience? It is one in which every experience "dissolves" into "illusion" through "conflict" with every other, to the point that the "conflict" (*Widerstreit*) never resolves itself into a truth. There is no harmony in this experience because it "swarms" (*wimmelt*) with "oppositions" (*Widerstreiten*) that are intrinsically "unreconcilable" (*unausgleichbaren*). Experience therefore is "rebelliously" (*widerspenstig*) set against coherence and harmony. We know what this experience is: it is the experience of war. And Husserl is suggesting that this experience is the only one through which we can reach the absolute consciousness which is, in fact, absolute temporalization.

In order to understand why we must pass through the experience of war to reach the level of absolute temporalization, we must extend Husserl's thought experiment. We must imagine a battle. As Husserl's description of the annihilation of the world suggests, a battle always swarms with conflicts. In other words, the battle consists in mixtures of bodies. The mixtures consist in accidents and chance encounters. Due to the chance mixtures of bodies on the battlefield, a soldier comes to be mortally wounded. Being caused by the mixture, the wound is an effect. It is the effect of the soldier risking his life in the abyss of the battle; he has risked and lost. Due to the mortal wound, the soldier has become aware, painfully aware that he is going to die. The awareness of his wound, however, blinds the soldier to the means and the purposes of the battle. And then, the blindness to the battle's causes releases the soldier enough to able to see the battle in its unlimitedness hovering above the battlefield. What does the soldier see? It is the vision of chaos, or, more precisely, the vision of life in its endless struggle with death. Can this vision really be conceived, can it really be thought? It must be thought because it is horrifying. Although the soldier is dying, the soldier has no choice but to start to think, and to think *against* the chaos. The experience of the battle is the event that forces us to think, and to think otherwise than how we have been thinking. Perhaps, Husserl would reject this extension of his description, but forcing us to be other, the thought experiment makes us break free of the vicious circle in which the transcendental would be copied off the empirical. The experience *converts* us to the phenomenological attitude.

### The Implications of Immanence

In *Ideas 1*, Husserl calls the transcendental level that we have reached through the annihilation of the world "immanence." As you recall from the opening of my presentation, the first sense of immanence is inner experience. And, at first glance, inner experience looks to be the form of auto-affection called hearing-oneself-speak. What follows expands on what we saw in Chapter 2, Section One. As we saw there, interior monologue is based on a process of temporalization. The process of temporalization has two consequences. On the one hand, temporalization introduces a delay into interior monologue so that hearing-oneself-speak is never immediate. On the other hand, the delay in time turns auto-affection into hetero-affection. Just as my present moment is never simply immediate, my interior monologue is never simply my own. Now, I would like to develop and determine some of the implications of the consequences that follow from the description of the temporalization that functions below the appearances of interior monologue. One of the purposes of this book lies in systematizing "the implications of immanence," but, I am not certain that they can be systematized or be exhausted. I am going to outline ten implications.

The *first* implication seems to be that temporalization is a structure consisting of two contradictory forces: singularization and universalization. On the one hand, singularization forces a present moment, like the sharp point of sword, to insert itself into the flow of time. On the other hand, however, universalization forces the flow of time, like a charging army, to overrun the singularity of the moment. Time temporalizes or endures by means of the force of universalization and the force of singularization, the force of repetition and the force of event. These two elements of repetition and event are irreducibly connected to one another but without unification. In other words, these two forces are necessarily bound to one another and necessarily disunified or non-coincidental, cracked apart like a wound and yet sown back up like a suture. The limit between the two forces is a sort of synthesis that is nevertheless divisible, differentiated, and uncloseable. Being always out of joint, we can call this limit within the experience of time "anachronism" (Derrida 1993: 65–6). (We shall return to the idea of anachronism in the Conclusion below.)

The *second* implication elaborates on the characterization of the two forces. It seems to be self-evident that every experience I have, no matter what its content, takes place in the form of the present. Even when I recall something or when I anticipate something, I recall or anticipate in (or into) the present. The self-evident nature of that claim – any experience whatsoever is present experience – has always implied that one is unable to experience one's own death or one's own birth. Both of these events would seem to involve a passage from the past as such and not the past as a past present or a passage into the future as such and not the future as a future present. But could there be such an experience of non-presence *as such*? If we imagine a variety of experiences, it seems that the answer to this question would have to be "no." I cannot experience my death or my birth *as such*. Yet, this impossibility does not imply that we have no other experience than the experience of the present as such. So, let us again, as we did in Chapter 2, go through an imaginative variation of experience. We can fill the experience with any content and, no matter what the content of experience is, we always find something like temporal dispersion or multiplicity (to speak like Bergson). In other words, as we test the experience, we find that in the present there is *always* a "before" (or a retention). If we go back further into the past and make that before present (it now being a present past), there is always another "before" prior to that other before. The difference between the now and the before is irreducible. It goes on forever. Likewise, as we test the experience, we find that in the present there is always an after (or a protention). Once again, if we go out further into the future and make the after present, there is always another after later than the other later. The difference between the now and the after is irreducible. It too goes on forever. While we cannot speak of us having an experience of our own death as such, the realization that there is always another after seems to multiply death within life. You can see that we are already very close to fundamental violence. But you can also see already that the apocalyptic thinking of the worst is mired in illusions since the fact that there is always another after later than any particular after seems to multiply life (and therefore birth) within death. As we intimated a moment ago with the battle, the two forces of singularization and universalization are really the inseparable forces of life and death. On the one hand, temporalization includes the force of spontaneity and production (life); on the other it includes the force of repetition and reproduction (death). In fact, due to this unstoppable reproduction, we can say that within subjective lived-experience, there is always necessarily something a-subjective and deadly.

The two forces of life and death brings us to the *third* implication of immanence. Inseparable and never unified, the two forces are necessary elements within the structure of temporalization, a structure that is, following the reduction, transcendental and absolute. Being so, the structure of temporalization (the battle) is prior to any regional division in knowledge or experience. Thus the two forces are *at once* essential necessities and practical necessities or even ethical imperatives. Not only do we have no choice but to universalize and to singularize, but also we *must* choose to universalize and to singularize. In French, this paradoxical double necessity would be expressed by the common idiom "il faut." The closest equivalent to this idiom in English, I think, uses the verb "to have." When I say to you that "you have to do that," it remains (without adding in more context) indeterminate between you being required to do it because of a theoretical, logical, or natural necessity or because of a practical, ethical, or cultural imperative. "You have to do that" expresses a paradoxical necessity – it is necessary both at once essentially or structurally *and* ethically or morally. *Importantly*, the paradoxical double necessity implies that all the *other* implications of immanence are at once essential (or theoretical) *and* ethical (or practical).[5]

Therefore, we come to the fourth through the ninth implications. *Fourth*, temporalization, as the absolute itself (the ultimate transcendental level of immanence), implies, not absolute knowledge (as Hegel thought), but absolute non-knowledge. In short, there is no pure presence or presence as such. Due to temporalization, all experience as the experience of the present is never a simple experience of something present over and against me, right before my eyes in a clear intuition; the force of repetition is always there. Repetition refers back to what has passed away, distant, and no longer present — and it anticipates ahead to what is about to come, from a distance, and is not yet present. The present therefore is always complicated by non-presence, which means that we really don't know what happened and what is going to happen. *Fifth*, if the experience of the present is always complicated in the way we were just describing, then nothing is ever given as such in certainty. Whatever is given is given as other than itself, as already past or as still to come. What becomes "foundational," we might say, is this "as." Or what becomes "foundational" is the "of" in "the thought of" so that "the thought of" becomes the thought of nothing present *as such*. Instead of the certainty of something given as such in full presence, we have the "maybe" of something given incompletely. *Sixth*, the fact that the "of" in "thinking of" has become foundational, this fact disturbs the traditional structure of transcendental philosophy. In traditional transcendental philosophy, there is supposed to be a uni-directional relation between foundational conditions and founded experience. In other words, an empirical event such as what is happening right now is supposed to be derivative from or founded upon conditions that are not empirical. Yet, temporalization determines that the empirical event is a non-separable part of the structural or foundational conditions. Or, in traditional transcendental philosophy, the empirical event is supposed to be an accident that overcomes an essential structure. But we see now that this accident cannot be removed or eliminated. *Seventh*, if the "accident" cannot be eliminated, if the "accident" has always already taken place, then we cannot speak of an origin in the traditional sense, a principle (or *arché*), a unitary starting point, complete in itself, an unprecedented beginning. Instead, the origin is always origin-heterogeneous, that is, the origin is heterogeneous from the start or what starts is itself heterogeneous to the very idea of origin. Likewise, if the "accident" cannot be eliminated, if "accident" always remains, then we cannot speak of an end in the traditional sense, a purpose (or *telos*), a unitary stopping point, complete in itself, with nothing left over. Instead, the end is always end-heterogeneous, that is, the end is heterogeneous finally or what finishes is heterogeneous to the very idea of end. Origin-heterogeneous and end-heterogeneous provide conceptual determination for the image of time that we presented at the beginning: a straight line extending infinitely in both directions. The present endlessly divides itself and that division never comes to a beginning in a subject and never to an end in an object.[6] Then, *eighth*, if there is no original principle and if there is no final purpose, then every experience contains an aspect of lateness and an aspect of earliness. It seems as though I am late for the origin since it seems already to have disappeared; it seems as though I am early for the end since it seems still to come. Every experience then is not quite on time or in the right place. Experience, the experience of unlimited time, is "out of joint." Being "out of joint," commanding in ways that are irreconcilable, the experience is one of powerlessness, but, more explicitly, it is one of violence and injustice. Then, *ninth*, with this "out of joint-ness" being foundational, there can be strictly no unified "I" or "auto" or "self." Instead of a unified "I," we find a "we" whose unity remains incomplete, whose border remains divisible, and whose interior is contaminated by others. There can be no one voice, no my voice as such; there is only a clamor or murmur or cries from this "we" that is at war with itself. This analysis completes the elaboration of "the implications of immanence" that we saw in Chapter 2. We have seen nine implications; there is, however, one more.

## III. The Event of the Experience of Shame

The *tenth* implication of immanence is that the absolute and irreducible violence involved in temporalization has an affective register. As we have passed through the first nine implications of immanence, you should have started to say to yourself – this claim, it seems to me, is the truth of our inner monologue – "I am at war with myself." In other words, one should have become more and more aware of the irreducible violence and injustice at the bottom of experience – acutely aware like the horrifying vision of the wounded soldier. But is this acute awareness strictly horror? Through the investigation of the implications of immanence, one has become aware that one cannot ever fully respond to the two necessities. When one is commanded to universalize, one violates the imperative by singularizing and when one is commanded to singularize, one violates the imperative by universalizing. This double violation makes one be indistinguishable from the forces inflicting the violence; they are there in you, they are you; and, at once, it makes one be indistinguishable from the forces that suffer violence; they too are there with you, they are you. How could one not feel responsible for the suffering – and feel compassion for the suffering? Exposed to and responsible for the murmurs, the whispers, and the cries, how could one not feel *shame* at the intolerable suffering and abominable violence? Therefore with this tenth implication of immanence, we must speak of fundamental shame.

The key to what I am calling fundamental shame lies in the undecidability of the two forces at war in temporalization. Each force commands categorically and unconditionally: "Universalize!" "No, singularize!" "Singularize!" "No, universalize!" The compulsion of these commandments forces one to decide for one or the other. Thus, the experience so described justifies Aristotle's claim that one feels shame only for one's own voluntary actions. One *is coerced* to decide, but the decision itself is *free* due to the undecidability between the commandments. The shame comes upon one, however, because, to decide to obey one commandment necessarily implies the disobedience of the other. No matter how one decides, one will be inadequate to the task of stopping the violence; one will be unable to stop compromising with the violence. No matter what happens, one will feel shame. The feeling is irreducible. The irreducibility of shame seems to contradict something else Aristotle says about shame. He claims that shamefulness is more appropriate to young people. Aristotle thinks this because, being ruled by their passions, young people are more prone to make mistakes – while elders, having better control of their passions, should not make shameful mistakes (Aristotle 1982: 249–51, Book, IV, ix).[7] We can, however, pervert this Aristotelian insight about shame and the ages of life. We can say that, no matter what one's age, the experience of shame, in the face of irreconcilable commandments, makes you become young again. Shame gives you the potentiality of the child, with the entire future opened-up in front of you. We must not fail to take seriously Deleuze (and Guattari's) claim in *What is Philosophy?* that "the feeling of shame [*honte*] is one of philosophy's most powerful motives" (Deleuze and Guattari 1994: 108). Deleuzians are often disappointed with this comment, because they think it betrays Deleuze's endorsement of Spinoza's joyful affects. Yet here, Deleuze is echoing Spinoza, who says that "the person who feels ashamed [*pudor*] has a desire to live honorably" (Spinoza 2002: 350, *Ethics*, Book IV, proposition 58). The experience of fundamental shame is *the* event because shame motivates one to change. It gives you the potentiality to become otherwise.

There is, however, a different affective register in reaction to fundamental violence. This reaction is fear, a feeling, as Aristotle knew, that is closely related to shame. Like shame, fear too motivates. Because I cannot stop others from entering in or from going out – recall that all limits are essentially porous – because I cannot stop the contamination of me, I attempt to repress their passage in or out. Out of fear of contamination (and therefore out of desire for purity), I try, or better, will the extermination of the others. Yet, because I am powerless to stop the contamination completely – others always continue to come in or to exit – I increase the will to extermination. And, moreover, I increase it to such a point that I start to approximate suicide. The contaminating others are inside me. I hear the murmur of their voices in my head. The war is in me. To stop the voices, I must silence myself; to stop the war, I must stop myself. As we saw earlier, the worst reaction – done out of fear – is a silencing and suicidal tendency, a hyperbolic tendency. At the limit, it is complete apocalypse. Here, with complete apocalypse fear – this fear is the heart that beats in the worst violence – seems to have been transformed into anxiety. No longer are we afraid of one thing, of anything in particular. We have become afraid of everything in general, of all the others. The worst reaction is, as Freud would say, a massive substitute formation. And, yes, this unlimited, indeed hyperbolic anxiety then looks to be a kind of madness.

What if this fear, however, evolves not from madness but from a kind of reasoning? What if this fear is not fear of the unknown, but fear of the known? With this question we come to the genuine stakes in the reversal of Platonism. Platonism thinks it knows what the primary *arché* is and what the ultimate *telos* is. If one thinks that one is going to lose the origin and not reach the purpose, one feels fear. We can imagine then that this fear is based in the supposed knowledge of an original principle and an ultimate end. It is fear based in the supposed knowledge of a prelapsarian origin and a post-lapsarian purpose. This fear arises when one thinks one knows absolute values that allow one to decide. The decision then drives the will to exterminate that which is not adequate to these supposed absolute values. In the experience of powerlessness, here in fear, one still thinks one knows what is best. This experience of powerlessness, however, has not reached the experience of undecidability. It still has not reached the experience of *the* event. It still has not felt shame, since shame, as a motivation for becoming otherwise, converts itself into courage, the courage not to will – but to let be.

## IV. Conclusion: Is it Happening?

What has been at issue throughout this chapter has been the experience of the event, which is the acute awareness of the fundamental and irreducible violence. It is the experience of the irreconcilable commandments of singularization and universalization. It is the acute awareness of undecidability. It is the experience of absolute non-knowledge. Then, as we have seen, beyond fear, we feel shame; shame at not being able to will, shame at not being able to stop the violence, shame at not being able to keep the others out or to hold them in. We feel shame at our lack of power. The necessity of these two forces is so strong that we are powerless *not* to obey their command. However, the shame motivates one to be otherwise. Instead of repressing the forces out of fear, we can, out of shame, let the forces be and become. Where does this power expressed in the "can" come from? It comes from the necessities themselves: if we are unable not to obey the commandments, *then we are able to obey the commandments*. In other words, unable to stop universalization, we are able to let it happen; unable to stop singularization, we are able to let it happen. If the worst violence consists in the reaction of repressing all the others coming into me, in the reaction of not letting all the others *in*, if we can define it, in other words, as *unconditional inhospitality*, then the least violence would be the reaction of letting all the others in unconditionally, that is, the least violence or perhaps the "best" as *unconditional hospitality*. Or, if the worst violence consists in the reaction of repressing all the others coming out of me, in the reaction of not letting all the others *out*, in other words, as *unconditional capture*, then the least violence would be the reaction of letting all the others out unconditionally, that is, the least violence or the "best" as *unconditional flight*. While we have invoked the Heideggerian idea of *Gelassenheit* through the verb "to let," this unconditionality would be anything but tranquil. It would have to have the courage to speak out and say: "Let all of them in, let all of them out, open all the prisons and hospitals, open them, no matter what!" If we can say that, then we can say it is happening, then we can say it is coming – even though, because of the straight line of time, we do not know strictly just what went by and precisely just what is coming. Never knowing strictly just what happened and never knowing precisely just what is going to happen, the question, "Is it happening?" remains therefore strictly unanswered and precisely unanswerable. I would like to add one more comment. I do not think that the unanswerability of the event happening is a cause for pessimism. I think it is a cause for something like hope since the unanswerability requires that we continue to try to find our way to the very least violence.

## Notes

1  Heidegger's important analysis of auto-affection appears in §34. Merleau-Ponty cites the Kant book in *Phenomenology of Perception* (Merleau-Ponty 2012: 561n29). Deleuze refers to the Kant book in 1956–57. Gilles Deleuze, *Qu'est-ce que fonder?* Cours hypokhâgne, Lycée Louis le Grand, 1956–1957, http://www.webdeleuze.com/php/sommaire.html. Heidegger's Kant book inspired Foucault's thesis on Kant's anthropology. Michel Foucault, *Introduction to Kant's Anthropology*, trans. Roberto Nigro and Kate Briggs (New York: Semiotext(e), 2008). Derrida refers to the Kant book in *Voice and Phenomenology* (Derrida 2011: 71). For more on Foucault's Introduction to Kant's Anthropology see my "The Origin of *Parrēsia* in Foucault's Thinking: Truth and Freedom in *The History of Madness*," (co-authored with Daniel J. Palumbo) in *Understanding Foucault, Understanding Modernism*, ed. David Scott (forthcoming with Bloomsbury Press).
2  Jean Hyppolite, *Genesis and Structure of Hegel's Phenomenology of Spirit*, trans. Samuel Cherniak and John Heckman (Evanston: Northwestern University Press, 1974), p. 143.
3  See Heath Massey's important study of Bergson's influence on Heidegger. Heath Massey, *The Origin of Time: Heidegger and Bergson* (Albany, NY: The SUNY Press, 2013).
4  This historical development towards immanence is based on my *Early Twentieth Century Continental Philosophy* (Bloomington: Indiana University Press, 2011).
5  Concerning the priority of both theory and practice (inseparable within the absolute foundation), I disagree with Martin Hägglund's view of Derrida. See Martin Hägglund, *Radical Atheism: Derrida and the Time of Life* (Stanford: Stanford University Press, 2008), pp. 96–7. Eddis N. Miller

(*Kantian Transpositions: Derrida and the Philosophy of Religion* [Evanston: Northwestern University Press, 2014]) agrees that Hägglund's interpretation of Derrida is a misconstrual: "Any attempt to completely empty Derrida's texts of all concrete ethico-political commitments can only result in a serious misconstrual of these texts. Such misconstrual is at work in Martin Hägglund, *Radical Atheism: Derrida and the Time of Life*" (p. 48). However, I am not really interested in squabbling about the correct reading of Derrida. No matter what, Hägglund's book is an important corrective to overly Levinasian readings of Derrida.

6   With these conceptual determinations of unlimited time, we are no longer speaking of phenomenological intentionality and its relation to the object. See Foucault 1970: 300. Also, Derrida 2011: 84–5.

7   While Aristotle here distinguishes between *aidos* (modesty or bashfulness, which is more appropriate to the young) and *aiskhyne* (disgrace or shame), it is clear that he thinks that the two emotions are connected.

## 4

# The Flipside of Violence, or Beyond the Thought of Good Enough

In one of his earliest and most significant texts, his 1964 "Violence and Metaphysics," Jacques Derrida says the following. The context for this quotation is Derrida's discussion of Levinas' thought of the other in relation to Husserl's phenomenology of the other. Derrida says:

> Every reduction of the other to a *real* moment of *my* life, its reduction to the state of an empirical alter-ego, is a possibility, or rather an empirical eventuality, which is called violence; and violence [that is, empirical or real violence] presupposes ... necessary eidetic [or ideal] relationships. [However,] there is a transcendental ... violence, an (in general dissymmetry) whose *arche* is the same ... This transcendental violence institutes the relationship between two finite ipseities. In effect, the necessity of gaining access to the meaning of the other (in its irreducible alterity) ... on the basis of an intentional modification of my ego (in general) ... and the necessity of speaking of the other as other, or to the other as other, on the basis of its appearing-for-me-as-what-it-is, that is, as other ... this necessity [of appearing or being a phenomenon] from which no discourse can escape, from its earliest origin – this necessity is violence itself, or rather the transcendental origin of an irreducible violence ... (Derrida 1978: 128)

The central idea in this quotation is twofold. On the one hand, Derrida is arguing that empirical or real violence presupposes eidetic or ideal relations such as the other appearing as what it is, as other. And, on the other hand, and, more importantly, Derrida is arguing that these eidetic necessities are themselves violent since they essentially force the other to be the same and no longer to be other: as he says, "there is a transcendental violence whose *arché* [or origin] is the same." In other words, what is most important about this quotation is that Derrida is arguing that violence is essentially irreducible. Thus we cannot, according to Derrida, speak of relations that are "absolutely peaceful." As we know, Derrida develops the idea of transcendental violence throughout his forty year career. And, for many of us, Derrida's idea of transcendental violence (and there are similar ideas in Foucault and Deleuze) has provoked a lot of thought. Recently, however, questions have been raised about the imagery of violence that one finds in certain kinds of contemporary philosophical discourses that are commonly called "poststructuralist," "postmodernist," or "deconstructive," that is, discourses in which Derrida was directly involved or which he inspired.[1] In this chapter, which is virtually the center of this book, I would like to respond to these questions. Then we shall be able to move from violence to speaking out.

The questions raised seem to consist in three types. The first and most important question goes like this: in the discourses that we commonly call "poststructuralist," "postmodernist," or "deconstructive," in a word, what we call "continental philosophy," the imagery of violence is so widespread that it is not clear whether those who compose the discourses really know that of which they speak when they use the word "violence." Obstacles, exclusions, and prohibitions, all of these are described through images of violence. Yet, the question is: is it really the case that these sorts of relationships are violent? Is blood really shed? Do these relations necessarily require the imagery of violence? Or are we who compose this sort of deconstructive discourse just confused? In short, through the charge of rampant confusion, this kind of question challenges the very legitimacy of the discourse.[2]

The second type of question concerns vigilance. It is closely related to the first, and it is perhaps just as important. It goes like this: when deconstructive discourses adopt the imagery of violence, calling it "originary," "transcendental," or "foundational," is deconstructive discourse "vigilant" enough in regard to what we might call "real," "physical," or "historical" violence?[3] Even though the sort of philosopher who raises this second type question about "real" violence acknowledges the necessity of violent imagery in deconstructive discourses, this sort of philosopher demands more vigilance so that the imagery of violence does not give off the impression of a tacit endorsement of "real" violence.

Then, there is a third kind of question, which is somewhat different to the first two. Here the question arises because, as we have already noted, the violence is irreducible[4] ("originary", "transcendental", or "foundational"), and if so then it seems any attempt to reduce violence is futile. The apparent futility resulting from the irreducibility of violence implies, as the argument goes, that nothing can be done. Consequently, the apparent futility seems to imply that there can be nothing like a moral principle in the strongest sense, which, I think, would have to be something like a categorical imperative, an unconditional imperative of non-violence or peace.[5]

Before I respond to each of these three questions directly in three sections of this chapter, I think we need to understand the background for the development of a fundamental discourse colored by imagery of violence. This background comes from the history of philosophy and especially from two landmarks in that history: Plato and Nietzsche. In particular, we must see how they speak about life. Here, however, as we have seen in Chapters 2 and 3, it is really Nietzsche's doctrine of eternal return that is most important. The eternal return doctrine sets up all the reflections on time in what I have called "the great French philosophy of the sixties" (that is, Derrida, Deleuze, and Foucault).[6] Then, after the historical background, in a second step (the second section, which responds to the first type of question), I would like to present a kind of "logic" (based in the structure of time) demonstrating why the imagery of violence is necessary for a transcendental investigation of the conditions for or the genesis of experience. Of course, I am going to argue here that the imagery of violence is necessary. However, I am less certain that necessity and appropriateness are identical. In her 1969 book, *On Violence*, Hannah Arendt had questioned the transfer of a set of concepts appropriate to one region to another region.[7] Starting therefore from a brief consideration of Arendt's book, I will take up the second kind of question concerning the need for vigilance (the third section, which responds to the second kind of question). There is no question that we need to be vigilant against real, empirical, or physical violence. However, thanks to an insight from Deleuze, I shall argue that we need to be even more vigilant. We need to be vigilant against all the forms of thinking and therefore forms of behavior that confine us, forms in which we have comfortably settled down.

Following this call for even more vigilance, we shall, in the third step (fourth and concluding section, which responds to the third kind of question), attempt to turn this fundamental violence around; we shall attempt to reverse it or "flip it over," hence the title of this chapter, "The Flipside of Violence." Indeed, as a response to the third kind of question concerning the imagery of violence in deconstructive discourses, the one that calls for a moral principle, I shall try to formulate something like a moral principle. However, unlike the sort of principle that this third kind of question calls for – one that allows for its untroubled application – the principle we find (if we can call it a principle), while unconditional and thus something like a categorical imperative, is unstable and troubling. This imperative makes us promise the impossible, which in turn makes us stop thinking that "the best guarantee" is "good enough,"[8] hence the chapter's subtitle, "Beyond the Thought of Good Enough." It is this impossibility that makes us be troubled, almost insanely troubled by the inescapable images of violence. However, before we reach this near madness, we must consider Plato and Nietzsche.

## I. The Soul and Life, Plato and Nietzsche

We begin with Plato for the obvious reason that his dialogues are the first truly philosophical discourse on the soul, but also a discourse with imagery of violence. Just as obvious, we shall look briefly at the two most famous discussions of the soul, the great myth of the *Phaedrus* and Book IV of the *Republic*. As you recall, the great myth of the *Phaedrus* presents not a direct discourse on the soul; instead Socrates there presents a "figure" (*eikon*) of what the soul is (Plato 1982a: 471, 246a). According to Socrates, the soul resembles a chariot, with a charioteer and two winged horses. For mixed souls, that is, human souls, the two winged horses are of a different kind, one good, the other evil.

The soul is trying through the winged horses to ascend to the banquet of the gods where one can view being or reality. But if the evil horse is not "well trained", then the ascent is difficult for the charioteer. Moreover, when many mixed souls attempt to ascend, there is rivalry and competition, resulting in many horses becoming lame and losing wings (248a). The *Republic* Book IV presentation of the soul is equally well known. Like the charioteer and two winged horses image of the *Phaedrus*, the *Republic* presents the soul as having what looks to be tripartite composition: the rational part (*logos*); the desiring or appetitive part (*epithumtikon*), which is irrational; and the spirited part (*thymos*). The *Republic* psychological discourse is less figurative than that of the *Phaedrus* since, in Book II, Socrates suggests to Glaucon that, in order to investigate justice in the individual, they first investigate justice in something bigger, which is the city (368c–369b). Then they will use the "likeness" (*homoiosis*) of the bigger in order to understand the smaller. So, in the *Republic*, Book IV, the discourse on the soul has moved away from the "likeness" of the larger image, the city, to the smaller, to what the soul in the individual really is. However, in Book IV, in order to explain the distinctive nature of the spirited part of the soul, Socrates makes use of a story (Plato 1968: 119, 439d). It is the story of Leontius who, when encountering corpses after an execution, has a strong desire to look at them; but at the same time he feels disgust and makes himself turn away from the vision of the corpses. Eventually however, his desire to look at the corpses "overpowers" (*kratos*) him and he looks. Socrates comments on this story by saying that it "certainly indicates that anger [that is, *thymos*] sometimes makes war [*polemos*] against the desires as one thing against something else" (Plato 1968: 119, 440a).

I would like to stress only two points about these two famous Platonic discourses. On the one hand, while the Platonic structure of the soul looks to be tripartite, it is really dualistic: there are the two horses, and then there are the rational part and the irrational part. The image of the charioteer and what is called "thymos," which look to be a third part, in fact function as means of synthesis or unification between the two parts. Yet, and this is my second point, in *Republic*, Book IV, *thymos*, as something like a synthetic third term, appears to be the place of war. And of course, one cannot overlook the imagery of violence in the *Phaedrus* with the so-called "bad horse" requiring "training," with horses getting injured in the ascent. Thus, over two thousand years before the rise of what we call "deconstructive discourse," we find violence within the very first psycho-philosophical discourse in the West. Perhaps, on the basis of this historical fact, we have to conclude that images of violence necessarily accompany every reflection on the soul and therefore on life. Certainly, Nietzsche thought that wherever there is life, there is violence.

We find the identification of life with violence in paragraph 11 of the second essay in *On the Genealogy of Morals*. In paragraph 11, Nietzsche says, "To talk of 'just' and 'unjust' *as such* is meaningless; an act of injury, violence, exploitation or destruction [*Verletzen, Vergewaltigen, Ausbedeuten, Vernichten*] cannot be 'unjust' *as such*, because life functions *essentially* in an injurious, violent, exploitative and destructive manner, or at least these are its fundamental processes [*Grundfunktionen*] and it cannot be thought of without these characteristics" (Nietzsche 1997: 50). Here, Nietzsche is describing life itself in terms of opposing forces, trying to take possession of one another. Importantly, in this description, Nietzsche indicates a necessity to life being violence (*Vergewaltigen*), and destruction or annihilation (*Vernichten*): life "*cannot* be thought of without these characteristics" (my emphasis). In short, Nietzsche is saying that violence is irreducible in life. As in Plato, in Nietzsche, life is fundamentally *polemos*; the opposing forces are brought together, so to speak, "synthesized," on a battlefield. Of course, this paragraph (11) and the one that follows it (paragraph 12) in *On the Genealogy of Morals* concern Nietzsche's idea of the will to power. But, we should notice that the "message" (if we can speak this way) of *On the Genealogy of Morals* is that the slaves, the weak, and therefore the powerless, have a sort of power that can undo the masters, the strong, and therefore the powerful. In fact, while the doctrine of the overman remains obscure, it seems that the overman (beyond the forms of thinking, such as those based in resentment, that define man) is someone who has incorporated this weak form of power.

We have mentioned two of the three most famous Nietzschean doctrines. In fact, if we look at the published version of Nietzsche's most important book, *Thus Spoke Zarathustra*, we see that, after the prologue which announces the death of God, the first book concerns the overman; the second book concerns the will to power; and the third book concerns the eternal return doctrine. The order of the three books indicates that the eternal return doctrine is most important; it is the very climax of *Thus Spoke Zarathustra*. Indeed, if the order of the books indicates a kind of priority or a movement toward the fundamental, then we have to realize that the eternal return doctrine is the basis for life.[9] Life is eternal return. In Book Three, in the paragraph called "The Vision and the Riddle," we find the clearest but also the most paradoxical presentation of the eternal return doctrine. The description of the doctrine and its images are well known, and we mentioned them above in Chapter 2. Nevertheless, I would like to draw our attention to three points in relation to the description and the images. *First*, Zarathustra stands under an archway called "the moment" (*Augenblick*). That the archway carries this name means not only that the eternal return doctrine concerns time, but also that it concerns a singular moment, in a word, difference. But, *second*, the archway crosses a road that extends endlessly in both directions, which Zarathustra calls "eternity." However, this image of an endless straight road implies that time does not wind itself into a circle. It does not return to a selfsame identical origin, *arché*, or principle, and thus it does not advance toward a selfsame identical end, *telos*, or principle. Time then is anarchical and a-teleological. *Third*, even though time is eternal in the sense of having no primary origin and no ultimate end, time is still a return or a repetition. The eternal return doctrine does not reduce time to an unlimited series of disconnected points. The return in the doctrine's name is supposed to account for the similarity of moments. This identification of life with time explains why Nietzsche's thought had such a tremendous influence on Derrida, Deleuze, and Foucault. All of their reflections on "difference and repetition" flow out of the eternal return doctrine, and in particular out of time conceived as anarchy and a-teleology. Of course, while we are using the word "anarchy" in the literal sense of having no origin or no principle, its popular meaning suggests nothing less than violence.

## II. The First Time is the Last Time (the response to the first kind of question)

We were just speaking of the tremendous influence of Nietzsche's eternal return doctrine on twentieth century French thought. However, it is impossible to underestimate the influence that Husserl's phenomenology exerted, directly and indirectly, through its discovery of the structure of time. What Husserl calls the "living present" is the absolute foundation of all of experience, all knowledge, all assertions of truth, all relations to objects and others. As we have seen, in his investigation of time-consciousness, Husserl shows that the present that we are actually living is divided between a primary form of memory called "retention" and a primary form of anticipation called "protention." For Husserl, these two primary forms are invariants across all experience. That retention and protention are irreducibly invariant implies that, no matter what experience occurs, there will always be a sense of it repeating something else that has already passed away and there will always be a sense of it anticipating something else that is still to come. In other words, retention generates a repeatable meaning which makes recognition possible, while protention generates a horizon of the same meaning within which recognition occurs. Thanks to this terminology, we can see already that Derrida's claim in "Violence and Metaphysics" is faithful to the phenomenological description of time. No matter what, if I am to have access to anything or anyone other, the other must appear. And insofar as it must appear, it must appear as something, as having a meaning. Thus it must appear as fulfilling a repeatable form. In order to have access to the other, the other must appear in the horizon of the same and thus, in order to be what it is, the other is deprived, *necessarily*, of its alterity. In short, the terminology, which is eidetically necessary for us to be able to understand time, suggests a violation of the other's alterity, in a word, it suggests violence.

*Moreover*, although Husserl speaks of the primal impression, of the moment that is happening right now, we have to see that this moment is stretched out between the immediate past and the immediate future. The present moment is differentiated, split apart, tortured by these two opposing movements. Immediate memory and immediate anticipation are irreducibly invariant, which means that all experience, no matter how apparently tranquil, is at bottom warlike. What Husserl calls "the primal impression" is, as we said of Plato's view of the soul, a battlefield. We need to introduce one more implication of Husserl's great discovery of the structure of the living present. Because retention and protention are irreducibly invariant across all experience, because these two opposing phases are fundamental or transcendental, because we cannot find anything like a present or a presence that is not contaminated by these two invariants, we cannot speak of an original starting point for the movement of time and we cannot speak of a final ending point for the movement of time. Like Nietzsche's eternal return doctrine, Husserl's structure of the living present implies anarchy and a-teleology.

The idea of time as anarchical and a-teleological is hard to understand. We can approach this difficult idea by thinking of artworks and in particular, of theater performances. Theater performances are not technological production, or, more precisely, not technological reproduction. In technological manufacturing, there must always be a model that is first; and on the basis of the model, there are the products that are second. The products, of course, are different from each other — they are individuals or particulars — since I can enumerate them. However, these different products are copies of the model and thus they must resemble or imitate the model as closely as possible. In manufacturing, clearly, no one wants to make products that do not function exactly the same. This maintenance of identity is what manufacturing quality control does: the copies must be identical and function identically. To speak like Deleuze, we can say that technological repetition is a repetition that does *not* make a difference. However, in French, of course, the word "répétition" means not only "repetition," but also "rehearsal," as in a theater rehearsal. Even the English word "re-hearsal" has the prefix which suggests repetition. If we think about theater rehearsals, one has to wonder what is being repeated. The idea of the rehearsal implies first that it is a copy or image of something. Yet, what is being rehearsed is nothing that precedes it insofar as what the performers are repeating or practicing in fact comes after the rehearsal: the main performance, "the premiere." Notice that the word "premiere" literally means "first." If we speak about a copy or image and the original on which the image is based, then with the rehearsal we have an original that comes second. But we still say, as the prefix "re" implies, that the rehearsal repeats something. If we say that the rehearsal repeats the script, then we have to say that the script refers to the idea that the author had for the performance. But, if we say that the rehearsal repeats the idea, then we also have to say that the idea is realized only in the performance that comes after the rehearsal. So, again we have a repetition which repeats something that comes after. In other words, unlike technological reproduction, a theater performance is a "creative repetition"; here we have a repetition that *indeed* makes a difference. An event such as the writing of *Hamlet* was based in no determinate model, no exact foundation, and no self-identical origin; therefore its subsequent theater productions, while repetitions, are able to be different from one another. Each performance is not a particular (that could be subsumed under a self-identical concept); each is an event or a singularity.

The idea of creative repetition seems to suggest no violence. However, images of violence are necessary because, *first of all*, creative repetition includes novelties, events, or singularities. Despite the apparent regularity of time (time as it is organized by representations and concepts), time is filled with singularities. As evidence of singularities, we can point to aha-experiences; realizations; surprises; experiences that are intense to the point of pleasure or pain – like a boiling point or a blinding light. Perhaps, the most banal evidence for singularities in time are dates on the calendar isolating the uniqueness of each day. In order to be able to account for these unique dates and unique experiences, we must think that there is something in the structure of time that is always singular, always event-like, and always new. As we saw, Nietzsche called the singularity within time the "moment" (*Augenblick*). How are we to think of the singular moment?

By attempting to answer the question of how to think of the singular moment, we are trying to avoid the confusion charged in the first kind of question. In order to avoid confusion, we must insist on taking the meaning of the terms we are using in a *proper* sense. We must think of a singular moment properly, as a singularity worthy of that name. The logic that we are now going to lay out consists in four steps. (1) *To begin*, if we conceive singularity in the most proper way possible (as novel, event-like, unique), then, most formally and abstractly, we must describe a singularity as a *first time*. More substantially and concretely, however, we must say that the force of the moment disappoints; its eruption interrupts and disrupts expectations; it fractures them and breaks expectations apart. The moment changes and transforms; but it also deforms and un-forms, it undoes and destroys. The singular moment eats its way in; it intrudes like a guest. (2) *But also*, we have to recognize that, if the moment is properly singular, unique, event-like, and novel, then as a first time a singularity is also and necessarily a last time. We must conceive a first time as a last time. In order to be a first time properly, in order to be *unlike* any other time, there can be no other time like it ever again. If there were another time *like* the first time, then this similarity would impress, depress, and repress the singularity; it would push the singularity away and replace it. Due to this similarity, we would not be able to say that we experienced an event – and perhaps we have to wonder whether we ever truly experience an event as such, whether it is ever possible to speak of an event since as soon as we speak we engage in generalities. The moment then becomes something lost, imprisoned, entombed, and archived. Indeed, we have to say that the flow of time, *on the one hand*, consists in singularities, *but also* (with this "but also" we are referring to a strange kind of non-unifying synthesis that we discussed in the last chapter) we have to say that time, *on the other hand*, consists in generalities. We must say that time also consists in generalities for the following reason. If there is something like a singularity in time, then, as we saw in our discussion of Husserlian temporalization, it cannot not appear without a horizon of expectation formed by past experiences. These past experiences form a horizon of expectation because they retain some feature or trait of the experience that is repeatable or iterable, which is a generality. (3) *Here*, we pass from the description of singularities to that of generalities. Again, in order to avoid confusion, we must think of a force of generality worthy of that name. If we think of generality properly, then we must describe generality, most formally and abstractly, as a feature or a trait that endures at all times; it is omni-temporal; it repeats indefinitely, to infinity, even universally. More substantially and concretely, however, we must say that the force of generality expresses and extends; it moves away and goes over; it breaks free and opens; it transcends and transgresses. The generality eats its way out and escapes like a criminal fleeing a prison. (4) *Finally*, we return to our earlier description of creative repetition. This description of generality means that, even as a generality extends its sameness indefinitely, at the same time, a generality worthy of its names makes possible or generate more events; and, as they come, these events worthy of the name, at the same time, make possible or generate more generalities.

At the root of this four-part logic, we find the most fundamental reason necessitating the imagery of violence – the irreducibility of negativity in life, in lived-experience. Many philosophers have recognized the irreducibility of negativity in experience.[11] But here, thanks to the invariant structure of time, we have a negativity based in the past and future being synthesized but without unity, the strange synthesis we mentioned earlier: the battlefield. In other words, the limit between past and future is porous. This negativity is based on an eidetic, structural, fundamental, or transcendental *inability* to keep out events and on an eidetic, structural, fundamental, or transcendental *inability* to keep in generalities. The first time cannot *not* be a last time, and vice versa. Expressed abstractly and transcendentally as a first time and a last time, the fundamental negativity of experience does not mean that every experience is one of bloodshed. We must not be confused on this point. However, the fundamental and irreducible negativity of experience (the in-ability or disability) implies necessarily that every experience contains within it the *essential possibility* of what we call "real violence" (Derrida 1988: 42–3). *Most simply*, because experience is fundamentally passive and receptive, I am necessarily open to what is coming. I am unable to stop what is coming and coming in. As soon as I open my eyes – and we should notice that even when my eyes are shut during sleep, I am still open since if I were not open I would not be able to be awoken (Merleau-Ponty 2012: 166–7) – something enters in. Because of this openness or non-closedness, this porosity, the structure of experience essentially includes the possibility of real intrusion, real violation, and real violence. As Derrida has already implied in "Violence and Metaphysics," the essential porosity of the limit is the very condition for real violence. Again, we must stress that this logic does not mean that every experience I have is one of bloodshed. Not every experience implies that I have suffered a mortal wound. However, the structure of experience implies that as soon as I am born, I am dying. As soon as I experience, I am open to every possible event that is coming, the most possible of which being my death. Or we can think of this structural death in this way: as soon as I experience, I remember and anticipate, through which a form is generated that is repeatable indefinitely beyond my finite life. I am fundamentally unable to enclose this generality within the time of my life; it survives while I am unable to do so. Because of this survival in the literal sense of going over and beyond life, I am unable to stop what is going and going away, what is taking and being taken away – such as my life.

## III. More Vigilance (the response to the second kind of question)

If there is one claim that truly clarifies the logic that we have just laid out it is this: within the structure of time, we find the *essential possibility* of real violence. This explains why images of violence are necessary in the descriptions of time. Yet, to say this again, the essential possibility of violence, and the images of violence it requires, what we are calling "transcendental violence," is *not* real violence. Despite this unequivocal assertion, we realize that we must still be vigilant. We must constantly remind ourselves that transcendental violence is not real violence. We must not let the imagery of violence used in transcendental discourse dull us to real violence and bloodshed. However, it seems to me that this kind of call for vigilance in relation to the difference between real violence and transcendental violence (that is, the essential possibility of real or actual violence) is not enough. We really need to be even more vigilant.

Again the demand for vigilance comes from a confusion. There is, for instance, a danger of confusing biological discourse with that of political action. In other words, the danger is the importation of imagery and thinking that is appropriate to one region – the region of biology – into another region – the region of human action – in which it is inappropriate. Indeed, this dangerous confusion of biology and political action is the danger that Arendt pointed out in *On Violence* (Arendt 1969: 74). As she says, "None of the properties of creativity is adequately expressed in metaphors drawn from the life process" (Arendt 1969: 82). However, beside the confusion of regions of discourse, there is also the danger, which I think might be worse, of confusing the discourse of a founded region with fundamental discourse. This is the danger Husserl pointed to early in his career: the danger of a vicious circle between the psychological or empirical with the transcendental or foundational. And Heidegger's constant reflections on the ontological difference concern the same vicious circle danger. It is Deleuze, however, who gives this dangerous confusion its clearest expression. In *The Logic of Sense*, Deleuze says, "The foundation can never resemble what it founds" (Deleuze 1990: 99). Deleuze's "principle" for the formulation of a foundation means that we must never import images into the foundation that originate in founded regions. It is this principle that forbids us from importing life-processes, including images of violence, into the foundation, in this case, into the essential structure of time. Here we must be especially vigilant. While the structure of time that we have laid out requires violent images, we must recognize that those images, imported from a founded region, remain inappropriate to the foundation. The vigilance we are speaking about now is a vigilance to continue to find new and different ways to think. I have deliberately removed the object from this phrase "to think" in order to indicate that the vigilance now required demands that we think beyond any constituted object or given subject, beyond any real fact or ideal essence, beyond anything at all.[12] Only through this thinking of nothing (in particular) will we be able to criticize and move beyond the current forms of thinking that confine us. The vigilance we are now speaking about demands of us that we constantly tell ourselves that these formulations, these images, these ideas and concepts are *not good enough*. Only with the recognition of this insufficiency of our current forms of thinking will we be able to find new modes through which we can discover ways to combat real violence and real injustice. This recognition of insufficient thinking brings us to the third kind of question raised about transcendental violence.

## IV. Conclusion: The Flipside of Violence (the response to the third kind of question)

As you recall, this third kind of question, in effect, rejects the apparent futility of eliminating violence. Instead, it asks us to return to moral principles, which are themselves based on stable foundations.[13] Let us reexamine the foundation we have been discussing throughout and especially reexamine it in light of Deleuze's principle of non-resemblance. At the beginning of our investigation, we quoted a long passage from Derrida's "Violence and Metaphysics." In that quotation, Derrida says, "[These] necessities [that is, the eidetic necessities such as the other appearing to me as other] are violence itself, or rather the transcendental origin of an irreducible violence … " Derrida continues in this way: "[These] necessities are violence itself, or rather the transcendental origin of an irreducible violence, supposing … that it is somehow meaningful to speak of pre-ethical violence. *For* [my emphasis] this transcendental origin, as the irreducible violence of the relation to the other, is *at the same time* [my emphasis] non-violence, since it opens the relation to the other" (Derrida 1978: 128, Derrida's italics). I would like to stress three aspects of this quotation. (1) *First*, we should notice that here Derrida speaks not only of "this transcendental origin" or of "irreducible violence," but also of "pre-ethical violence." That is, the violence of which we are now speaking is not the violence that we normally imagine. In short, it is not violence that is willed. If this violence does not resemble the violence we normally and currently imagine, then how are we to think of it? You can see, I hope, that the foundation (transcendental violence) that Derrida is trying to formulate does not violate Deleuze's principle of non-resemblance. The non-resemblance between this violence and normal or "real" violence explains why Derrida wonders if pre-ethical violence makes any sense. (2) Then, *second*, we should notice that, after Derrida wonders about pre-ethical violence making any sense, he says "for" (*car*). The explanation for this wonder about the meaningfulness of pre-ethical violence really lies in the following sentence. In fact, the explanation lies in the phrase "at the same time" (*en même temps*). (3) *Third*, "for at the same time," the irreducible violence of the relation to the other is nonviolence.[14] So, the foundation or structure that Derrida is formulating for us is self-contradictory, between violence and non-violence. The irreducibly violent relation to the other, Derrida says, "opens [*ouvre*] the relation to the other," the very relation that is non-violent. Being violent and non-violent, this foundation cannot therefore be stable.

However, are we able to generate a principle, even perhaps, a moral principle, from this unstable, self-contradictory "foundation"? If we are going to do so, minimally it would have to exhibit the same self-contradictory structure of violence and non-violence. However, the self-contradiction expressed in the structure also includes the terms same and other. This opposition gives us a clue about what the principle might be. Another clue comes to us from the development of Derrida's thinking. Immediately following the quotation we have been examining, Derrida says simply that "it is an *economy*," and highlights the word "economy" (Derrida 1978: 128).[15] We know that, as Derrida's thinking develops, he becomes more and more interested in the literal meaning of the word "economy," as the law of the home (from the Greek "oikonomia"). The word "economy" then comes to be associated with the problem of hospitality (Derrida 2000a). However, in 1967 (the publication date of *Writing and Difference*, in which "Violence and Metaphysics" is collected), the word "economy," undoubtedly, must be charged with Marxist connotations. It is not until 1993, of course, that Derrida writes a book on Marx, *Specters of Marx*. Near the end of *Specters of Marx*, we find this strange sentence: "tout autre est tout autre" (Derrida 1994: 173; Derrida 2008a: 82–3).[16]

To conclude, let us investigate this sentence. The key to this sentence lies in the copula, which is both predicative and existential. What is wholly other *is* (the existential copula), and thus since it is *something*, it is not purely wholly other; and yet, what is wholly other *is* (the predicative copula) wholly other, and thus asserting itself as such the other is wholly other. In other words, the quality of "wholly-other" is attributed to the wholly other (predicative), and yet the wholly other exists as something that is the same as everything else (existential). Clearly, the sentence is self-contradictory.

We can elaborate on this analysis in the following way. The sentence "tout autre est tout autre" is *first of all* a tautology: "every other is every other." Here, with the tautology, we have an assertion of existential equivalency. There is no difference between anything: "every other is simply the same as every other." With this tautological rephrasing, with this sameness, we have the violence toward the other. The assertion does not respect the other's alterity as such; it represses the other's singularity within the generality of the "every." But, there is a *second* way of understanding the tautology: "tout autre est tout autre" could be rendered in English as "wholly other *is* wholly other." This rephrasing is still a tautology since on either side of the copula, one finds the same phrase. Nevertheless, despite the apparent tautology, this rephrasing stresses the attribute of wholly otherness. The stress of the copula could even lead us to add an exclamation mark at the end of the sentence. Now it would seem to be saying: "Make no mistake! The wholly other is truly, really, unequivocally wholly other!" Rephrased in this way, the sentence provides a clear expression of otherness. Now the sentence says nothing but alterity. It now respects the other's alterity as such, and the violence of the expression seems to have been removed. Nevertheless, the two versions of "tout autre est tout autre" together confront us with the same self-contradiction we have seen before: between sameness and otherness, between violence and non-violence. Yet, there is a *third* way to render the sentence. "Tout autre est tout autre" could mean that "each and every other is wholly other." With this, we approach something like a principle, even a moral principle. If we accept the language of respect for the other introduced already in the interpretations of "tout autre est tout autre," and if one then accepts the third rendering in which every single other must be considered as wholly other, and finally if one also accepts the addition of the exclamation mark, then we are confronted with an imperative that says the following: that every single other – all of them – must be treated with respect. The imperative is unconditional, since it includes all others, every single one of them. The unconditional status of the imperative even commands us to promise, to say this again, to respect every single one. The universality of the commandment includes not just those present, but also those who have already passed away and those still to come. The imperative commands us to promise to remember all the others who have passed away to and to anticipate all the others still to come. The imperative says: "Promise that you will treat every single other, all of them, everywhere and at all times, with respect!" The promise is perhaps even the promise of perpetual peace.

The question now is obvious: can this promise be kept? Immediately, one will say "no." However, the reason for the impossibility of keeping the promise does not lie in the factual conditions of me being unable to find every single other. The reason for the impossibility is structural. No one is able to balance the singularity or finitude of experience with its generality or infinitude. I am able to let the other enter into me, but when I do, the opening makes the other the same as me. I am able to let a generality take flight, but that will always land in a singularity. In short, there can never be justice. And the impossibility of justice means that something like violence in experience, even in the most non-violent experience, can never be eliminated. This should, I hope, destroy any sense of good conscience. It should trouble us. It should not allow us to settle into the smug attitude in which we think that what we have thought, conceived, and done is "good enough." It should stop us from becoming comfortable. We must not think that, because we have a stable moral principle by means of which we can decide against violence, we can be done with violence once and for all. No, instead, and this is the aim of deconstruction, I must make myself experience, *acutely*, the imperative of the promise and, I must make myself experience, *acutely*, the impossibility of me keeping the promise. Then, I undergo this mad imagination of violence, the imagination of so much violence being done to every single other that I could not *not* feel insufficient. The *feeling* of insufficiency would then move me. It would move me to force myself to keep trying to keep the promise: eliminate violence of any kind, for every single other, found anywhere in the world or outside the world! This interminable effort to keep the promise is really the flipside of violence.

## Notes

1 Ann V. Murphy, *Violence and the Philosophical Imaginary* (Albany, NY: The SUNY Press, 2012). Erinn Gilson, "Review of Ann Murphy, *Violence and the Philosophical Imaginary*," in *Journal of French and Francophone Philosophy*, vol. XXI, no. 1 (2013), pp. 173–82. Gary Steiner, *Animals and the Limits of Postmodernism* (New York: Columbia University Press, 2013).
2 Gilson, "Review of Murphy," pp. 179–80.
3 Murphy, *Violence and the Philosophical Imaginary*, p. 117. See also Johanna Oksala, *Foucault, Politics, and Violence* (Evanston: Northwestern University Press, 2012), in particular, Chapter 2 "Foundational Violence." Oksala expresses concerns that foundational violence does not take into account "physical" and "historical" violence: "My central claim is, however, that the investigation of the constitutive role of physical violence must be thoroughly historical and must not rely on any ontologized notion of originary violence as such."
4 To be clear, everything I am saying here is opposed to violence, especially in light of violence's "stupidity," as James Dodd has called violence. James Dodd, *Violence and Phenomenology* (London: Routledge, 2009), p. 12. For another very careful account of violence in Derrida, see Samir Haddad, "A Genealogy of Violence, from Light to the Autoimmune," in *Diacritics* 4.2 (2011): 173–93.
5 Steiner, *Animals and the Limits of Postmodernism*, p. 131.
6 See Leonard Lawlor, *Thinking through French Philosophy* (Bloomington: Indiana University Press, 2003), and *Early Twentieth Century Continental Philosophy* (Bloomington: Indiana University Press, 2011).
7 The second question of violence echoes what Hannah Arendt says in her small 1969 book called *On Violence* (Arendt 1969), to which I shall return below.
8 Steiner, *Animals and the Limits of Postmodernism*, p. 154.
9 Even though Steiner recognizes the great influence of Nietzsche on Derrida and Foucault's thought, he does not take up the role that the eternal return doctrine plays in their thinking.

10 Derrida 2005: 2. The same phrase, "the first time is the last time" also appears in *Specters of Marx* (Derrida 1994: 10).
11 One immediately thinks of Hegel. But more recently Barbaras has stressed this negativity in his "privative anthropology." See Renaud Barbaras, *Introduction à la phénoménologie de la vie* (Paris: Vrin, 2008), p. 249.
12 See Heidegger's "What is Metaphysics," for the thought of the nothing (Heidegger 1998: 82–96). Also, see Foucault's "The Thought of the Outside" (Foucault 1998: 147–69).
13 Steiner, *Animals and the Limits of Postmodernism*, pp. 146, 164, and 210.
14 In more writings more recent than "Violence and Metaphysics," Derrida refers to the non-violent side of this relation with Heidegger's idea of *Zusage*, acquiescence. See Derrida 1989a: 129n5. He also speaks of as an address that implies friendship or even an "I love you" in *Politics of Friendship* (Derrida 1997: 215–16). Indeed in *Politics of Friendship*, Derrida speaks of this prior friendship as a "temptation," the temptation "of the book you are reading [that is, of *Politics of Friendship*]." He adds, however, that it is a temptation that the book also resists. The temptation and the resistance to the temptation implies, even in 1994, both non-violence and violence at the same time.
15 By comparing the 1967 *Writing and Difference* version of "Violence and Metaphysics" to the original 1964 version in *Revue de métaphysique et de morale*, we see that the sentence "c'est une économie" is a 1967 addition. My thanks always to Robert Bernasconi who did the first real investigation of the differences between the two published versions of "Violence and Metaphysics."
16 I first tried to analyze this sentence in *Derrida and Husserl* (Bloomington: Indiana University Press, 2002), pp. 221–2.

# Part II: Three Ways of Speaking

# 5

# Auto-Affection and Becoming: Following the Rats

As we pointed out in Chapter 1, globalization defines the epoch in which we are living right now. As we noted, the word "globalization" means that the earth has been or is trying to be enclosed within a globe. Enclosing the earth in a globe means that all the ways out have been closed, so that one species, the human, is able to dominate all the other species. What justifies, what gives us the right to dominate the animals? The answer to this question is well-known: humans believe they have the right to dominate because humans believe that they possess a special kind of subjectivity. The concept of subjectivity that we think we possess has its conceptual origins in Descartes' "cogito," but the concept of the "I think" develops into the Kantian idea of autonomy. The Kantian idea means of course that I am self-ruling; I give the moral law to myself, unlike the animals upon which nature imposes its laws. But in order to give the law to myself, I must tell it to myself. Kantian autonomy therefore is based on auto-affection. What makes me, as a human, autonomous is my supposed ability to hear myself speak at the very moment I speak. Because the voice seems to be purely immediate and mine, I hear myself speak in pure presence. This supposed pure self-presence gives humans a dignity that far surpasses that of animals. It justifies the human right to domination.

But, Derrida has shown in *Voice and Phenomenon* that auto-affection is never pure self-presence (Derrida 2011: 60–74). And, Deleuze in *Difference and Repetition* has shown that, when Kant introduces receptivity into the self, this puts a crack in the self (Deleuze 1995: 84). These arguments show that human auto-affection is really and always hetero-affection; that within thought there is something that cannot be thought and yet demands to be thought. It seems to me that these arguments against the purity of auto-affection cannot be reversed or ignored. As we quickly see, they provide us with the means to criticize our current times (Deleuze and Guattari 1994: 108), the times in which all living things are enclosed in a globe for human use, the times in which a kind of war is being waged against animal life. What must we do to stop (or at least slow down) this war, what must we do to bring about some change in the collective human relation to animals? To put this as dramatically as possible, we must stop being human. But such a dramatic claim means that we must undermine human auto-affection; indeed, we must enlarge the concept of auto-affection. In thought, in my interior monologue, when I hear myself speak, I also inseparably do *not* hear myself. What do I hear if not my "self"? I hear the other voices of the animals. When I hear myself speak, I also inseparably hear the gnashing of the teeth of an animal in the agony of death. The voice of the animal is in me, and thereby I undergo the ways that animals change or *become*. We have gone from auto-affection to becoming, hence the title of this essay. We could even say that we have gone from Derrida's thought to that of Deleuze (or to that of Deleuze and Guattari).

We shall return to Derrida's thought at the end, and, as we shall see, the intersection of Derrida's thought with that of Deleuze provides us with a double strategy in regard to the collective human relation to animals. But, primarily in what follows, we shall focus on the concept of becoming that Deleuze and Guattari develop in the Tenth Plateau of *A Thousand Plateaus* (Deleuze and Guattari 1987). The Tenth Plateau is the longest chapter in the book, ninety-seven pages in the original French edition; it is also remarkably complicated. What I am going to do is lay out a kind of plan for becomings in general. First, we shall identify the agent, the condition, the positive definition of, and the motive for becoming; these are respectively: aging, desubjectification, minority, and affects. Like Levinas (Levinas 1981: 14 and 38), Deleuze and Guattari recognize the power that aging has to unmake the molar form of the subject, making the person susceptible to the affects of love and shame, affects which motivate the person to become minor. All becomings in Deleuze and Guattari are defined by becoming-minor. But then, we shall formulate the negative definitions, the prepositions, the structure, and the criterion for becoming; these are respectively: becoming is not imitation; the prepositions are "before," "in," and "for" ("devant," "en," and "pour" in French); becoming consists in a zigzag structure, and the criterion is writing. In Deleuze and Guattari, becoming is never a process of imitating, and yet the one who becomes finds oneself before another who ends up being in oneself. With the other in me, however, I am not substituting myself for another; the structure of becoming is not reciprocal. It is a zigzag in which I become other so that the other may become something else, but this becoming something else is possible only if a work (*œuvre*) is produced.[1] It seems to me that no one has sufficiently recognized this fact: for Deleuze and Guattari, a becoming is successful only if writing results.[2] Without the tangible result of a creation, becoming fails and becomes a bare repetitious circle of the same behavior, or worse, suicide. But then third, after having laid out the general plan for becomings, we shall examine a particular kind of becoming, becoming rat. At the end, as the subtitle suggests, we shall follow the rats.

Why rats? Early in the Tenth Plateau, Deleuze and Guattari distinguish three kinds of animals: individuated animals, the family pet, with its own little story; animals with attributes which are taken up into myths; and animals who travel in packs, inspiring tales (Deleuze and Guattari 1987: 240–1). Deleuze and Guattari valorize the animals who travel in packs, and this valorization of the pack animals is why rats play such an important role in the Tenth Plateau.[3] The Tenth Plateau opens with the "tale" of the rat named Ben, the tale presented in the 1972 film called "Willard" (Deleuze and Guattari 1987: 233). But rats appear four other times in the Tenth Plateau (Deleuze and Guattari 1987: 240, 258, 262, and 275). If we want to understand becoming in Deleuze and Guattari, then we must understand becoming rat. As we shall see, when I become rat, the rat becomes a "feverish thought" in me, forcing me to think. And, in response to the gnashing rat thought, I do not start to look like a rat. No, instead, I start to write like a rat, which is to write in the style of the rat's agony, to fabulate a tale of rats – so that the work produced will call forth a new people. Writing like a rat, we might be able to call forth a people who themselves have the feverish thought of the rat in them, forcing them to think differently. Perhaps this thoughtful people would say, "This right that I seem to have is not justified." Then perhaps we would see coming, a people who would no longer enclose the world in a globe.

## I. The Agent, Condition, Positive Definition of and Motive for Becoming (Aging, Desubjectification, Minority, and Affect)

To be blunt, if we want to change our relationship to the world, to others, and to animals, we must understand how it is possible for us to change, in other word, how it is possible to enter into the experience of becoming. Deleuze and Guattari suggest that the cause or "agent" of becoming may be the experience that drugs produce in us (Deleuze and Guattari 1987: 283, see also Deleuze and Guattari 1994: 165). Now while such a suggestion may seem infamous, one must recognize that hallucinogenic drugs change our perceptions (Deleuze and Guattari 1987: 278). Nevertheless, for Deleuze and Guattari, taking such drugs does not constitute a *successful* becoming. The failure is due to the fact that the drug user, and especially the addict, enters only into a cycle. He or she gets high; then he or she comes down; and then the drug user wants to get high again; gets high again; and then comes down; and so on. This cycle or circle is all that happens, which means in fact that nothing happens. For Deleuze and Guattari, becomings are never processes of beginning *again*, they are never processes that move only in a circle: get high; come down; get high again. We can also see this cyclic behavior in the alcoholic's idea of the last glass (Deleuze and Guattari 1987: 438). The last glass is based on a subjective evaluation of how much the alcoholic is able to bear. Deleuze and Guattari say, "What can be tolerated is precisely the *limit* at which, as the alcoholic sees it, he or she will be able *to start over again* [*recommencer*] (after a rest, a pause ... )" (Deleuze and Guattari 1987: 438). Nothing therefore with the alcoholic happens but the same thing over and over again; recommencement is not an event.

Although the concepts of limit and recommencement are very important for understanding *A Thousand Plateaus* – early in the book, they say that the body without organs is a limit and that one is always attaining it (Deleuze and Guattari 1987: 159) – Deleuze and Guattari oppose the concept of limit to that of threshold. The threshold lies beyond the limit, beyond the last glass; crossing the threshold, they say, makes the alcoholic change, to become suicidal or to stop drinking. For Deleuze and Guattari, either choice would break out of the circle. The two choices however are clearly not identical; it is the choice between choice and non-choice (Deleuze 1989: 177). The choice to commit suicide by drinking oneself to death is to choose to have no more choices, while the choice to stop drinking allows one to choose again and differently. The choice of more choices – to get drunk by drinking water[4] constitutes what Deleuze and Guattari call an event (or a line of flight).

But still, when the threshold has been crossed, we can ask "what happened?" The character of the alcoholic does not allude to Proust (although he is mentioned in relation to the concept of threshold: the narrator crosses the threshold and chooses to stop having love affairs and to start writing); the alcoholic refers to F. Scott Fitzgerald. In the Eighth Plateau, Deleuze and Guattari tell us that "what happened?" is the question that Fitzgerald keeps coming back to, at the end, after having said that "all life of course is a process of breaking down [*démolition*]" (Deleuze and Guattari 1987: 198; Deleuze 1989: 50). With the idea of demolition or destruction or unmaking, we come to the true agent (it's not drug experimentation) and condition of becoming. According to Deleuze and Guattari, in a life, there is a type of cracking that is micrological, like the small, almost imperceptible cracks in a dish (Deleuze and Guattari 1987: 198).

These cracks in a life are the cracks of aging. Such cracks are not big molar blows like the blow of losing all of your money in the stock market. The micrological cracks in a life refer us to this sort of experience: you wake up one morning and you realize you have gray hair, and now it's over, you're old; or you wake up and realize that you no longer love the person in bed with you. What has exactly happened is nothing assignable or perceptible; these are molecular changes, "such that when something occurs, the self [*moi*] that awaited it is already dead, or the one that would await it has not yet arrived" (Deleuze and Guattari 1987: 198–9). The micrological cracks of aging, these experiences in which one is finally aware that one has lost something of oneself, are the agent of becoming. But aging also indicates the necessary condition for becoming: the condition in which one's molar form is destroyed, the condition, in other words, of "desubjectification" (Deleuze and Guattari 1987: 159).

The condition of the molar form of the subject being destroyed has however a positive side which we have already encountered, the choice of having more choices.[5] But Deleuze and Guattari also call the positive side of desubjectification "rupture," the word being their French translation of Fitzgerald's English "clean break" (Deleuze and Guattari 1987: 199). The clean break which aging causes – again aging is the *agent* of becoming, while the destruction of the molar form is the necessary condition – does not mean that now one remains forever young. It means that, having shed the form of an adult, one is able to become something other than an adult man. One becomes a child, but that means that one frees the potentialities that the molar form of adult man was enclosing. Deleuze and Guattari say, with a rupture,

> I am now no more than a line. I have become capable of loving, not with an abstract, universal love, but a love I shall choose, and that shall choose me, blindly, my double, who has no more self than me [*n'a pas plus de moi que moi*]. One has been saved by love and for love, by abandoning love and self [*moi*]... One has become like everyone [*tout le monde*: the whole world], but in a way in which no one [*personne*] can become like everyone [*tout le monde*: the whole world]. (Deleuze and Guattari 1987: 199–200)

By means of this quote (whose importance we should not underestimate), we see that becoming involves love; but love in Deleuze and Guattari is no longer a feeling between persons; it is no longer a personal feeling (Deleuze and Guattari 1987: 240; also pp. 105–6). Love is now an affect.[6] As Deleuze and Guattari say, a feeling (*sentiment*) is the sense (*sens*) of a form and its development, the formation of a subject; it is introceptive. In contrast, an affect is informal, setting out ways (instead of the development of a form); an affect is a projectile (instead of a feeling that is introjected), a relation outward to the double (Deleuze and Guattari 1987: 399–400). But since the double is not an "I" or an ego, since it is not a molar unified self or subject, the double is really a multiplicity. Insofar as the love they are describing is not restricted to a feeling between persons, insofar as the love they are describing is a love of multiplicity, we see as well that becoming in Deleuze and Guattari is hyperbolic; it is the love of the whole world (*tout le monde*).[7] And as love of the whole world (a utopian love), this love frees the potentiality of everyone (*tout le monde*).

So, while aging is the agent which puts in place the condition of the demolished molar form of the subject, the motive or motor of becoming is the affect (the affect as the motor of desubjectification just as the function, to which we shall turn in a moment, is the motor of deterritorialization). But we must extend the idea of the motor of becoming. The imperceptible events of aging undo the molar form of oneself, which allows one to choose a clean break, in other words, to choose to become. And this choice of becoming is a choice to love the whole world; this is a love, we just saw, that differs from the abstract universal love of persons. This love is no longer a feeling of one molar person or ego for another molar person or ego; it is in short no longer human love, no longer the love of man. Thus, as Deleuze and Guattari would say, it is a love of the minor. As is well known, all becomings in Deleuze and Guattari are becomings minor, but let us look at their exact definition in *A Thousand Plateaus*.[8] First, they tell us that there are "no becoming-man ... because man is majoritarian par excellence."[9] Then they state the positive definition: "all becoming is a becoming-minoritarian" (Deleuze and Guattari 1987: 291). A minority, for Deleuze and Guattari is not defined by statistics; it is not "quantitative" or a "definable aggregate" (Deleuze and Guattari 1987: 105 and 291). Women are a minority for Deleuze and Guattari, not because there are fewer women than men in a given population. Women are a minority because "the body is stolen first from the girl ... The girl's becoming is stolen first ... The girl is the first *victim*" (Deleuze and Guattari 1987: 276, my emphasis). The positive definition of becoming therefore is not really a minor existence; it is that this minor existence is "oppressed" (Deleuze and Guattari 1987: 247), "wronged" (*indûment*) (Deleuze and Guattari 1987: 159; Deleuze 1989: 215); minor existence is one that is undergoing, as Deleuze and Guattari say in *What is Philosophy?*, "abominable sufferings" (Deleuze and Guattari 1994: 110). Abominable suffering is what defines a minority for

Deleuze and Guattari. And the affect felt before this extreme suffering is "the shame of being a man" (Deleuze and Guattari 1994: 107). The affect of shame at being a man, at being human all too human, with our oppressions, our clichés, our opinions, and our desires, is really the *motive* for change.[10]

## II. The Negative Definitions, the Prepositions, the Structure, and the Criterion for Becoming

We have just seen one negative definition of becoming; there is no becoming major, no becoming man. But there are several more negative definitions. As we can see with the micrological process of aging, for Deleuze and Guattari, a process of becoming does not terminate in a molar form; in micrological aging, one, a subject, does *not* grow up to be an adult, a girl does *not* grow up to be a woman. So, when speaking of becoming animal, they say, "Becoming can and should be qualified as becoming-animal even in the absence of an endpoint [*un terme*] that would be the animal which one has become" (Deleuze and Guattari 1987: 238). So, the experience of becoming is *not* an experience directed toward or oriented by a final form. The lack of finalism is why Deleuze and Guattari separate becoming from history (Deleuze and Guattari 1987: 296). But they go further. If there is no final form into which one transforms oneself, then becoming is *not* based in imitation, resemblance, or analogy. The adverb "like" (or, in French, "comme") does not define becoming. In becoming animal, one does not end up looking *like* a horse or a dog or a rat. Indeed, Deleuze and Guattari reject both the faculty of imagination (which is able to provide analogies of proportion) and the faculty of the understanding (*l'entendement*,

*Verstand, intellectus*) (which is able to provide analogies of proportionality) (Deleuze and Guattari 1987: 234). Since becoming is not a process of imitating, there is no eminent term by means of which one could measure or judge what is undergoing the becoming. That there is no eminent term or standard explains why Deleuze and Guattari separate becoming from memory, from what they call "gigantic memory," memory as the faculty that always recalls one major idea such as man (Deleuze and Guattari 1987: 293). As we shall see, although becoming is not this kind of memory, it maintains a relation to a strange kind of memory. Nevertheless, just as the experience of becoming is *not* an experience of "gigantic memory," it is *not* an experience of recognition. As Deleuze and Guattari say, "The animal, flower, or stone one becomes are ... *not* molar subjects, objects, or forms that one knows *from the outside of us* [*on connaît hors de nous*] and that one *recognizes* [*reconnaît*] from experience, through science, or by habit" (Deleuze and Guattari 1987: 275, my emphasis). Since the experience of becoming is not recognition, becoming is also *not* a relation of representation. In becoming I do not become the representative of what I am becoming; it is not a relation of one thing (me) standing in *for* another (the animal, for example). Finally, since the experience of becoming is not a representation, it is also *not* perception in the standard sense; it is *not* a relation in which the subject and the object remain outside of one another. Therefore to summarize, in Deleuze and Guattari, becoming is neither a circular process of recommencement nor a process that comes to an end. Moreover, it is not a process governed by an eminent form or endpoint; it is not a relation of recognition in which the subject and the object would be *outside of* one another, and it is not a representative relation of one thing standing in *for* another.

The negative definitions that we have just presented contain prepositions, in particular, "outside of" (*hors de*) and "for" (*pour*). There is in fact a logic of prepositions at work in Deleuze and Guattari's experience of becoming, where pre-position must be taken in its literal sense, as prior to the positioning of a subject over and against an object. Deleuze and Guattari always use the preposition "devant" when they speak of becoming. Their use of this preposition refers neither to an experience of being over and against, outside of one another, nor to the subject-object relation. Already in *Difference and Repetition*, Deleuze had explained what the preposition "devant" means: "Each time that we find ourselves before [*devant*] or in a limitation, before [*devant*] or in an opposition, we must ask what such a situation supposes. The situation of being before supposes a swarm of differences, a pluralism of free differences" (Deleuze 1995: 55). Then in *A Thousand Plateaus*, Deleuze and Guattari say, "Perception will no longer be in the relation of a subject and of an object, but rather *in* [*dans*] the movement serving as the limit of that relation ... Perception will confront its own limit; it will be *among* [*parmi*] things, in [*dans*] the set of its own proximity" (Deleuze and Guattari 1987: 282). In the experience of becoming, when one is fascinated by something before oneself, when one contemplates something before oneself, one is *among* it, *within* it, together in a zone of proximity. "Before," therefore, in fact, means "among" and "within."[11] But before what? In becoming animal (or child or woman or minor), I find myself fascinated *before* something I cannot recognize, before something that has lost its molar form, something singular. For Deleuze and Guattari, as is well known, singularities are always in a multiplicity, in a pack (Deleuze and Guattari 1987: 239). The pack always looks back (*regarder*) and emits sounds. And it is this gaze from the singular animal and its cries that place the animal *within* me: one in the other. But the structure of "one in the other" does not mean, for Deleuze and Guattari, that becoming consists in a reciprocal relation. It is not the case that humans become animals and animals become human, as if the two would exchange places, one standing in *for* (*pour*) the other; it is not, as we said, a representational relation. Deleuze and Guattari present the crucial preposition for becoming in *What is Philosophy?*: "we become animal so that [*pour que*] the animals become something else" (Deleuze and Guattari 1994: 109). The preposition "pour" then becomes "pour que." Or, the "pour" of representation becomes the "pour" of "in their favor," "for" not "against."

Instead of a reciprocal or even chiasmic relation, Deleuze and Guattari describe becoming as a zigzag structure (Deleuze and Guattari 1987: 278). In order to understand the zigzag, we must focus on what they call "functions." In *A Thousand Plateaus*, Deleuze and Guattari distinguish functions from forms. Being molar, a form is composed of many functions. Functions themselves are informal; they have only little, micrological "details" (Deleuze and Guattari: 292) or "traits" (Deleuze and Guattari: 141). A face, for example, has a form, but it is composed of many traits or features, a mole or a tic for example (Deleuze and Guattari 1987: 188). A poem, for example, has a form, its verses and the spatial arrangements of words and punctuation. But within the poem, there are functions of rhyme and alliteration. These poetic traits may be extracted and repeated differently than they were in the poem; repeated into a different milieu or territory or repeated more rapidly or more slowly, they may be used differently and then they produce different outcomes. Deleuze and Guattari, of course, call this extraction and emission of traits "deterritorialization" (Deleuze and Guattari 1987: 141).

Because the traits are informal, each function is plural or even undecidable (Deleuze and Guattari 1994: 20). For instance, the function of disguising oneself contains at least two possible uses: exhibition and concealment. We see the undecidability of the function of disguise in animals. Animals disguise themselves at times in order to exhibit themselves so that, through the exhibition, they are able to attract something that can serve as a mate; at other times, they disguise themselves in order to conceal themselves so that, through the concealment, they are able to attack something that can serve as nourishment. A warrior therefore – this is Deleuze and Guattari's example (Deleuze and Guattari 1987: 277–8) – dresses himself for battle in a way that he may hide from the enemy. Although the warrior extracts the function of disguise from the animals, he does not become an animal. The warrior becomes a woman, since women too disguise themselves. Let us recall the formula for becoming from *What is Philosophy?*: one becomes something else so that this something also becomes something else. All becoming, Deleuze and Guattari say in *What is Philosophy?*, is double (Deleuze and Guattari 1994: 109). So, the warrior becomes woman so that woman may become something else. What does the woman become? The woman does not become a man. Disguising herself, she becomes an animal who exhibits herself, not so that she may attract a mate, but so that she may be able to attack an enemy. In its undecidability, the animal function of disguise is at the center of becoming woman, but in this becoming it is not the case that man becomes woman and woman becomes man. Man becomes woman and then woman becomes animal. But woman must become animal so that animal as well becomes something else. What does the animal become? There is no clear answer to this question, except to say that the function of disguising has other possible uses, other possible territories, than the ones we have outlined here. Perhaps, disguising is a function of marking, a function of tracing; disguising is perhaps a way of writing. Then we could say that the animal becomes a tale.

Writing brings us to the criterion for a *successful* becoming. Repeatedly in *A Thousand Plateaus*, Deleuze and Guattari speak of the prudence that is required in becoming. Because the destruction of molar forms is required – recall the agent of becoming is aging – it is always possible that one will not be able to go farther than destruction. It is always possible to become suicidal. We saw that the alcoholic can chose to drink himself to death or he can stop drinking and thereby have more choices. Deleuze and Guattari seem, however, to think that the choice of more choices is not enough; becoming has to go further. Let us backtrack into the experience of becoming. In order for the experience to happen, the condition of desubjectification must have been put in place by aging; then it is possible for me to experience a rupture and cross a threshold or a borderline, thereby entering into proximity with what I am becoming. Because of the borderlines – crossing the borderline from warrior to woman, from woman to animal, and from animal to something else – it is possible, they say, "to conceive of the possibility of laying [the borderlines] out [*étaler*] on a plane, the borderlines [*les bordures*] following one another by tracing [*en traçant*] a broken line" (Deleuze and Guattari 1987: 251). What is important in this quote is the verb "tracer," which means an action of drawing or of writing. The action of drawing or writing traces out a map, which in *A Thousand Plateaus*, Deleuze and Guattari call "the plane of consistency" (Deleuze and Guattari 1987: 251). They say:

> All the becomings are *written*, like sorcerers' *drawings*, on this plane of consistency, which is the ultimate Door, through which they find their way out. This is the only *criterion* to prevent them from bogging down, or turning to nothingness. The only question is: does a becoming go this far? Can a multiplicity flatten in this way all its *conserved* dimensions, like a flower that would hold onto its whole life up as far as its being dried?" (Deleuze and Guattari 1987: 251, my emphasis)

For Deleuze and Guattari, the criterion for a successful becoming therefore is that something is written down, that by writing the becoming down one "conserves" the formulas that will allow others to become and cross thresholds. In *What is Philosophy?*, the plane of consistency is also called "the plane of immanence *of concepts*" (Deleuze and Guattari 1994: 35, my emphasis). So, the criterion that a becoming is successful is that something like a concept is constructed, something like a work (*œuvre*). We come to the model of becoming that Proust provided: "to write is to become" (Deleuze and Guattari 1987: 240).

## III. Following the Rats

We have seen that aging is the agent of becoming insofar as it produces micrological cracks in the self. Aging sets up the necessary condition for becoming, which is the condition of having one's molar form of the subject destroyed (desubjectification). Desubjectification then opens one up to be affected by the abominable sufferings of others, with the result that the affects of love and shame motivate one to become other than man. Such a becoming non-human, becoming-animal for example, is not defined by the imitation of the molar form of the animal. Instead of a resemblance relation, the relation that defines becoming is pre-positional. I find myself positioned before the animal, but being before in fact means I am in proximity with the animal. I am among the others and they are in me. But just as imitation does not define becoming, neither does representation define the preposition of one *for* another. Instead, becoming consists in a zigzag structure: we become animal so that animal becomes, not human, but something else. The zigzag is set in motion by emission and extraction of a function (deterritorialization). And finally, beyond the destruction of the molar form, deterritorialization, in order to be successful, must use the animal function to produce something else. It must take the micrological function of the rat, for example, and write "like" a rat.

When Deleuze and Guattari speak of becoming-rat, they do not refer to Proust; they refer instead to Hugo von Hofmannsthal, to his "The Lord Chandos Letter."[12] Fictionally penned at the beginning of the seventeenth century (von Hoffmannsthal wrote it in fact in 1902), "The Letter" is supposed to have been occasioned by the receipt of a letter from Francis Bacon; Chandos then is writing back to Bacon. "The Letter" opens with Chandos saying, "I hardly know if I am still the person your precious letter is addressing. I am now twenty-six. Am I the same person ... ?"[13] He is not; Chandos says, "I have completely lost the ability to think or speak coherently about anything at all."[14] Then he describes his current existence, in which there are moments in which mundane objects are filled "with a swelling tide of higher life." But he worries that Bacon will not understand these moments. So he illustrates with the story of him spreading rat poison in the milk cellar of one of his dairy farms. Afterward, that evening, Chandos says that he went out riding. "Suddenly," he writes, this cellar unrolled inside me, filled with the death throes of the pack of rats. It was all there. The cool and musty cellar air, full of sharp, sweetish smell of the poison, and the shrilling of the death cries echoing against the mildewed walls. Those convulsed clumps of powerlessness, those desperations colliding with one another in confusion. The frantic search for ways out. The cold glares of fury when two meet at a blocked crevice ... I tell you, my friend, this was in me ... The soul of this beast I saw within me bared its teeth at its monstrous destiny.[15]

It is on this description of the rats dying in Chandos that Deleuze and Guattari focus. They say,

> Chandos falls into fascination before [*tombe en fascination devant*] a 'people of rats' [*un 'peuple de rats'*] who are in agony [*qui agonisent*], and it is in him [*en lui*], across him [*à travers lui*], in the interstices of his overthrown self [*dans les interstices de son moi boulversé*] that "the soul of the animal bares its teeth at its monstrous destiny" [*l'âme de l'animal montre les dents au destin monstrueux*]: not pity ... as he makes clear; still less an identification. It is a composition of speeds and affects involving entirely different individuals, a symbiosis; it makes the rat a thought in [*dans*] the man, a feverish thought [*une pensée fiévreuse*], at the same time as the man becomes rat, a rat who gnashes and is in agony [*rat qui grince et agonise*] ... Then a strange imperative is born in him: either stop writing or write like a rat [*comme un rat*]. (Deleuze and Guattari 1987: 240; also Deleuze and Guattari 1987: 275)

In this quote, we see the pre-positional logic that we had described earlier. Chandos falls into fascination "before," "devant" the "people of rats," but it is "in him," "en lui" that "the soul of the animal bares its teeth at its monstrous destiny." The rats have become in him a "feverish thought" of rats gnashing their teeth in agony. How has this feverish thought entered into

Chandos? It is clear that aging has set up the necessary condition for becoming: desubjectification. The rupture with his past self opens him up for the affect, which Chandos tells us – and Deleuze and Guattari reiterate this – is not pity. On the one hand, the animals, through their death throes, are in the process of losing their molar form, but, on the other hand, Chandos too, due to aging, is in the process of losing his molar form. The double informality allows for the affect to pass from one to the other. Chandos says that the affect is "a vast empathy." But we can see that the affect is something like the shame of having to poison animals. The result of the affect, however, is, as Deleuze and Guattari conclude in the quote above, that Chandos experiences a strange imperative: either stop writing or write like a rat. Although Deleuze and Guattari do not mention this, at the end of "The Letter" Chandos speaks of writing and thinking in a language that is not English or Latin or Spanish or Italian, a language "of which I know not one word," Chandos says, "a language in which mute things speak to me."[16] The formula for this becoming therefore is: the rats become a thought in man, "a feverish thought," while the man becomes a writer who writes like a rat.

The result of this becoming, writing, is not surprising since we have seen that the criterion for a successful becoming is the production of a diagram, a map, a score, a concept, or, most generally, a work. What is at stake in the imperative that Chandos undergoes is literature, to write literature like a rat.[17] But what is at stake in literature is the production of a people. As Deleuze and Guattari say in both *A Thousand Plateaus* and in *Kafka: Toward a Minor Literature*, "literature is the affair of the people" (Deleuze and Guattari 1987: 346; also Deleuze and Guattari 1986: 18 and 84). The purpose of literature in the production of a people tells us what the "so that" of Chandos' becoming rat is. Chandos becomes rat *so that*, writing like a rat will call forth a people. This "so that" does not mean that writing like a rat aims to produce, as the French translation of "The Letter" says, "un peuple de rats," "a people of rats"; it does not aim to endow rats with human qualities or to endow humans with rat qualities; this attribution of characteristics is the work of myths. No, writing like a rat would fabulate a rat legend (Deleuze 1989: 275), it would be a rat tale. Like any tale, its question would be: what is going to happen? If it is a good tale, no one would be able to predict the ending. But undoubtedly it would be a tale of the rat's struggle with death. Writing like a rat then would be to write in the style of agony, in the style of an "agon," a contest, or struggle, against death: "agony against all the deaths" (Deleuze and Guattari 1994: 160). What would this style look like? The least we could say is that, writing like a rat (like any animal-writing) would be a writing that struggles to escape from the dominant forms of expression. Instead, it would extract the function of teeth gnashing, the phonic traits of teeth gnashing, in order to reiterate them at a speed that is faster than or perhaps slower than the gnashing of rat teeth in the agony of death; it would extract the vibrant traits of eyes in order to reiterate them at an intensity that is stronger or weaker than the color of the rat eyes in the agony of death. Writing like a rat would create a new syntax of gnashing, a new chromatics of color. Its aim would be to create a vision or an audition that has never been seen or heard before.[18] It would create the outside of language, the outside in the sense of a new land. There would be a character, a persona, who exhibits a profound empathy with the whole world. This character would therefore present a new possibility of life. The character's hyperbolic love would infect, like a rat, everyone (*tout le monde*) with the feverish thought of the rat's agony. And it is this infection that would produce a people contaminated with the feverish thought of the struggle against death. Writing like a rat – it would write a folktale – would produce a people who thought feverishly.[19] Such a people would indeed be an immense change from our current times.

## IV. Conclusion: Auto-Affection and Becoming

We started with globalization. As the word suggests, globalization means that the earth has been enclosed within a globe; perhaps, by enclosing, globalization, we would have to say, is a kind of peace. But this peace, which is the peace of pacification, is in fact war by other means. The enclosure of globalization means that one species, the human, dominates all the other species. What justifies this domination is the belief that humans possess a kind of subjectivity that animals do not possess, a form of auto-affection that, as the belief goes, is truly "auto," uncontaminated by any other: "I hear myself speak at the very moment I speak."

Let us now examine the experience of auto-affection, as we have examined it in previous chapters. Here, however, we shall focus on how auto-affection intersects with Deleuze and Guattari's idea of becoming. So, let us do, again, the phenomenology of interior life. When I engage in interior monologue, when, in short, I think, it seems as though I hear myself speak at the very moment I speak. My interior voice is not required to pass outside of myself; it is not required to traverse any space, not even the space of my body. So, my interior monologue seems to be immediate, immediately present and not to involve anyone else. As we know, interior monologue *seems* therefore to be different from other kinds of auto-affection like me touching myself. Of course, this belief is based on a simplification of interior life. The temporalization of auto-affection means that the hearing of myself is never immediately present in the moment when I speak. But the conclusion that hearing myself is not immediately present also means that the experience of auto-affection resembles the experience of aging. There is a delay in time which turns my speaking in the present moment into a response to the past. Because of the delay in time, there is a past that always precedes me, a past that has always started without me, from the very moment of my birth. No matter how young I am, I have always already aged. It is always later than I think so that my hearing myself speak is like a rendezvous which I had forgotten but which I have just remembered. That auto-affection involves a strange sort of memory leads to the other problem with the belief that interior monologue is my own. Beside the irreducible agedness involved in the experience of auto-affection, there is the problem of the voice. In order to hear myself speak at this very moment, I must make use of the same phonemes as I use in communication (even if this monologue is not vocalized externally through my mouth). It is an irreducible or essential necessity that the silent words I form contain repeatable traits. This means that, when I speak to myself, I speak with the sounds of others. In other words, it means that I find in myself other voices, whispering to me from the past. There is not a Platonic memory of one form, but there is a memory of multiplicity, the many voices are in me. The problem therefore with the belief that interior monologue is my own is that others' voices contaminate the hearing of myself speaking. Just as my present moment is always already old, my interior monologue contains a kind of indirect discourse. Here, with these other voices in me, our phenomenology of inner experience intersects with Deleuze and Guattari's idea of becoming.

We have in fact been pursuing a double strategy. On the one hand, we have been trying to undermine the claim that humans are superior to animals by criticizing, by means of the delay in temporalization and the traits in language, the belief that human auto-affection is pure "auto." On the other hand, we have been trying to become animal, to put the animals in us so that we humans change our relation to animals. Both strategies, as we have just seen, intersect; we could even say that the two strategies are the intersection of Derrida's thought with that of Deleuze and Guattari. Based on the two strategies, we can now say, as Derrida would, "l'animal que donc je suis," "the animal that therefore I am." The animal that I am, that I have in my "I think," is like a specter who haunts me. The haunting I undergo is relentless. The thinking is so feverish that I feel myself being late. Is this lateness the feeling of bad conscience (as in Derrida) or the feeling of shame (as in Deleuze and Guattari)? It does not matter. All that matters is that, since I am late for my rendezvous, I am in a hurry to catch up, hurrying along and following, "l'animal que donc je suis," "the animal that therefore I follow." But following the animals never means imitating the animals. Following the animals means writing like the animals. As we have suggested, this kind of writing – write like a rat – would challenge and question common sense. It would question what we call the truth. Therefore, it would be a writing that fictionalizes, that fabulates, that writes tales (Deleuze and Guattari 1994: 168).[20] Only through tales – again, they would be a kind of folktale – are we able to call forth a collectivity. Is this collectivity a people (as in Deleuze) or a democracy (as in Derrida)? Again, it does not matter. All that matters is that, since the collectivity would be called forth by rat-writing, the collectivity would have a different relation to the animals than we do. Perhaps this collectivity to come would be themselves a people who thought feverishly. Haunted by the specter of the agony of animals which they find within themselves, perhaps they would say "This land that I seem to possess is not my own." They would say, "Let's open all the doors and destroy the walls." Perhaps they would be a people who loved the world so much that they wanted to let everyone, without exception, enter in, and to let everyone, without exception, exit out. Perhaps, we could call this people to come "the friends of passage."

## Notes

1 Perhaps Proust is the model for all becomings in Deleuze and Guattari; in *A Thousand Plateaus*, they say that "another outcome [*issue*] [other than annihilation] was possible, or was made possible by Proust," and that other outcome was the work (*œuvre*) (Deleuze and Guattari 1987: 272 and 439).
2 Daniel W. Smith seems to recognize the fact that the production of a work is the criterion for a successful becoming in his Preface to his English translation of Gilles Deleuze, *Essays Critique et Clinique* (Deleuze 1997). See Preface, p. xli, when Smith speaks of literature in Deleuze. Ronald Bogue also seems to come quite close to recognizing this fact in the final chapter of his excellent *Deleuze on Literature* (London: Routledge, 2003). Claire Colebrook too seems to recognize this fact in her *Gilles Deleuze* (London: Routledge, 2002), when she says, "We can think of art and philosophy as becoming-molecular or becoming imperceptible. We do not actually want to be a molecule or animal, for this would mean not writing at all" (p. 128). Then she says, "freedom requires moving beyond the human to affirm life. Literature, for Deleuze, is essential here."
3 Donna Haraway criticizes (in fact she is dismissive of) Deleuze and Guattari for the valorization of animals that travel in packs as opposed to house pets such as dogs. But she fails to see that Deleuze and Guattari also say that "it is also possible for any animal to be treated in the mode of

the pack or swarm . . . even the cat, even the dog" (Deleuze and Guattari 1987: 294/241). See Donna Haraway, *When Species Meet* (Minneapolis: University of Minnesota Press, 2008), p. 29.

4  This phrase refers to Henry Miller; see Deleuze and Guattari 1987: 286. But we must stress here the role that asceticism plays in becoming; see Deleuze and Guattari 1987: 247. A crucial example of becoming can be found in Foucault's third volume of *The History of Sexuality*. Foucault says, "One familiarizes oneself with the minimum. This is what Seneca wishes to do according to a letter written a time before the Saturnalia of the year 62. Rome is 'in a sweat' and 'licentiousness is officially sanctioned.'" Seneca asks himself if one ought to take part in the festivities or not; what puts one's restraint to the proof is to abstain from the festivities and to break with the general attitude. But not to isolate oneself is to acting with a still greater moral force; the best is 'without mixing with the crowd, to do the same things, but in a different way [*mais d'une autre manière*].' And this 'different way' is that to which one forms oneself ahead of time by means of voluntary exercises, periods of abstinence, and poverty cures" (Foucault 1986: 60).

5  One should note that aging plays a crucial role at the end of Part I of *What is Philosophy?* (Deleuze and Guattari 1994: 110–11). Here too aging (or history) opens up the possibility of becoming.

6  For more on love in Deleuze and Guattari, see John Protevi, "Love," in *Between Deleuze and Derrida*, ed. Paul Patton and John Protevi (New York: Continuum, 2003), pp. 183–94, especially pp. 188–9.

7  See Tamsin Lorraine, *Irigaray and Deleuze: Experiments in Visceral Philosophy* (Ithaca: Cornell University Press, 1999), pp. 183–4.

8  See Philippe Mengue, *Deleuze et la question de la démocratie* (Paris: L'Harmattan, 2003), p. 178. Here Mengue recognizes the importance of the intolerable in Deleuze's final texts. Ronald Bogue, *Deleuze on Music, Painting, and the Arts* (London: Routledge, 2003), p. 35. Here Bogue recognizes that all becomings are minor, but does not see the essential requirement of suffering. Paul Patton, *Deleuze and the Political* (London: Routledge, 2000), pp. 78–83. Patton's discussion of becoming remains one of the best available. Claire Colebrook, *Gilles Deleuze*, p. 143. Elizabeth Grosz, "A Thousand Tiny Sexes: Feminism and Rhizomatics," in *Gilles Deleuze and the Theater of Philosophy*, ed. Constantin V. Boundas and Dorothea Olkowski (London: Routledge, 1994), pp. 187–211.

9  See Véronique Bergen, *L'ontologie de Deleuze* (Paris: L'Harmattan, 2001), p. 79.

10 See François Zourabichvili, "Deleuze et le possible" in *Gilles Deleuze, une vie philosophique*, sous la direction de Eric Alliez (Le Plessis-Robinson: Institut Synthélabo, 1998), pp. 335–57, especially p. 351.
11 Derrida too has stressed this preposition (Derrida 1992a: 70).
12 In *A Thousand Plateaus*, they refer to "The Lord Chandos Letter" three times; see Deleuze and Guattari 1987: 240, 258, 275. On p, 240, they say: "Hofmannsthal, or rather Lord Chandos, falls into fascination before [*tombe en fascination devant*] a 'people of rats' [*peuple de rats*] who are in agony [*qui agonisent*], and it is in him [*en lui*], across him [*à travers lui*], in the interstices of his overthrown self [*dans les interstices de son moi boulversé*] that "the soul of the animal bares its teeth at its monstrous destiny" [*l'âme de l'animal montre les dents au destin monstrueux*]: not pity but participation against nature. Then a strange imperative is born in him: either stop writing or write like [*comme*] a rat . . . If the writer is a sorcerer, this is because to write is to become, to write is traversed by strange becomings, which are not becomings-writer, but becomings-rat, becomings-insect, becomings-wolf, etc. . . . Many suicides by writers are explained by these participations against nature, these nuptials against nature. The writer is a sorcerer because he lives [*vit*] the animal as the only population before which [*devant laquelle*] he is responsible in principle. The German pre-Romantic Karl Philipp Moritz feels responsible, not for [*des*] the calves that die, but before [*devant*] the calves that die and give him the incredible feeling of an unknown Nature [*l'incroyable sentiment d'une Nature inconnue*] – affect. For the affect is not a personal feeling, nor is it a characteristic; it is the actualization [*l'effectuation*] of a potency [*puissance*] of the pack that throws the self into upheaval and makes it reel [*qui soulève et fait vaciller le moi*]. Who has not known the violence of these animal sequences [*séquences*], which uproot one from humanity, if only for an instant, making one scrape at one's bread like a rodent or giving one the yellow eyes of a feline? Terrible involutions which call us towards unheard-of becomings." On p. 258, they say: "When Hofmannsthal contemplates the agony of a rat, it is in him [*en lui*] that the animal 'bares his teeth as this monstrous destiny.' This is not a feeling of pity, as he makes clear; still less an identification. It is a composition of speeds and affects involving entirely different individuals, a symbiosis; it makes the rat a thought in [*dans*] the man, a feverish thought [*une pensée fiévreuse*], at the same time as the man becomes rat, a rat who gnashes and is in agony [*rat qui grince et agonise*]." On p. 275, they say: "You become animal only molecularly. You do not become a barking molar dog, but, by barking, if it is done with enough heart, with enough necessity and

composition, you emit a molecular dog. Man does not become wolf, or vampire, as if he changed species; the vampire and werewolf are becomings of man, in other words, proximities between molecules in composition, relations of movement and rest, speed and slowness between emitted particles. Of course, there are werewolves and vampires, we say this with all our heart; but do not look for a resemblance or analogy to the animal, since this is the animal-becoming in actualization, this is the production of the molecular animal (whereas the 'real' animal is trapped [*pris*] in its molar form and subjectivity). It is in us [*en nous*] that the animal bares its teeth like Hofmannsthal's rat, or the flower opens its petals; but this is done by corpuscular emission, by molecular proximity, and not by the imitation of a subject or a proportionality of form." In *What is Philosophy?*, they allude to von Hoffmannsthal, without mentioning him by name; Deleuze and Guattari 1994: 109 "Artaud said: to write *for* [*pour*] the illiterate – to speak for the aphasic, to think for the acephalous. But what does 'for' mean? It is not 'for their benefit,' or yet 'in their place.' It is 'before' [*devant*]. It is a question of becoming. The thinker is not acephalic, aphasic, or illiterate, but becomes so. He becomes Indian, not in order to become the Indian – perhaps 'so that' [*pour que*] the Indian who is Indian becomes himself something else and tears himself away from his agony. We think and write for the animals themselves. We become animal so that the animal becomes something else. The agony of a rat or the slaughter of a calf remains present in thought not through pity but as the zone of exchange between the human and the animal in which something of the one passes into the other. This is the constitutive relationship of philosophy with non-philosophy. Becoming is always double, and it is this double becoming that constitutes a people to come and the new land [*terre*]." In *A Thousand Plateaus*, they refer to the following French translation: *Lettres du voyageur à son retour*, traduit de l'allemand par Jean-Claude Schneider (Paris: Mercure de France et Gallimard, 1969). I am using the following English translation: *The Lord Chandos Letter and Other Writings*, selected and translated from the German by Joel Rotenberg (New York: New York Review Books, 2005).
13 Von Hoffmannsthal, *The Lord Chandos Letter and Other Writings*, p. 117.
14 Ibid., p. 121.
15 Ibid., pp. 123–4.
16 Ibid., pp. 127–8.
17 J. M. Coetzee through his character Elizabeth Costello writes a variant of the Lord Chandos Letter, "Letter of Elizabeth, Lady Chandos." Elizabeth Costello's letter stresses the role of language in this experience. See

J. M. Coetzee, *Elizabeth Costello* (New York: Penguin Books, 2003), pp. 227–30.

18 I am following the three aspects of the minorization of major language that Deleuze presents in "Literature and Life," in Deleuze 1997; see also Deleuze 1989: 5.

19 See Deleuze and Guattari 1978: 355, where Deleuze and Guattari speak of "a Stateless woman-people."

20 In many places, Deleuze appropriate Bergson's idea of a fabulation function (which in English is also called "the story-telling function" or "the myth-making function"). See Deleuze 1989: 269–70; also Deleuze 1995a: 174. For the Bergson reference, see Bergson 1977: 108–9. The English translation of *The Two Sources* renders "la function fabulatrice" as "the myth-making function"; this translation does not harmonize well with Deleuze's use of this Bergsonian idea since Deleuze stresses that the fabulation is used against the dominant myths of a society. In *Cinema 2* (Deleuze 1989: 269–70), Deleuze says, "It is thus necessary to go beyond all the pieces of spoken information; to extract from them a pure speech-act, creative story-telling [*fabulation créatrice*] which is as it were the obverse side of the dominant myths, of current words and their supporters; an act capable of creating the myth instead of drawing profit from or business from it."

# 6

# The Origin of *Parrēsia* in Foucault's Thinking: Truth and Freedom in *The History of Madness*[1]

Published in 1961, the *History of Madness* is a monumental study of madness in the "Classical Age" (that is, in the seventeenth and eighteenth centuries, primarily in France). In its original form, the *History of Madness* displays a debt to phenomenology as it was interpreted in France after World War II. This debt is most apparent in Foucault's use of the word "experience," a use that Foucault later will call "enigmatic" (Foucault 1972: 16) and "floating" (Foucault 1984: 336). It is perhaps the vestiges of phenomenological thinking in the *History of Madness* that leads to Derrida's 1963 criticism of Foucault, a criticism that makes Foucault remove the book's original title ("Folie et déraison"; "Madness and Unreason") and its original preface for the *History of Madness*' 1972 reissue.[2] In his 1973 course at the Collège de France, *Psychiatric Power*, Foucault himself states that the *History of Madness* made use of three notions that were not very helpful for the investigation of madness: violence; institution; and the family. All of these notions, Foucault says, should be replaced with notions of power (Foucault 2006a: 14–15).[3] Self-criticisms such as these found in *Psychiatric Power* have led commentators to speak of periods in Foucault's thinking, indicating thereby that one must understand the trajectory of Foucault's thinking as discontinuous.

Despite the debt to phenomenology, the *History of Madness* displays a remarkable level of innovation. In it, we find a restructuring of the relation of theory and practice, a restructuring that anticipates Foucault's idea of an apparatus (*dispositif*).[4] Similarly, Foucault's analysis of the gaze in the birth of asylum (Foucault 2006: 437–43) anticipates his famous analysis of light in Bentham's panopticon prison in *Discipline and Punish* (Foucault 1977: 200–2). Moreover, the *History of Madness* presents the three axes by which Foucault himself defines his thinking at the end of his life: knowledge; power; and ethics. The *History of Madness* concerns the formation of domains of knowledge which constitute themselves as specific knowledge of "mental illness"; the organization of a normative system built on a whole technical, administrative, juridical, and medical apparatus whose purpose was to isolate and take custody of the insane; and the definition of a relation to oneself and to others as possible subjects of madness (Foucault 1984: 336). Finally, and most importantly, as its original title indicates, the *History of Madness* provides a history of the relation between unreason and madness. Even though Foucault removed *Folie et déraison* from the book's cover, this relationship is the book's core theme. The 1961 analysis of madness and unreason anticipates Foucault description of his work in 1984 as a history of thought (Foucault 1984: 334). Thus, one is able to juxtapose, to the discontinuity thesis, a continuity thesis: Foucault's thinking follows an unbroken path from unreason to *parrēsia*, his last great concept.

In what follows, we intend to follow this path from unreason to *parrēsia* (an ancient Greek term that is rendered in French as "franc-parler" and in English as "speaking freely" or "speaking frankly"). We intend to show that the three characteristics by means of which Foucault defines speaking frankly in his 1983 lecture course, *The Government of Self and Others*, can be traced back to his analysis of delirium in the central chapter of the *History of Madness* called "The Transcendence of Delirium" (Foucault 2006: 208–50). As we shall see, both the discourse of delirium and the speaking that speaks the truth frankly are intensifications of freedom. In order to be able to demonstrate the connection of *parrēsia* back to unreason or delirium, we must return to Foucault's secondary thesis, the one that accompanied the submission of the *History of Madness* as his primary thesis in 1961: Foucault's *Introduction to Kant's Anthropology*.[5] In addition to our continuity thesis (from *parrēsia* to unreason), we are also arguing that it is impossible to understand the *History of Madness* without understanding Foucault's *Introduction*. Here, we see Foucault reconstruct the structure of Kant's thought, going from the level of the a priori of knowledge, as it is presented in *The Critique of Pure Reason*, to the level of what Foucault calls "a priori of existence," presented in Kant's *Anthropology from a Pragmatic Point of View*, and finally to the "fundamental level" of what Kant himself calls "transcendental philosophy" in his *Opus Postumum*.[6] It is only by following Foucault's reconstruction of the fundamental level that we are able to see that, for Foucault, the central concern of his thinking is the relation of truth and freedom. When we are able to see that the fundamental level, for Foucault, concerns the relation of truth and freedom, then we are able to see unreason or delirium as an act of freedom in relation to truth; and then we are able to see the act of unreason as the origin of *parrēsia* in Foucault's thinking. *Parrēsia* as "the highest exercise of freedom" (Foucault 2010: 67) originates from the "absolute freedom" of unreason (Foucault 2006: 157). In order to approach the origin of *parrēsia* in Foucault's thinking, let us first set up the context for seeing it.

## I. An Entire Readjustment of the Ethical World: Summary of the *History of Madness*

What we intend to do now is chart the most crucial moments in Foucault's "archaeology" of unreason in the *History of Madness* (Foucault 2006: xxviii). "Archaeology" is a technical term in Foucault's thought. It designates, as he says in the 1969 *Archaeology of Knowledge*, "a description that questions the already-said at the level of existence" (Foucault 1972: 131). Archeology therefore in *The Archaeology of Knowledge* investigates the background of linguistic or theoretical acts such as the statement of the truth of madness as well as practices such as the confinement of the mad. In *The History of Madness*, in 1961, its use seems to be less rigorous and more indeterminate. As with his use of "experience," his use of the term "archaeology" looks to be closer to its use in phenomenology where it means a "dismantling" of constructed forms in order to reveal the original act that constituted the forms. This act would be a combination of immanence (subjective and internal) and transcendent (objective and external). Therefore, we are able to view Foucault's history of madness through these phenomenological terms; Foucault is recounting a history that moves from transcendence to immanence. Moving from a transcendent god to immanent human experience, the movement is, as Foucault says, one of "desacralization" (Foucault 2006: 90).

The *History of Madness* is divided into three parts, the first of which begins with madness in the Middle Ages and Renaissance.

In this opening epoch, madness was a great peril, the mad man a tragic figure of the end of the world that constantly threatened, haunted, and fascinated man's imagination. But it was also a figure of irony and derision, the error and folly of man in the world (Foucault 2006: 13). This liminal ambiguity of the characters of madness and the mad man is played out in the paintings of Brueghel and Bosch, especially Bosch's the "Ship of Fools," on one side, and the literature of Brant's *Narrenschiff* and Erasmus's *The Praise of Folly* on the other. Figural art and language, image and word, which for a long time were complementary, begin to come apart and take different directions. In particular, rather than portraying in a dark flash the tragic end of the world that threatens man, the discourses of Brant and Erasmus take hold of man and show him his moral truth. Madness is no longer tied to the truth of the world, "but rather about man and the truth about himself that he can perceive" (Foucault 2006: 23). Madness becomes the object of a moral discourse in which it is tied to all of man's various errors, faults, and defects. Madness's truth is grasped and criticized in this objectifying discourse. The derisory surface of irony covers over the profound threat of apocalypse.

The division between the tragic vision of the world and the critical consciousness of madness marks the beginning of a separation that will only continue to widen in the Classical Age. The experience of madness that felt the imminent threat of an apocalyptic end recedes into the shadows, while the experience of madness captured in the language that criticized the conduct proper to man's nature is put under a brighter and more clarifying light (Foucault 2006: 27). It is with the great confinement of the Classical Age, instituted by Louis XIV's 1656 edict of Nantes that established the Hôpital Général in Paris, that this division takes on a concrete institutional form.

For Foucault, confinement is a "decisive event" in the history of unreason (Foucault 2006: 77). It is the event in which madness comes to be perceived against the same social and moral horizon as poverty, idleness, and libertinage. It is the event in which madness came to be seen as one type of unreason among others with which it had a shared kinship. Now against this moral horizon, madness would take on new meanings, meanings distinct from those it had in the Middle Ages and Renaissance. Madness was now part of the ethical decision of the Classical Age: it was the decision within which certain groups, all of which could be classified under the title "unreason," were divided from other groups, those placed under "reason." Confinement was the practice that concretely accomplished the ethical decision that animated the moral perception of the Classical Age.

Confinement was not a medical establishment. It was "a semi-juridical structure, ... an instrument of order, of the new bourgeois and monarchical order that was beginning to take shape in the France of that time" (Foucault 2006: 49). The shift in meaning of libertinage in the first half and the second half of the seventeenth century is a good example of this. (We should not overlook the fact that, for Foucault, eighteenth century "free thinking" echoes Greek *parrēsia*.)The shift of meaning manifests a "certain kinship of immorality and error" (Foucault 2006: 97). Libertinage was a kind of skepticism that demonstrated the constant threat of madness in the search for a reasonable ordering of the heart's passions. But by the second half of the seventeenth century, the libertine's free thinking comes to be seen as a consequence "of a licentious life" (Foucault 2006: 98). In order to bring him back to the truth, one must limit his freedom by curbing his unreasonable passions and desires. And so the libertines were confined. Confinement then served the purpose of moral reform. It brought "one back to the truth through moral constraints" (Foucault 2006: 96).

Confinement is the concrete manifestation of *an entire readjustment of the ethical world*. It is the immanent space of the movement of desacrilization; the gesture that divides reason from unreason. Through this readjustment the figures of unreason – those who have transgressed the ethical limits of bourgeois society – appear and can be grasped by objective knowledge. What the example of the libertine shows us is that an ethical perception and moral condemnation is at the foundation of the objective knowledge of madness that begins to develop in the Classical Age. The observation and study of the nature of madness is now possible because it is understood as the alienation of man's reason from itself. Man's natural passions and desires turn his reason against itself, against what is otherwise understood as his truth. Libertinage shows us that what the medical knowledge of madness identifies as the nature of man is in fact the *result* of a reorganization of social space along the lines of an ethical perception. All of the figures who appear in confinement are those who challenged, in one way or another, the sovereignty of reason. As such they can all be classified under the term "unreason."

For the Classical Age, reason belonged to what was human in man's nature. Madness, then, was man's loss of his humanity and his return to the immediacy of his animality (Foucault 2006: 148). This animality was not, however, the space of a determinism from which the mechanisms of madness could be derived. It was instead "*a space of unpredictable freedom* where fury was unleashed" (Foucault 2006: 150; original emphasis). The unpredictable freedom of the mad person's animal fury threatened Classical man's essentially rational nature with its violent counter-nature. In the Classical Age, madness was felt as a negativity that threatened the natural order of reason.

Within the walls of confinement, madness begins to stand out against the other forms of unreason. The threat of madness's animal fury meant that reason could at any moment be scandalized by madness. Madness could reveal the violent unpredictable animality that lies underneath man's calm rational order. But madness was confined because its fall into animal fury is the consequence of a moral abandon. Ethical choice and animal fury, the Classical Age's experience of madness understood the mad person as both at once. The mad person was on the immoral side of an ethical decision, but was also at the same time an example of the human being's animal nature, one into which we could all possibly slip.

We can now see that the movement of desacrilization that we've been following is also a movement of internalization. Madness is no longer a transcendent threat but an immanent one. Madness threatens man's reason from within. The concrete gesture of confinement institutionalizes this movement through a division of reason from unreason on the basis of a moral perception. The figures of unreason captured behind the walls of confinement form the background against which madness can be taken up as an object of knowledge.

A paradox animates Foucault's analyses in Part Two: while there is no difficulty in recognizing the mad person in all of his various manifestations, the medical knowledge of the Classical Age is unable to grasp madness as such. Reason is able to say with no hesitation what is not reason, what is its other, and yet its putative opposite, madness, is absent. Reason has a double relation to madness then: it is a norm against which the mad person can be recognized in his conduct and language; and it is the subject of knowledge, the one who takes hold of madness as an object. In short, there is reason as structures of the reasonable and reason as structures of the rational, and madness is either fully present or totally absent in relation to one or the other (Foucault 2006: 182).

Unreason is the void, the chasm between the truth of the mad person recognized in an instant and the truth of madness analyzed according to its virtual phenomena (Foucault 2006: 205). It is precisely that experience that unifies what otherwise appears to us as contradictory or paradoxical. And what appears to us as contradictory and paradoxical is that madness, as the manifestation in signs, words, and gestures of what is error, illusion, phantasm, and dream – that is, the manifestation of non-being in appearance, the undeniable logic of a delirious imagination – madness can only say of itself through reason that which is the negation of reason. "A rational hold on madness is possible and necessary," Foucault writes, "*to the extent that madness is non-reason*" (Foucault 2006: 243; original emphasis). Unreason is the singular experience that underlies this paradox of the Age of the Understanding.

As the seventeenth and eighteenth centuries progress, the two perspectives on madness slip into one another as the mad person becomes more and more an object of knowledge. The mixture of the two perspectives, however, does not take place because nineteenth century positive psychiatry accounts for this paradox of unreason through a progressive series of teleological developments. Instead, madness is separated from unreason and brought to the surface of an already constituted discursive truth, while unreason sinks into the background where it is eventually forgotten.

The various attempts to understand madness theoretically are accompanied by various attempts at a cure. Neither of these levels is purely and simply medical. Extra-medical practices, those animated by an ethical perception, begin to understand madness as the *"psychological effect of a moral fault"* (Foucault 2006: 296; original emphasis). For the medical practice of the Classical Age, there is no distinction between physical and moral treatments, at least not until "the problem of madness is displaced towards an interrogation of the responsible subject" in the first half of the nineteenth century (Foucault 2006: 325). Here therapies that focus on the physical body become the cure of innocent determinism, while moral therapies treat "blameworthy freedom" (Foucault 2006: 325). But one can isolate a difference in nature between the two kinds of treatment: those that aim at transforming qualities of passions, in which "the essence of madness is taken as nature and as sickness," and those that use discourse to restore madness to its truth, madness here taken as unreason, or delirium (Foucault 2006: 339).

We can see the unity of these two approaches in the treatment whose method was a return to the immediacy of nature. The thought was that the illusion and delirium of madness could be cured by returning madness "to its own truth," since its truth, as an illness, is nature; and "to its closest contradiction" since "delirium as appearance without content" is the contrary of the plenitude of nature (Foucault 2006: 334). In this treatment the mad person is returned to the truth of nature by freeing him from his passionate, delirious freedom through a return to "the gentle constraints of nature," while avoiding the wild fury of his counter-natural animality (Foucault 2006: 335–6). The liberation of madness through the laws of nature – laws that are in fact mediated by morality – brought him back to the man of reason (Foucault 2006: 338).

This treatment, which took place within confinement, is an example of the continuing movement of desacrilization – of the flattening out of madness onto the surface of its visible phenomena and natural truth – that leads to the establishment of positive psychiatry in the Modern Age. It is an example of how the space of confinement, without ever changing its external structures, undergoes an internal reorganization and a change in its meaning. In the first half of the seventeenth century confinement was an undifferentiated space of exclusion and banishment of reason's other. By the time of the start of the nineteenth century, it begins taking on positive moral values, those in which madness is perceived solely on the surface of its natural phenomena and comes to be seen as entirely pathological (Foucault 2006: 338). Part Three traces out the slow but eventual "detachment" of madness from unreason that makes positive knowledge of madness possible. And the practice of confinement is the concrete a priori condition of this possibility. More specifically, positive knowledge of madness occurs when confinement takes on a medical value, when its purpose becomes to cure. But to get to this point, confinement must undergo a series of crises, which lead to a further rearrangement of its internal space, breaking it from the complex unity it had in the seventeenth century. This rearrangement is not merely practical, but it is infused with and carried along by political, economic, medical, and moral values. What is at stake in Part Three is the analysis and history of these crises and discontinuities. They form the broken line that leads to madness's final detachment from unreason.

In the new form of confinement, the mad are given a "restrained and organized freedom" (Foucault 2006: 435). In contrast to the first half of the Classical Age, in which the mad person's freedom was tied to his violent animality, now, at the end of the eighteenth century, appears "a gentle animality" (Foucault 2006: 435). This animality does not destroy in its violence the mad person's human truth, but "lets emerge one of nature's secrets" (Foucault 2006: 435). Confinement, then, becomes "as much a space of truth as a space of constraint" (Foucault 2006: 435). By giving the mad person a restrained physical freedom, the wanderings of his imagination are constrained by the reality they confront. As a result, freedom is aligned with man's nature. Madness, then, alienates man from his nature. The situation of madness in confinement becomes nature by "recurrence" (Foucault 2006, 438): the internal space of confinement is reorganized according to the forms that it itself gave birth to. The relationship of principle and consequence is inverted: what was once the space of appearance and error – in short, the negativity of unreason – has become the space of nature and truth, the privileged space for positive knowledge of madness.

The reorganization of the internal space of confinement, though, is not sufficient for the establishing of positive psychiatry in the nineteenth century. What was needed was also a reorganization of the social space external to confinement. This takes place through the scandalized conscience subjected to the gaze and judgment of others. During the Classical Age, the scandal of the mad person's animal and counter-natural fury was hidden away in confinement to be at most made into a spectacle. Now, around the time of the French Revolution, bourgeois "revolutionary consciousness" makes into a public scandal the mad person's interior life, one which betrays the immorality at the heart of man. In this way, "psychological interiority was constituted on the basis of the exteriority of scandalized consciousness" (Foucault 2006: 449). The movement of desacrilization, which we saw is one of interiorization, we now see is also a movement of moralization. Everything that was transcendent, secret, and obscure in madness from the Renaissance through the Classical Age is flattened out to the horizontal surface of man's natural truth and the moral values of bourgeois society. It is only at this point that Pinel and Tuke could claim to "free" the mad from their chains so as to cure them in the asylum.[7]

Madness's positivity is now completely detached from the negativity of unreason, and as such can be offered up as an object of knowledge. The consequence of this movement of desacrilization is a fundamental shift in man's relation to truth. It is no longer the case that madness reveals to man *the* truth of the world, but rather madness reveals to man *his* truth. Man's relation to alterity through madness in the Renaissance and Classical Age was a relation to the transcendent otherness of death and the end of the world. Now, at the beginning of the nineteenth century, man's relation to alterity is a relationship to himself, mediated by the alienating character of madness. At the moment madness becomes an object of knowledge, madness becomes "the first great figure of the objectification of man" (Foucault 2006: 461). Man's relation to alterity is reduced to the circle of the same, to what Foucault, in the title of the *History of Madness*' final chapter, calls "the anthropological circle." As he says, "there is no question here of concluding" (Foucault 2006: 512). In the nineteenth century, the language of unreason, the speech of "free thinking," recedes into the background as madness comes to speak the truth of man in the reorganized space of the asylum. Unreason, according to Foucault reappears only in the poetic language of Hölderlin, Nietzsche, Nerval, and Artaud, in the work of those whose eventual madness meant the absence of work. What we aim to show now is how the expressive act of freedom by those who attempt to speak the drunken immediacy of the sensible, "the eternally recommenced courage of this ordeal," is also the instant in which the truth of madness – and thus the truth of man – escapes (Foucault 2006: 536). In this way we can understand the reciprocal transcendence of truth and freedom.

## II. The Repetition of *The Critique of Pure Reason* in *The Anthropology from a Pragmatic Point of View*: The Reciprocal Transcendence of Truth and Freedom

Kant's name appears only three times in the *History of Madness* (Foucault 2006: 123, 126, and 240n67). Nevertheless, the insights Foucault gains from his study of Kant organize structural moments in the movement of the *History of Madness*. Most clearly, the final chapter, "The Anthropological Circle," builds on the final section of the *Introduction to Kant's Anthropology*. Both of these, as we were just discussing, criticize contemporary philosophy's relation to anthropology.[8] In particular, Foucault criticizes the circular structure of contemporary philosophical thinking. Therefore, although the question that Foucault asks, in his *Introduction to Kant's Anthropology*, is the role of anthropology in Kant's thought, Foucault's real target in his *Introduction* is what he calls "contemporary philosophy," that is, French thought after World War II. On the basis of his reading of Kant's *Anthropology* in relation to both the critical project and what Kant, near the end of his life, calls "transcendental philosophy," Foucault accuses "contemporary philosophy" of a confusion that results in it suffering an illusion. In order for us to understand the criticism and in order to develop positive conclusions that will lead us to the *History of Madness*, we need to note only three points in Foucault's dense and detailed account of Kant's *Anthropology*.

First, in his investigation of the relation of critical thinking and anthropology, Foucault lays out a threefold movement that goes from the a priori of knowledge, that is, the critique as presented in *The Critique of Pure Reason*, to the a priori of existence, as presented in *The Anthropology* itself. And then, from the anthropological or existential a priori, Foucault takes us to the fundamental level, which is the concern of "transcendental philosophy." Each step along this path is a repetition. The nature of this repetition (or of repetition in general) is Foucault's central concern. Is the repetition a movement of the same or a movement of difference (Foucault 2008: 83 and 108)? Foucault thinks that, in Kant himself, the nature of the anthropologico-critical repetition is not clear (Foucault 2008: 108). However, in "philosophy since Kant," the repetition is precisely a circular movement of the same.

The repetitions therefore take place between three levels: the a priori of knowledge (critical thinking); the a priori of existence (anthropology); and the fundamental level (transcendental philosophy). The first repetition from critique to anthropology arrives at the level of existential a priori, a level that Foucault also calls "the originary."[9] Foucault defines this as an a priori that is structurally conditioning (or essential) but a structure that appears empirically in the course of time. We shall speak more about temporal dispersion in the third point below. Most simply, "the originary" refers to what is structurally prior and non-intuitable, and yet something given in an intuition and posterior. Its most general definition is the "already there" (Foucault 2008: 68). The combination of structural condition and empirically determined appearance makes the originary ambiguous. Lying between the level of the critique and the level of the foundation, the originary plays a crucial role in Foucault's criticism of "contemporary philosophy."

The second point we need to note is the nature of the fundamental. Foucault turns to Kant's *Logic*, in which Kant repeats the famous questions near the end of *The Critique of Pure Reason* – what can I know?; what should I do?; and what may I hope? – and adds a fourth question: what is man? According to Foucault, the fourth, additional, anthropological question repeats the first three questions at the fundamental level of "transcendental philosophy." Oriented by notions like source, domain, and limit, Kant in his "transcendental philosophy," according to Foucault, confronts two interrelated problems. On the one hand, there is the problem of the relationship between God, the world, and man. On the other hand, there is the problem of "the appurtenance of truth and freedom" (Foucault 2008: 104). The question of man in relation to the first problem receives the answer that man is in the middle as the synthesis between the world as the domain of existence and God as the absolute source. The answer in relation to the second question is that man is a "citizen of the world"; in the world, man articulates truth and freedom. Therefore, like the originary, man is ambiguous between being the synthesis between the world and an infinite God and being a citizen of the world. In both sides of the ambiguity, man must be defined by finitude.

The third important point is this: despite leading us into the fundamental level, anthropology is still empirical. While Foucault pursues anthropological empiricity through the themes of time and language, he determines time and language, and thus empiricity, and consequently the originary, as dispersion. Here however, Foucault is not interested in the question of the a priori. He is interested in the effects of temporal dispersion on truth and community. Because of the dispersion, truthful judgments are always threatened with loss. Synthetic activities can be failures and judgments erroneous since future appearances may falsify the judgments. Similarly, in language, the exchange of words and sentences proliferate meanings, which may have an effect on truth. But more seriously, for Kant, the proliferation might lead to disputes and threaten the social bond. As Foucault stresses, both the spontaneous act of synthesizing and the production of meaning are acts of freedom. Because these acts might result in the loss of truth and community, Foucault calls this freedom "dangerous" (Foucault 2008: 91). In the question of empiricity, we are really confronting the problematic relation of truth and freedom. However, binding *Können* to *Sollen*, Kant in the *Anthropology*, according to Foucault, proposes a moral obligation to seek the truth and to form a universal community (Foucault 2008: 64 and 71–2). In fact, because of the moral obligation, it is possible to see time indicating "the hypothesis and the hypothec of an exhaustive determination" (Foucault 2008: 90). The building up of truthful syntheses can lead the mind to "postulate" (hypothesis) that an absolute truth lies at the end of the temporal development, and the building up of truthful syntheses can lead the mind to think of the successes and errors as a kind of "deposit" (hypothec) toward the goal of absolute truth. To summarize, the three points are: repetition (and the originary); the fundamental (and finitude); and empiricity understood as dispersion (the relation of truth and freedom).

We are now able to examine Foucault's criticism of "contemporary philosophy."[10] To be clear, the criticism aims at the *movement* of "contemporary philosophy." In "contemporary philosophy," Kant's thought, according to Foucault, is made to return to its "fundamental rootedness" in the dispersion of empiricity. "Contemporary philosophy" investigates the dispersion of empiricity (human history and language), that is, it investigates the originary, as if it were the fundamental level, in order to form a concrete critique, one that is freed from the abstractness of the a priori. In other words, "contemporary philosophy," according to Foucault, repeats the divisions of Kantian critique into the a priori, the originary, and by repeating the division into empiricity, "contemporary philosophy" thinks it has provided the foundation for the division. What it has done, in reality, is mix the three sides of the division together within the level of the originary, that is, within the level of the anthropological. As the intermediary between the a priori and the fundamental, the originary takes on the privileges of the a priori and the meaning of the fundamental. Most importantly, in order to understand the movement of "contemporary philosophy," "the originary is developed," as Foucault says, "by going from the problematic of the necessary to that of existence *without making any difference between the two*" (Foucault 2008: 106; our emphasis). Through the originary, the analysis of conditions and the interrogation of finitude are the same. In other words, in this contemporary mode of thinking, one finds finitude not only in the conditions but also in existence. And, therefore, the movement of "contemporary philosophy" is circular. In Kant, as we saw, the mistakes and errors that threaten truth are treated as a kind of "deposit" (hypothec) toward an absolute truth. In short, the mistakes are given a teleological sense. Similarly, in "contemporary philosophy," as soon as the anthropological opening to the fundamental fails to provide the meaning and justification of the opening itself, the problematic of human existence attaches itself to "the hypothec of empiricity" (Foucault 2008: 106). In "contemporary philosophy," "the hypothec of empiricity" is interpreted not simply as teleological but also as dialectical. Instead of leading teleologically to a regulative idea, the "deposit" "returns" to an origin: original truth affirmed; truth lost or negated in errors; and finally, returning to the origin, truth rediscovered and reaffirmed. In this dialectic, truth is always alienated from itself (Foucault 2008: 122). Therefore, "contemporary philosophy's" movement, its kind of repetition, is the dialectic of the same and other.

On the basis of the criticism of "contemporary philosophy," we are able to draw two positive conclusions. First, through the recognition of the contemporary confusion, we can see now that, in order to reach the fundamental level, there must be difference, not sameness. Without stating it explicitly, Foucault places his work under the following transcendental or critical principle: the foundation can never resemble or be the same as the founded.[11] Any attempt to analyze the dispersion of time and language must be guided by this principle.[12] We can see this kind of foundation in *The History of Madness*, where Foucault differentiates between the practices in which the mad are confined and the medical and scientific conceptions of the mad. However, this difference is not a sameness or mirror relation between practices and theories. In fact, Foucault throughout *The History of Madness* insists that the scientific knowledge of madness is always engaged in practices aiming at a cure, while the practices of confining the mad are always connected to theories of the individuals (Foucault 2006: 172). This structure (of power and knowledge) is not simply bifurcated between the practices and knowledge; the two sides are "unfolded" from one another and dissymmetrical.[13] Therefore, this structure is *in* the dispersion of theories and practices, but it is different *from* the dispersion itself. Indeed, the archaeological excavation of this structure or apparatus is what Kant would have called "transcendental philosophy." The structure is really fundamental.

Second, above all else we must stress that, for Foucault, temporal and linguistic dispersion can never be overcome: "this dispersion that no confusion, dialectical or phenomenological, will have the right to reduce" (Foucault 2008: 106). Foucault will reiterate this claim in *The Archaeology of Knowledge* (Foucault 1972: 125 and 127). If dispersion cannot be overcome, then time or history must not be conceived as a circle. If one thinks that the movement of immanent desacrilization that we described above is a "return" to the sacred and transcendent, then one is suffering from an illusion. Although Foucault does not say this (but his numerous allusions to Nietzsche's eternal return doctrine suggest this comment), time must be conceived as a straight line. Of course, dispersion indicates a more complicated image than a straight line. Nevertheless, the image helps us see that the circular dialectic of finitude must be unwound. If it is, then we must not conceive errors as steps of mediation leading to the truth. We must not conceive events of error or truth as a kind of deposit made on the future appearance of truth itself. For Foucault, there is no truth of truth. There are only truth events. Most importantly, with time unwound, freedom (or power) is not bound to and closed in by the moral imperative commanding the pursuit of the truth. Of all the ideas that one is able to find in the *Introduction to Kant's Anthropology*, the most important idea is this: the problematic of the fundamental level is the relationship of truth and freedom (Foucault 2008: 106). More precisely, the problematic is "the reciprocal transcendence of truth and freedom" (Foucault 2008: 86) which, as we shall see, is the very heart of the *History of Madness*, which we find in the chapter called "The Transcendence of Delirium."

## III. The Transcendence of Delirium, or the Reciprocal Transcendence of Truth and Freedom

We are privileging the middle chapter of the *History of Madness*, "The Transcendence of Delirium," for several reasons. Although as we have seen, the Classical Age is the age of division, Foucault tells us the experience of delirium is discernible "within" the division, "in the order of speculative knowledge as well as in the order of the institution" (Foucault 2006: 250). Moreover, Foucault claims that delirium is the essence of madness; it is true madness (Foucault 2006: 238). In "The Transcendence of Delirium," Foucault "sketches out the structures that "properly [*propre*: or really] belong to madness" (Foucault 2006: 214). Finally, he tells us that the experience of delirium is unreason (*déraison*) itself (Foucault 2006: 243).[14] On the basis of these statements, it is clear that for Foucault himself this chapter is very important. Indeed, in the *History of Madness*' concluding chapter, he will re-use many of the formulas developed in "The Transcendence of Delirium."

Like the overall movement of the *History of Madness*, "The Transcendence of Delirium" description of the medical knowledge of madness in the Classical Age moves from what is exterior and to what is interior. Coming from the exterior, the body undergoes immediate causes such as accidents to the brain but also remote causes such as changes in the environment. Among the remote causes, we find in Classical Age medical theory the passions. According to Foucault, the passions are found among the more remote causes, and as one of the more invariant and obstinate cause of madness. As the point of contact between the soul and the body, and between activity and passivity, passion, according to the Classical Age, produces metaphorical relations between the body and the soul. These metaphorical relations can be rational. However, in the case of madness, a passion is able to produce or cause an image to appear in the mind, an image of an object of desire, for example. But also and at the same time, the passion makes "animal spirits" circulate through the body, turning the body into "a sort of geometrical figure of the passion" (Foucault 2006: 226). Then however, when the passion has been transposed into the corporeal space, the mind is no longer able to divert its attention from the image. The mind becomes finally more passionate for the desired object represented. Because passion coordinates the relations of the soul and the body, Foucault claims that in the Classical Age passion is not at the center point between the soul and the body. It is a bit prior to their relations. As prior, passion can be the starting point for the movement of madness. And despite the fact that the movement takes place within the union of the soul and the body, madness ends up dissociating the soul from the body, leading to an "irrational movement, and at that point, slipping away from the weight of truth" (Foucault 2006: 231). While passion can be the cause of madness, the determinism of passion is "the freedom offered to madness to penetrate the world of reason" (Foucault 2006: 228).

Starting with the passions which refer to the sensibility (Foucault 2006: 224–5), the movement Foucault describes goes on to the power of imagination. The imagination, of course, has the power to produce arbitrary images. Arbitrariness and arbitrary images are not mad and they even have a kind of innocence to them. Emerging from a dream, a reasonable man might observe that "I saw myself as dead." However, when one makes this observation, one is measuring the arbitrary image against reality, against "the weight of the truth." Consequently, one realizes that the image is false. In contrast, according to Foucault, in madness, one has the formation of the image, which is not yet madness. Madness occurs when the subject posits that he is dead as an assertion and valorizes the assertion as truth. As Foucault says, "Madness therefore goes beyond the image and yet is deeply embedded in it, for it solely consists of allowing the image to take on the value of total and absolute truth" (Foucault 2006: 232). The madman (the subject) is deeply embedded in the image because unlike the reasonable man, he does not measure the image and the assertion against reality. Yet, the madman is beyond the image, because in madness there is "the act of secret constitution" (Foucault 2006: 232).

According to Foucault, this act of constitution is an act of belief. The madman really believes that the image corresponds to reality. In the act of belief, the madman makes a judgment that he really believes is true. The discourse he then develops does not dispute the image. The discourse works the image over, hollows it out, and distends it throughout a process of reasoning, which rotates around the judgment. Again, a person might dream that he is dead. The death image is not madness. A person is mad who imagines himself dead; takes the image as true; asserts the supposedly true judgment that "I am dead"; and then reasons that, because he is dead, he has no need of food or heat, etc. Foucault stresses that the discourse developed around the supposedly true judgment is entirely rational, and medical theorists of the Classical Age recognize the "full rigor of logic" in the madman's reasoning (Foucault 2006: 233). The mad discourse is reason really underway; it is even a kind of "pure reason" since what has been constituted is an idea that corresponds to no existence (Foucault 2006: 234).[15] This idea is indeed "a total and absolute truth." Foucault calls such ideas "unreal" or "irreal" (*irréel*) (Foucault 2006: 231). The irreality or ideality suggests that the freedom of the constitutive act, belief, is a "vain freedom," where the word "vain" is being used in its sense of "emptiness." This vain freedom is the same "dangerous freedom," of which Foucault spoke in his *Introduction to Kant's Anthropology*. It is vain and dangerous because this freedom intends only the appearance of being, or, more precisely, only non-being (Foucault 2006: 232).

To reiterate, the movement of madness that Foucault is describing in "The Transcendence of Delirium" goes from external causes to the internal soul or mind. However, the movement really begins with the passions, which are prior to the actual relations between the soul and the body. As prior, we could say that the entire movement that Foucault sketches for us refers to passion.[16] As Foucault says, "passion is the general possibility of madness." However, the sketch provides more details. Passion refers first of all to the sensibility (Foucault 2006: 141), which receives impressions or causes from the external world. From the sensibility, we then go to the power of imagination. The power of imagination is the freedom to produce images, which lacking a judgment are neither true nor false. Now, from the viewpoint of the sensibility, the imagination produces images. However, from the viewpoint of imagination's, so to speak, "other side" (the side opposite to the sensibility), imagination is the freedom to believe, to assert, to affirm, and to judge the veracity of the image. Imagination is therefore a moment of synthesis in the movement of madness; this moment of synthesis is the side of the understanding. Then, from the understanding, we went to "pure reason," as Foucault says. The judgment and the image are surrounded by a rational discourse. Finally, because the rational discourse surrounds an image and a false judgment, the discourse is really that of unreason. Unreason (or delirium), however, is not madness. According to Foucault, what defines madness in the Classical Age is "the relation" between image, which is neither true nor false, and the reasoning, which has the simple form of logic. Foucault concludes that madness in the Classical Age does not therefore refer to changes in the body or the mind. It refers to the existence of a "delirious discourse" "beneath" (*sous*) the alterations of the body and the strangeness of behavior and speech, below the various relations of image and reasoning which might be phenomena of madness. As Foucault says, "Delirium is both madness itself, and beyond each of its phenomena, the silent transcendence that constitutes madness, in its truth" (Foucault 2006: 238). Delirium (unreason) is fundamental: the general possibility of madness. In this foundation, the synthesis of imagination is the root of transcendence.

Through this reiteration of the movement, we can see that the structure Foucault has sketched parallels that of Kant's faculties, going from the sensibility to understanding, to reason, via the imagination. Moreover, like his *Introduction to Kant's Anthropology*, Foucault moves from something like an a priori of knowledge (medical knowledge) to the fundamental, which is unreason, via the union of the soul and the body. Here again, this union (or disunion, which is madness) is made possible by the imagination. Most importantly, we can see now that what unreason or delirium most concern is "the reciprocal transcendence of truth and freedom." In the *History of Madness*, Foucault calls this freedom "absolute freedom" (Foucault 2006: 156–7). It is absolute because this freedom is relative to neither an external reality nor a moral value. This freedom is not "a semi-freedom" (Foucault 2006: 436). In particular, the synthesis enacted by this freedom is not a "moral synthesis" (Foucault 2006: 495). The irrational synthesis is a "bad use" of freedom (Foucault 2006: 439) which disrupts common sense knowledge and common sense morality.[17] The judgment produced by this synthesis is really delirious. The word "delirious" literally means a babbling or a raving, a way of speaking that deviates from "the straight path of reason" (Foucault 2006: 237).[18] This delirious speaking uses temporal and linguistic dispersion to unmake cognitive and moral syntheses. It unmakes truths already instituted. Nevertheless, as we saw, the delirium affirms "a total and absolute truth." Like absolute freedom, absolute truth means a truth relative to neither the correct truth of knowledge nor the good truth of morality. As such, it moves out in a straight line away from any given reality. This truth might be the illusion of madness or the transfiguration of humanity. No matter what, the free act of affirmation, that is unreason, is not only the constitutive act of madness; it also produces a truth that goes further than any truth that corresponds to a real thing. We should not forget that the madman could be "the moment of truth [and] speak the truth" (Foucault 2006: 210).

## IV. Conclusion: The Origin of Parrēsia in Foucault's Thought

At the end of the opening lecture in the 1983 course called *The Government of Self and Others*, Foucault speaks of two lineages that have evolved from Kant. Based in *The Critique of Pure Reason*, the first lineage is that of "the analytic of truth": the critical analysis of the conditions of possibility of true knowledge (Foucault 2010: 20). However, Foucault asserts there is a second lineage, which poses the following questions: "what is actuality [or present reality: *l'actualité*]?"; "what is the actual field of our experience?"; "what is the actual field of possible experiences?" (Foucault 2010: 20). The second lineage results in what Foucault calls "an ontology of the present, [or] of actuality." And in these closing minutes of the first lecture, Foucault confirms that he has linked himself to the second lineage. However, we see now that Foucault's link to an ontology of actuality begins in his *Introduction to Kant's Anthropology*. As we saw, in the *Introduction*, Foucault considers the relation between truth, as it is analyzed in Kant's critical philosophy, and freedom, as it is analyzed in Kant's pragmatic anthropology, moving finally to the fundamental level which in 1983 he calls "an ontology of the present."

Presented in 1983, this lecture is the basis for Foucault's 1984 text called "What is Enlightenment" (Foucault 1997: 303–19). This concerns how Foucault sees his own work in relation to what Kant says in his own text called "What is Enlightenment." Foucault's "What is Enlightenment," which remained unpublished during his lifetime, is cited frequently as the final definitive word on his thinking. It is important to recognize, however, that "What is Enlightenment" originates in the context of the course, *The Government of Self and Others* (Foucault 2010). This course, and with it *The Hermeneutics of the Subject* (Foucault 2005) and *The Courage of Truth* (Foucault 2011), concerns the ancient practice of *parrēsia*. Given this context, it is not implausible to claim that, when Foucault speaks of critique in "What is Enlightenment," he is attempting to retrieve the idea of *parrēsia* for the contemporary "philosophical *ethics*." This claim is even less implausible when we recognize that, although the word "francparler" does not appear in "What is Enlightenment," Foucault hints at it through his use of the verb "franchir": "I shall thus characterize the philosophical ethos appropriate to the critical ontology of ourselves as a historico-practical test of the limits that we are able to cross over [*franchir*], and thus as work carried out by ourselves upon ourselves as free beings" (Foucault 1997: 316). With the verb "franchir," Foucault harkens back to the idea of transcendence found in his first publications, but also it alludes (at least) to the act of freedom that is *parrēsia*.

In the lecture courses on *parrēsia*, Foucault isolates three characteristics, which he calls "the crux"; "the essence"; and "the heart" of *parrēsia* (Foucault 2010: 56, 64; and 66). For Foucault, "the crux" of *parrēsia* lies in the fact that *parrēsia* is an "irruptive event," that is, it is a speech act, a doing that produces unforeseen effects on the one who hears the frank-speaking. Speaking-frankly is based on no institution, no defined or coded context. Not producing a coded effect, *parrēsia*, as Foucault states frequently in *The Government of Self and Others*, produces an "unspecified risk," the worst of which is the death of the speaker. *Parrēsia* is dangerous. "The essence" of *parrēsia* lies in the fact that speaking-frankly requires something like a "personal relation between the person who utters and the statement." The personal relation is that the speaker authentically believes that what he is saying is genuinely true. The parresiastic statement is the affirmation of the affirmation (or the assertion of the assertion), which leads us to "the heart" of *parrēsia*. The assertion of the assertion means that the speaker asserts his or her own freedom and that is why we find "courage in the heart of *parrēsia*." It is why the Romans translated "parrēsia" as "libertas" (Foucault 2010: 46). *Parrēsia* therefore aims to "intensify" freedom; it is "the highest exercise of freedom" (Foucault 2010: 67).

The movement of unreason (or delirium) that Foucault sketches in "The Transcendence of Delirium" is structurally similar to the three characteristics of *parrēsia*. Like *parrēsia*, unreason does not produce a coded effect. It is an event that irrupts and disrupts instituted codes of knowledge and value. Of course, the irrational speech is dangerous. As the libertines knew, irrational discourse results in one being confined within a general hospital. Or, we could say – and the libertines knew this too – that irrational speech "crosses over" (*franchir*) the limits within which we find ourselves enclosed. Crossing over the limits might land us in an illusion – or in a truth that exceeds any truth that corresponds to reality. Unreason has a second characteristic that mirrors *parrēsia*. There is no unreason without the act of belief; unreason requires that one believe in what one is asserting. Here too, with unreason the subject binds himself to the assertion he is making: this is the truth and I am the person saying it. And finally, because of its dangers, unreason, this "dangerous freedom," would have to require courage.

For Foucault, in *The Government of Self and Others*, it is Plato who exhibits this courage. Plato had the courage to tell the truth to the tyrant of Syracuse, Dionysus. As is well-known, Plato's courageous speech act almost resulted in his death. In light of the *History of Madness*, we could say that when Plato said that he thinks Dionysus is not a good man, he was a bit irrational or even delirious. Here, with this anecdote about Plato we truly see freedom be intensified. Perhaps, Plato had broken through the confines of the Greek restrictions on freedom. Perhaps he had reached what Foucault, at the beginning of his career, called "absolute freedom." It is this absolute freedom that we seek within the "semi-freedoms," which regimes of power have constructed for us. Within the actuality of the present, we seek this freedom so that we might say a truth that is not a repetition of the same, but truly other: "truth is never the same" (Foucault 2011: 340).

## Notes

1. This chapter is co-authored with Daniel J. Palumbo
2. See Derrida 1978: 31–63.
3. For more on Foucault's relation to psychology, see Saïd Chebili, *Foucault et la psychologie* (Paris: L'Harmattan, 2005).
4. For more on Foucault's concept of apparatus, and for all of his concepts and terms see *The Cambridge Foucault Lexicon*, ed. Leonard Lawlor and John Nale (New York: Cambridge University Press, 2014).
5. Foucault's investigation of the relation of freedom to truth is inspired by Heidegger. Of course Foucault claims in one of his last interviews that his entire philosophical itinerary was determined by his reading of Heidegger – even though Foucault never wrote a book or even an article on Heidegger. We see Heidegger's influence (even though his name is never mentioned) most directly in Foucault's introduction to his own French translation of Kant's *Anthropology from a Pragmatic Point of View*. Foucault's "Kant book" builds on Heidegger's Kant book. For studies of Foucault's relation to Heidegger, see Alan Milchman and Alan Rosenberg, *Foucault and Heidegger: Critical Encounters* (Minneapolis: University of Minnesota Press, 2003). Béatrice Han's essay in this volume is particularly interesting. Béatrice Han, "Foucault and Heidegger on Kant and Finitude," in *Foucault and Heidegger*, pp. 127–62. See also Jean Zoungrana, *Michel Foucault. Un parcours croisé: Lévi-Strauss, Heidegger* (Paris: L'Harmattan, 1998), and Leonard Lawlor, "Heidegger and Foucault," in *The Bloomsbury Companion to Heidegger*, ed. François Raffoul and Eric Nelson (London: Bloomsbury, 2013), pp. 409–16.
6. Commentators have generally overlooked Foucault's *Introduction to Kant's Anthropology*. In an otherwise excellent book, Marc Djaballah does not discuss the *Introduction* at all. See Marc Djaballah, *Kant, Foucault, and Forms of Experience* (London: Routledge, 2008). Similarly, Fréderic Gros overlooks the *Introduction* in his *Foucault et la folie* (Paris: Presses Universitaire de France, 1997).
7. A Quaker, Samuel Tuke (1784–1857) organized the "York Retreat" near the end of the eighteenth century. It was famous for its "moral treatment" of the mad. Like Tuke, Philippe Pinel (1745–1826) reorganized the Bicêtre Hospital in Paris for a more "humane treatment" of the mad. In 1974, he ordered the removal of the chains from the mad at Bicêtre. This moment is captured in a painting by Charles Louis Muller called "Pinel Orders the

Chains Removed." Foucault devotes Chapter 4 of part three ("The Birth of the Asylum") to Pinel and Tuke. See Foucault 2006: 463–511.
8  Both this chapter and the final section anticipate Foucault's final two chapters in *The Order of Things* (Foucault 1970: 303–87).
9  Foucault appropriates this term from the phenomenological tradition and in particular from Heidegger's *Being and Time*.
10 This paragraph is based in the last two sections of Foucault's *Introduction* (Foucault 2008), see especially pp. 106 and 121.
11 Deleuze 1990: 99.
12 A few years later, Foucault will speak of "historical a priori" and "dispositions" (Foucault 1970: 157–9); much later he will speak of "apparatuses" (*dispositifs*) (Foucault 1977: 204–7).
13 Deleuze 1988: 111–13.
14 Deleuze speaks of a delirium proper to reason (Deleuze 1997a: 27; "délire" is rendered as "delusion").
15 See also Deleuze's account of the language of sadism in which the language of pure reason is violence (Deleuze 1997a: 20).
16 Here, we could say that Foucault's sketch of delirium intersects with Deleuze's Kant book, where Deleuze speaks of a higher form of the faculties, in particular in relation to *The Critique of Judgment* where the faculty of pleasure and pain is at play. See Deleuze 1984: 3–4, and 50–2.
17 Deleuze stresses constantly the need to disrupt the harmony of common sense and good sense. See Deleuze 1983: 103–10, and Deleuze 1995: 131.
18 For the good use of faculties in Kant, see Deleuze 1983: 92.

# 7

# Speaking Out for Others: Philosophy's Activity in Deleuze and Foucault (and Heidegger)[1]

There are many obvious intersections between Deleuze and Foucault: the relation of desire and pleasure; the structures of *agencement* and *dispositif*; and, the self-relation as the fold. These intersections are especially evident and determinable insofar as Deleuze wrote about Foucault and Foucault wrote about Deleuze. Yet, it is remarkable that *both* Deleuze and Foucault, each at the end of his life, wrote about philosophy itself. Of course, Deleuze's last great book (written with Guattari), appearing in 1991, is called *What is Philosophy?* Yet, Foucault's last two courses at the Collège de France from 1982 to 1984 aim to answer the same question. This final intersection of Deleuze and Foucault's thinking in the question of philosophy seems to have gone unnoticed. So, the question that we are going to address in this chapter is: What is philosophy for both Deleuze and Foucault? There is, however, a more precise way to formulate the question. On the one hand – this is a Deleuzian way to formulate the problem – the problem is the relation of philosophy to historical contingency. That is, today philosophy finds itself in the territory of capitalism. On the other hand – this is a Foucaultian way – the problem is the relation of philosophy to power. That is, philosophy always finds itself in a particular relation to power. Both ways of expressing the problem imply that essentially the problem amounts to this: What is philosophy's "reality" (Foucault's terminology [Foucault 2010: 229])? or, what is philosophy's "use" (Deleuze's terminology [Deleuze and Guattari 1994: 8–9])? In short, what is philosophy's activity?

It seems that the answer we find in late Deleuze and in late Foucault consists in a certain way of speaking. Philosophy's activity is linguistic. As we see in Deleuze and Guattari's *What is Philosophy?*, philosophy's use is "speaking for others" (*parler pour les autres*), and if we look at Foucault's final courses at the Collège de France its reality consists in what the ancient Greeks called "*parrēsia*" (speaking frankly, fearless speech, or even outspokenness). As we shall see in this chapter and in Chapter 8, these two philosophical linguistic utterances are connected. In *What is Philosophy?*, Deleuze and Guattari argue that speaking for others arises when we are in front of the intolerable suffering of others. As we have seen, this standing before them, in their suffering, fills us with the shame at being human all too human. Thus the feeling of shame motivates us to speak for them which, in turn, takes us beyond the merely linguistic and requires *parrēsia*; it requires that we speak frankly, that we speak out, and then, as Foucault would say, speaking for requires, beyond the passivity of the feeling of shame, the activity of courage. The use of philosophy comes to light when we convert shame into courage. Then we see that philosophy has a reality insofar as its speaking affects a change in reality. As Deleuze and Guattari say, what is at issue in speaking for is "becoming" (Deleuze and Guattari 1994: 109).[2] On the basis of the feeling of shame we must become other, enter into our own conversion of speaking and acting. We then speak for others so that they become other, so that they escape from their suffering and agony. We speak frankly and become outspoken when we take the risk to address the tyrant, the risk to expose the most naked and excessive uses of power, as those found for instance in the prisons.

There are two problems with which we must deal in order to understand the conversion of shame into courage (based on the association of "speaking for" with *parrēsia*). On the one hand, if it is indeed the case that what is at issue in speaking for is becoming, then we must reexamine the problem of return or *the* return (as in Nietzsche's eternal return doctrine) as we find it in early Deleuze and Foucault. The return necessary concerns the future of what is coming and of what is other. Foucault himself indicates that the problem of the return is at the center of both his own thinking and Deleuze's when he says, in "Theatrum Philosophicum," that "Time is what repeats itself; and the present ... does not stop recurring ... Being is a Return [*Retour*] freed from the curvature of the circle; it is Recurrence [*Revenir*] ... [freed] from the law of the Same."[3] Now, twice in this review essay, Foucault praises Deleuze for not denouncing metaphysics "as the forgetfulness of being." The allusion to Heidegger is obvious. Thus, we think that, if the project of determining the activity of philosophy for the later Deleuze and Foucault requires that we go back to the earlier problem of return, then the earlier problem of return requires us to look at the criticisms Deleuze and Foucault level at Heidegger's thought.[4] Heidegger's thought seems to express precisely the idea against which early Deleuze and Foucault fight: the idea of circular return. Immediately, we can say that philosophy's activity is not a circular return – not a return to an origin or foundation – as if it amounted to a promise being fulfilled. Thus philosophy's reality, its deed, its use, must amount to going beyond historical contingency without returning to a prior condition, or it amounts to going beyond the current regime of power within which it finds itself without returning to a prior regime. Its activity or reality must consist in a creative repetition that returns without end.

The second problem then appears on the basis of this concept of unlimited return. The very idea of speaking for others seems to imply a form of representation: when I speak for you, I represent you, and then I mediate you with me and with others on the basis of a reductive and homogenizing identity, similarity, and resemblance. In other words, when I speak for you, it looks as though your singularity disappears; you never appear as an event. There is only the repetition of a general concept. The representation then looks to be precisely a circular return. In fact, as early as the 1968 *Difference and Repetition*, Deleuze denounces speaking for others understood as representation; he says, "The misfortune in speaking is not speaking, but speaking *for others* or representing something" (Deleuze 1995: 52). The problem becomes more acute when we look at the 1972 exchange between Deleuze and Foucault called "Intellectuals and Power." There, Deleuze says, "We laughed at representation, saying it was over, but we didn't follow this '*theoretical* conversion' through – namely, theory demanded that those involved finally speak on their own account, *practically*." As is well known, Deleuze claims in "Intellectuals and Power" that Foucault was the first to teach us the fundamental lesson of "the indignity of speaking for others" (Deleuze 2004: 208, translation modified). How is it possible to reconcile this early indignity with speaking for others with Deleuze (and Guattari's) later endorsement of "speaking for" in *What is Philosophy?* Although we are not certain, it seems that it was Foucault and Deleuze's involvement in "Le Groupe d'Information sur les Prisons" in 1971–1972 that allowed them to start to think of "speaking for" in a new way.

The GIP's independence from any political party and from any enterprise (like a sociological study or a judicial inquest) freed the prisoners from representing something like a social type. The questionnaire that the GIP used, in particular, allowed the inmates to speak on their own account. Yet, the GIP spoke too, not only through the way the questionnaire was worded but also through its own publications. What the GIP did then in its publications was make the voices of the inmates "resound." Freed from representing a general concept, a social type, or a moral universal, this resonance looks to be more like a creative repetition than a representation. So, we are going to examine the GIP documents as a kind of *verification* of our interpretation of the late endorsement of "speaking for" and its association to *parrēsia*. Before we come to this "verification" through the GIP documents, we must take up the problem of the return in Deleuze and Foucault in relation to Heidegger. Through Heidegger, we shall be able to see that the conversion of shame into courage gives us a glimpse of how philosophy calls us to go over man.[5] We start with Heidegger and Deleuze.

## I. Return in Deleuze, Foucault – and Heidegger

Deleuze's most extensive early discussion of Heidegger appears in Chapter 1 of *Difference and Repetition*. As is well-known, in this chapter, Deleuze attempts to liberate difference from the demands of "the concept in general." The concept in general (or representation) leads us to conceive difference only for or in relation to something that serves as its foundation or ground. Indeed, difference becomes nothing but the negation of the foundation, a negation which, when it is itself negated, returns difference to the foundation from which it derived. In other words, in the representational concept of difference, difference is nothing but a bare repetition of the foundation; the dialectic is always circular. In this conception, difference relates negatively back to a foundation, which is the abstract identity of the concept (the third term of mediation). Therefore, difference is no longer conceived in terms of itself or "in itself," hence the title of *Difference and Repetition*'s first chapter. It is within the context of this reconception of difference and its relation to negation that Deleuze introduces his note on "Heidegger's Philosophy of Difference." In the note Deleuze makes five points, which I now outline in brief.

The *first point* is that the "not" in Heidegger does not express the negative; rather it expresses the difference between being and beings. The *second point* is that the difference between being and beings is not the "between" in the ordinary sense.[6] Instead, it must be understood as "the fold," the "Zwiefalt." Difference understood as the fold is constitutive of being. In other words, being, in Heidegger, differentiates the being off from a sort of background of obscurity. In this way, Deleuze gives a new sense to Heidegger's expression "ontological difference": being is the active "differenciator" of beings (Deleuze 1995: 65, also p. 117).[7] The *third point* is that the "ontological difference corresponds to the question." In other words, Deleuze makes an equivalency between being and questioning. As equivalent to a question, being actively constitutes beings as differences, as if they were so many different answers to a question that remains open and consequently unanswerable. As a kind of non-being, difference (or the question) – this is the *fourth point* – "is *not*," as Deleuze says, "an object of representation."[8] The "turn beyond metaphysics," according to Deleuze, amounts to insisting that metaphysics cannot think "difference in itself." The Heideggerian "turn," for Deleuze, is a resistance to conceiving difference as a third term "between" being and beings, it is a "stubborn" resistance to mediation. Finally, the *fifth point*: "Difference cannot, therefore, be subordinated to the Identical or the Equal, but must be thought as the Same, in the Same." Through the Same, Heidegger is trying to think a "gathering" that is not reducible to empty indifferent oneness.

It seems that Deleuze intends these five points to show how certain readings of Heidegger are really misunderstandings (probably he has in mind those of Sartre and Merleau-Ponty). In particular, Deleuze's five points aim to outline a more accurate reading of the Heideggerian "not": "the Heideggerian NOT refers not to the negative in being, but to being as difference; it refers not to negation but to the question." Deleuze's defense of Heidegger is so strong here that he says that he considers the Heideggerian "correspondence" between difference and the question, between the ontological difference and the being of the question, "fundamental." Despite this attachment, Deleuze suggests that Heidegger's own formulas for the "not" might be to blame for the misunderstandings of his later work. Indeed, through a series of questions, Deleuze distances himself from Heidegger's thinking. In particular, he is not certain that speaking of the Same (or gathering), rather than Identity, is really enough to think original difference.[9] Deleuze asks, "Is Sameness enough to disconnect difference from all mediation?" The distance that Deleuze takes from Heidegger's thought, however, really comes down to the status of the being (*das Seiende* or *l'étant*), not the status of being (not *das Sein* or *l'être*). The question for Deleuze is the following: "Does Heidegger make the conversion by means of which being [*l'être*] must be said only of difference and in this way being [*l'être*] revolves around the being [*l'étant*]?" In other words, "Does Heidegger conceive the being [*l'étant*] in such a manner that the being [*l'étant*] is removed from all subordination in relation to the identity of representation?" Deleuze concludes, "It seems not, given [Heidegger's] interpretation of Nietzsche's eternal return" (Deleuze 1995: 66).[10]

Whether or not Deleuze's claim about Heidegger's interpretation of Nietzsche's eternal return doctrine is correct – in *Difference and Repetition* (but already in the 1962 *Nietzsche and Philosophy* [Deleuze 1983: 220n31]), it is clear that Deleuze thinks that Heidegger does not understand the eternal return doctrine – it tells us a lot about how Deleuze conceives his own thinking in relation to that of Heidegger. When Heidegger interprets the eternal return doctrine as being "metaphysical," Deleuze thinks that Heidegger is claiming that it is a founded repetition. That is, it is the repetition of an identity that predetermines all the answers to the question, as if for Nietzsche the repetition was a repetition of permanence, as if repetition did not produce a multiplicity of new answers, as if therefore there was no true becoming. In contrast, what Deleuze sees in the eternal return doctrine is a very specific kind of repetition, one that, as he says, "makes a difference" (Deleuze 1995: 60). The repetition to which the eternal return refers, in Deleuze's interpretation of Nietzsche, is a repetition that repeats no identity; it is foundationless insofar as it repeats the being (*l'étant*), but the being – an individual thing – is not conceived as a copy of an original or a copy of a model. The being is conceived as a singularity or as an event. A singular event, for Deleuze, is a true "commencement" so that the repetition of the eternal return is a "recommencement." Being based in a commencement, in an event, the recommencement is not determined and therefore has the potential to produce more differences, more events, more novelties, more answers to the question (Deleuze 1995: 200–2). The repetition is creative.[11] Therefore, insofar as Deleuze thinks that Heidegger does not understand Nietzsche's eternal return doctrine, he thinks the real issue between his own thinking and that of Heidegger is the idea of foundation: founded repetition versus unfounded repetition. Heidegger, for Deleuze, remains attached to "the primacy of the Same" (Deleuze 1995: 321n11). As we shall now see, Foucault also thinks that Heidegger remains attached to the primacy of the same.

The main occurrence of Heidegger's name in Foucault's published works appears in *The Order of Things*, in Chapter 9, "Man and his Doubles."[12] Although this is among the most difficult texts Foucault ever wrote, its basic idea is well known: the idea of man. Unlike human nature in the Classical Age which is correlated "term by term" to nature, man in the Modern Age is defined by a kind of ambiguity or doubling of finitude. First and foremost, man's finitude appears to him in the positive content of certain disciplines such as biology and man's finitude appears to him in the way man knows in these disciplines.[13] In other words, finitude is repeated from the positive content of knowledge into the conditions for that positive knowledge. In Chapter 9, after having defined "man's primary characteristic" as repetition (the repetition of the positive and the fundamental), Foucault then extends the repetition of finitude into three other "doubles" that define man: "the transcendental repeats the empirical, the *cogito* repeats the unthought, the return of the origin repeats its retreat" (OT 326/316).

It is in the section that concerns this fourth repetition, the retreat and return of the origin, that we find the one occurrence of Heidegger's name. The section overall, however, concerns man's relation to the origin. Foucault provides a tripartite description of this relation. *First*, Foucault speaks of the origin retreating from man into the past. In Modern thought, according to Foucault, man always finds himself alive against the background of life, labor, and language that began long ago. In short, man's origin is the "already begun" (OT 341/330), which means that man is not "contemporaneous" with the origin. Because of this non-contemporaneity, it is not possible to attribute, according to Foucault, an origin to man. Then *second*, because man seems to have no origin, to be virtually outside of time, he also appears to be that being from which all the chronologies of life, labor, and language have derived. Therefore, the origin of things always retreats or withdraws to a beginning earlier than man, while man retreats from things as that from which all the durations of things can begin. This double retreat, however, makes possible, according to Foucault, a "third retreat" (OT 343/332). So, *third*, taking up the *task* to call into question everything that pertains to time, Modern thought contests the origin of things in order to discover the "origin without either origin or beginning."[14] Time then would be, as it were, "suspended" in thought – in the sense that making this timeless origin be visible thought would seem to have made time stand still. And yet, thought itself would not be able to escape from time because it is not contemporary with the originless origin of time. In the Modern Age, thought can never be contemporary with the origin. However, as Foucault stresses, the suspension of time in thought is able to make the relation of thought and origin "flip over." Previously, the origin withdrew from thought into the past; now, however, it withdraws from thought going out into the future. In other words, after finding itself coming too late for the origin, thought now projects the origin out in front as what is still to be thought.

Although Foucault does not say this, the task for thinking that aims at suspending time amounts to Heidegger's retrieval of the meaning of being as time. According to Foucault, however, this retrieval is a retrieval of the same.[15]

As with Deleuze's claim about Heidegger's interpretation of the eternal return doctrine, with Foucault we cannot find one clear argument to support the claim that Heideggerian retrieval is a retrieval of the same.[16] A clue seems to appear, however, when Foucault says in "Man and his Doubles" that "[the origin] is promised to [man] in an imminence that will perhaps be forever snatched from him" (OT 345/334–5). The clue seems to be this: it is difficult to conceive promising in any other way than as something to be kept; as something to be kept, a promise must be fulfilled.[17] Then as something to be fulfilled, it seems that promising must always be based in a lack. The same dominates this retrieval or return or repetition because the promising, to which Foucault seems to be referring, is conceived as a deficiency (OT 353/342).[18] The withdrawal of the origin produces a deficiency, but the deficiency, it seems, produces something like an outline or a figure in relief that the future will fill in. In other words, what is to come is determined as what is going to fill in this lack. The still coming future will be the same as what was outlined with the withdrawal of the origin into the past. There seems, however, for Foucault, another and stronger step in this "argument," if we can call it an argument and if we understand it correctly. Foucault speaks of "the insurmountable relation of man's being to time" (OT 346/335). Thus it seems that the lack is a lack in "man's own being," which means that the return of the origin – promised and not yet fulfilled – is a fulfillment of *man's being*. Man is the figure in relief made by the withdrawal. The return of the origin therefore is a return of the same being as us. And then, we see that what is at issue in the question of return is really a going beyond or over man.

## II. The Conversion of Shame into Courage

Therefore, for both Deleuze and Foucault, as we just saw, Heideggerian repetition, return, or retrieval does not reach the true repetition, because Heidegger, it seems, conceives repetition as a repetition of the same. Thus the true repetition, for both Deleuze and Foucault, is what we called above a "creative repetition", a phrase which seems to be contradictory since repetitions repeat and therefore cannot be creative. Yet, one can understand the phrase if one thinks of the artwork. As we discussed in Chapter 4, an event such as the writing of *Hamlet* was based in no determinate model, no exact foundation, and no self-identical origin; therefore its subsequent theatre productions, while repetitions, are all able to be different. We know of course how important Oedipus and Hamlet are in Deleuze's *Difference and Repetition*. We know how important the tragic is in both early Deleuze and in early Foucault. The importance of tragedy and the artwork in Deleuze and Foucault means that they both oppose the repetition of the same with the repetition of the different, and this means that they oppose the being of man with the being of language.

There is no question that Foucault, in *The Order of Things*, opposes the being of language to the being of man.[19] There, Foucault notes that at the end of the Classical Age, language loses its status as the transparent medium between things and order, as the transparent medium between speaker and hearer. No longer occupying the middle, language, for Foucault, no longer functions transitively and no longer has a destination, an end or *telos* or *eschaton*. Then language no longer folds back over itself into a circle. The being of language in Foucault is "radical intransitivity", through which language is liberated from its finitude, allowing it to take on an indefinite potentiality (OT 313/300). It seems that for Foucault the indefinite potentiality of language (when it is liberated from transitivity) implies that language is capable of producing events. Thus, we must say that, despite Deleuze's so-called "vitalism," it is language that inspires his reflections on sense and event in *Difference and Repetition* and in *The Logic of Sense*. In fact, in *The Logic of Sense*, he says, "We will not ask therefore what the sense of an event is: the event is sense itself. The event belongs essentially to language, it *is* in an essential relation to language" (Deleuze 1990: 22). Always, however, for Deleuze, the linguistic event (sense or more generally a work, like an artwork) arises out of an affective encounter, out of the vision of what is "terrible," as "the soldier" sees in Stephen Crane's *The Red Badge of Courage* (Deleuze 1990: 101). This vision of the terrible opens the way to go beyond or over the being of man.

Going over man brings us to the question of philosophy in the final Deleuze and Foucault. In *What is Philosophy?* Deleuze (with Guattari) speaks of shame as one of the most powerful motives of philosophy (Deleuze and Guattari 1994: 108). This shame is what one feels when confronted with the suffering of others. And for them, it seems that the shame in relation to the suffering of others (alluding apparently to Nietzsche, they call this "the shame at being human"[20]) motivates one to "speak for" (*parler pour*) others. But then Deleuze and Guattari ask: What does it mean to speak for others? They say that speaking for others is speaking "before" others. They change the preposition from "pour" to "devant." One feels shame when one stands "before" (*devant*) the victims of the Holocaust (and here of course they are speaking of Heidegger's political "mistake"). But beyond the feeling of shame "before" (*devant*) the suffering of others, they say that what is at issue in "speaking for" is becoming (Deleuze and Guattari 1994: 109). Here "devant" seems to change its meaning from "before" to "being in advance of." In advance of, for example, the animals who are suffering, one must become animal. In other words, from the shame before, one must take the first step in advance of the animals, and become animal. The change in meaning of the "devant" seems to imply that the ones who are becoming are the avant-garde. But then, Deleuze and Guattari return to the preposition "pour." Earlier in Chapter 5, we saw the role of the "pour que" in Deleuze and Guattari. Here again we see that one becomes animal "so that" – "pour que" – the animals become something else or other. The "pour que" of becoming puts the animals back in front and reduces we who are becoming to being only means. We who are becoming non-human, we who are speaking for others and before others who are suffering and in agony amounts to making, helping, or better, *letting* the animals become something else and something other. "Speaking for" tries to help them change so that they are no longer suffering or are in agony. This speaking so that others become other is really what responsibility would be for Deleuze and Guattari. And it seems this kind of responsibility would require courage.

The speaking that helps others become other (others to come), then, leads us to Foucault. In his final courses at the Collège de France, Foucault, as we mentioned at the beginning, lectured on the ancient Greek notion of *parrēsia*, translated as "free-speech," "fearless speech," or even "outspokenness" (CF-GSO1, 61/63).

In particular, in *The Government of Self and Others I*, Foucault stresses that *parrēsia* is *not* a performative utterance.[21] *Parrēsia* is always something *more* than a performative. As examples of performative utterances, Foucault speaks of "I baptize you" and "I apologize," but he could just as well have spoken of "I promise." In contrast to performative utterances such as "I promise" – here we see the connection to Heidegger – "there is," Foucault says, "*parrēsia* at the moment when the statement of [the] of truth constitutes an irruptive event opening up an undefined or poorly defined risk for the subject who speaks." Involving a non-defined or badly defined, indeed an unforeseeable, risk for the speaker, this kind of event provides no outline of what is coming. It is truly different from promising, and thus it is genuine becoming. But the undefined risk for the speaker means that the speaker must act *courageously*.[22] Therefore, if we combine these two ideas, one from the late Deleuze, one from the late Foucault – that is, respectively, speaking for and *parrēsia* – we can then convert the shame before intolerable suffering into the courage to speak out. In fact, as we shall see now, it is precisely this combination of ideas that seems to animate Deleuze and Foucault's work in "Le Groupe d'Information sur les Prisons" in 1971–1972.

### III. Speaking Out For Prisoners

In order to verify the interpretation of "speaking for" and its association with *parrēsia* that we just presented, we are going to reconstruct the contours of what the GIP was, what it did, and what it accomplished. So, *first*, we must ask for what purpose was the GIP established. While its activities ran over 1971 and 1972, its roots go back to events in the autumn of 1970.[23] In

September 1970 and then again in January 1971, several imprisoned members of a Maoist inspired movement called "Gauche prolétarienne" went on a hunger strike in order to be recognized as political prisoners (rather than being treated as common criminals.) Daniel Defert, who was a member of the group charged to prepare the lawsuits for the imprisoned (the group was called "Organisation des prisonniers politiques" [OPP]), proposed to Foucault to generate a commission of inquest concerning the prisons. It was "at this moment," as Foucault says, that he "concerned himself" with the prisons (Foucault 2001a: 1072). It seems that Foucault accepted Defert's proposal because such an inquest was the logical next step following *The History of Madness*: from the confinement of the mad to the imprisonment of common criminals and political dissidents.[24] However, while Defert seems to have proposed a "commission of inquest" (making use of a judiciary term), Foucault created an "information group," hence the name he gave to the group: "Le Groupe d'Information sur les Prisons."[25] As Foucault says in the "GIP Manifesto," which he read aloud on 8 February, 1971, "Hardly any information has been published on the prisons. The prisons are one of the hidden regions of our social system, one of the black boxes of our life. We have the right to know, we want to know" (Foucault 2001a: 1043). Foucault's transformation of the inquest commission into an information group explains why Deleuze says, much later, after Foucault had died, in the short interview called "Foucault and Prison," that "Foucault had been the only one, not to survive the past [Deleuze mentions the past of May 1968], but to invent something new at all levels" (Deleuze 2006: 272). According to Deleuze, the GIP was an entirely new kind of group and thus starting it was, as he says, "like taking a step into darkness" (Deleuze 2006: 273).

What made the GIP entirely new, according to Deleuze, was its "complete independence" because it concerned itself only with the prisons; it was "localized" (Deleuze 2006: 276–7) or even "singular."[26] It was not based on an ideology, or, more precisely, it was not based in something like a universal moral value; it was not a totalizing movement.[27] It had nothing to do with a political party or a political enterprise. What was at issue for GIP was not a sociological study of prisons; it was not reformist; it did not want to propose an ideal prison (Foucault 2001a: 1072). What was at issue was "to let those who have an experience of the prison speak," "literally to hand over the speaking to the inmates" (Foucault 2001a: 1043 and 1072).[28] The inmates were to speak "on their own account" (*pour leur compte*) (Deleuze 2004: 206), and "in their own name" (Deleuze 2004: 209).[29] As the GIP "Manifesto" says, "We shall not find the information [we are seeking] in the official reports. We are asking for information from those who, somehow, have an experience of the prison or a relation to it" (Foucault 2001a: 1043). Clearly, here we see that the GIP sought to avoid, as Deleuze says in "Intellectuals and Power," "the indignity of speaking for [*parler pour*] others" (Deleuze 2004: 208).

In fact, the GIP tried to avoid the indignity of speaking for others by distributing a questionnaire to the inmates, but it was not allowed to distribute the questionnaire inside the prisons. So, every Saturday, Foucault tells us in an interview published in March 1971 (Foucuault 2001a: 1046), he and other members of the GIP went to the visitor gate of La Santé Prison and distributed the questionnaire to the families of inmates who were waiting in line. The first Saturday, Foucault says, the families gave the GIP members a cold welcome. The second time, people were still distrustful. The third time, however, was different. Someone said that "all that is just talk, it should have been done a long time ago." Then suddenly, exploding with anger, a woman starts to tell her entire story: she speaks of the visits, the money she gives to the inmate she is visiting, the wealthy people who are not in prison, she speaks of the filth in the prisons.[30] Thus the woman speaks in her own name, on her own account. And, when she starts to tell her story, it seems that the GIP has succeeded in letting those who have an experience of the prison speak. The GIP had given speech over to the inmates. As Deleuze says, "This was not the case before" (Deleuze 2006: 277).

What was made known by the questionnaire? The questionnaire was composed of eleven sections. The section topics and the questions contained in them are not surprising. They concerned the conditions of visitations; conditions of the cells; the food; what sort of exercise; what sort of work; knowledge of rights; the types of discipline and punishments used in the prisons. However, two questions seem remarkable. On the one hand, under the category of "Visites," the questionnaire asks whether its respondent can describe the conditions of visitations, and, in particular, "those conditions which appear to you to be the most intolerable." On the other hand, under the category of "Discipline," and after asking about solitary confinement, the questionnaire asks the respondent what is "most intolerable after being deprived of freedom." The apparently one extant copy of the GIP questionnaire is, in fact, filled in by an unknown former inmate. In response to the question of what constitutes the most intolerable conditions of the visits, the former inmate had written that it is "the 'screws' [that is, the police] behind your back who are trying to see whether you expose family letters. It's shameful." The answer to the second question of what is most intolerable after solitary confinement is: "One is, all the same, on solid ground [after being freed from solitary confinement]. [But] one has suffered." These answers indicate that what the inmates spoke of was shame and suffering and it was (and is still?) the intolerable.[31] The knowledge of intolerable shame and suffering explains why Deleuze says that Foucault "was very shocked by the results [of the questionnaire]. We found something much worse [than bad food and poor medical treatment], notably, the constant humiliation" (Deleuze 2006: 273). The pamphlet that GIP published was called "Intolerable." And Foucault says in an interview that "simply, I perceive the intolerable" (Foucault 2001a: 1073).

We come now to the *second* question: what did the GIP do? This question itself contains two others questions: What did GIP do with the information about intolerable suffering, shame, and humiliation? What did the inmates and families become as a result of what GIP did? These two questions are inseparably connected because, as Foucault reports, the GIP wanted that "there is not too much difference between those making the inquiry and collecting the information and those who are responding to the inquiry and providing information" (Foucault 2001a: 1046). In a rare occasion, Foucault then speaks of an "ideal": "The ideal for us would be that the families communicate with the prisoners, that the prisoners communicate among themselves, that the prisoners communicate with public opinion. That is, we'd like to break apart the ghetto" (Foucault 2001a: 1046). All that the GIP was doing was providing the "means" (*moyens*), the means to express, the means to communicate, the means to make the information circulate "from mouth to ear, from group to group" (Foucault 2001a: 1046–7).[32] By being simply a "means" to express the intolerable in its "raw state" (Foucault 2001a: 1073), the GIP broke apart the ghetto-like difference, but it also made the intolerable "echo" (Foucault 2001a: 1045).[33] In "Foucault and Prison," Deleuze will also speak of the "echo" made by the GIP. In fact, he says that the GIP "amplified" the inmates' voices, its means made their voices "resound" (*retentissement*) (Deleuze 2006: 280). In fact, in this late text, Deleuze says that "the goal of the GIP was less to make [the inmates] speak than to design a place where people would be forced to listen to them, a place that was not reduced to a riot on the prison roof, but would ensure that what they had to say passes through" (Deleuze 2006: 277). The conclusion we must draw is that in the GIP, the ones doing the inquiry became "means," or, as Deleuze would say, "relays" for the voices of the inmates (Deleuze 2004: 206–7). But then, moving to the side of the ones responding to the inquiry, we must notice that they too were no longer simply inmates or prisoners. In a 1972 text for *Le Nouvel Observateur*, Deleuze says the inmates themselves are judging the forms that their collective actions must take within the framework of the specific prison within which they find themselves (Deleuze 2004: 204). In the same text, Deleuze recounts that a new kind of public gathering is taking place. It has nothing to do with "public confession" or with a "traditional town meeting." Instead, former prisoners are coming forward and saying what was done to them, what they saw, physical abuse, reprisals, lack of medical care (Deleuze 2004: 205). In fact, Deleuze reports that at one such gathering the prison guards tried to shout down the former inmates. The inmates however silenced the prison guards by describing the brutality that each one had committed. The inmates used the very sentence that the prison guards had used to intimidate the inmates: "I recognize him" (Deleuze 2004: 205). Thus, at the least, the inmates became speakers. But they also became writers by responding to the questionnaire. The importance of writing is seen in the fourth GIP pamphlet (from late 1972), which published, without correcting punctuation or spelling (that is, in their "raw state"), letters written from prison by a certain "H.M." In the short commentary that he wrote to accompany the publication of the letters, Deleuze claims that H.M.'s letter bear witness to complementary or opposed personalities, all of which, however, "are participating in the same 'effort to reflect'." In fact, Deleuze says that H.M.'s correspondence "is exemplary because its heartfelt reflections express what a prisoner is exactly thinking" (Deleuze 2004: 244). Thus we must conclude that the amplification of the inmates' voices was done so that the prisoners became thinkers.

We come then to the third question: What then happened? As Deleuze says in "Foucault and Prison," the GIP was a "thought-experiment" but like all experiments it had mixed results (Deleuze 2006: 273). On the side of the ones responding to the questionnaire, there were risks. Accompanying the uprisings that continued over the two year period, there was a rash of suicides in the prisons as a kind of last ditch protest. In fact, H.M. committed suicide and the fourth GIP pamphlet was devoted to suicides in the prisons. On the side of the ones collecting the information, the GIP side, there were risks too. In a 1971 interview Foucault speculated that the authorities might react to the GIP's actions by throwing all of its members in jail (Foucault 2001a: 1073). Most importantly, however, soon after the GIP was disbanded in 1972, the prison authorities clamped down on the prisons again. As Deleuze reports in "Foucault and Prison," Foucault came to believe that the GIP had been a failure (Deleuze 2006: 279). Foucault had the impression that the GIP had served no purpose. "It was not repression," Foucault says in Deleuze's words, "but worse: it was as if someone speaks but nothing was said" (Deleuze 2006: 277). Yet, Deleuze insists that the GIP had been a success in a different way. Although it did not succeed in bringing about long-lasting concrete changes in the French prisons, the GIP did produce "new conditions for statements." It was successful, according to Deleuze, insofar as it made possible "a type of statement about the prison that is regularly made by the inmates and the non-inmates, a type of statement that had been unimaginable before" (Deleuze 2006: 280). In other words, we could say that the GIP's success appeared not in the prisons themselves, but in the statements, concepts, and books it made possible. For instance, the former inmate Serge Livrozet wrote a book called *De la prison à la revolte*, for which Foucault wrote a preface (Foucault 2001a: 1262–7; also Deleuze 2006: 276–7).[34] While the GIP documents constantly state that they are not trying to raise the inmates' consciousness (*pas de prise de conscience*) (Foucault 2001a: 1044), and, while Foucault constantly says that the GIP is not providing the inmates with knowledge (Foucault 2001a: 1289), it did in fact give the inmates and their families a new way of relating to themselves. The GIP not only was a relay for the inmates' voices, but it was also a relay for thinking.

We are now in a position to be able to summarize the three stages that we have just outlined. First, because the GIP was a localized and therefore non-totalizing movement, because it was specific to the prisons, it was freed from anything like a universal moral value or a general concept. As always, Deleuze and Foucault's thinking is opposed to generalities and universals. GIP was no different; it was non-representational. It was merely an information group. Second, when the inmates and their families started to speak, their voices emerged not as a representation of some abstract idea. Their voices emerged – the voices became audible and the inmates and their families became visible – as an event, as a singularity.[35] Their voices emerged from the "darkness" of the background (*un fond*), from the depth (*la profondeur*), of the prisons. Their emergence was not grounded on the foundation of a principle (*pas de fondement*). They spoke not for another, but on their own account, or, to capture the French expression, they "spoke *for* their own account" (*parlent pour leurs comptes*). What did they say? They spoke of intolerable suffering and shame. Third, when the inmates and their families spoke of their intolerable suffering, the GIP also spoke and spoke out. However, since the voices of the inmates did not represent a type, because the GIP did not represent a universal, the GIP's speech did not represent the inmates.[36] Even though the GIP gave, as they themselves said, to the inmates the "means to express themselves," it did not mediate. Instead, as we saw, they "amplified" or made "resound" the inmates' voices. The GIP reacted to the intolerable by making or letting the inmates' voices "echo." In other words, when it re-sounded the inmates' voices, it produced a foundationless repetition, a recommencement of a commencement. Amplifying the audibility and visibility of the inmates and their families, we find ourselves "before" (*devant*) them. In other words, through its means, the GIP opened a space in which we are forced to listen to the agony of others, in which we feel shame at being human, and then we find ourselves in a space in which we are forced to become intolerant of the intolerable. What is at issue is not representation, but becoming. Not only did the GIP communicate knowledge, it also communicated the feeling of intolerance. And, the echoing-"speaking out" (*parrēsia*) required courage since it involved risks: the members of the GIP might find themselves imprisoned. But, as we saw thanks to Deleuze's "Foucault and Prison," Foucault thought that the GIP was a failure. The inmates spoke, the echo resounded, but it was like no one had said anything, it was as if no one had listened. Nevertheless, caused by "the moment" of the 1970–71 hunger strikes, by "the moment" when Defert asked Foucault to establish the group, the "effectuation," as Deleuze would say, left behind a "counter-effectuation." It left behind, as a kind of remainder, *works*. It left behind the book called *Discipline and Punish*; it left behind the concept called "power."[37]

## IV. Conclusion: Philosophy's Activity as Speaking Out For Others

While Foucault gave us a new concept of power, it was Heidegger who led thought for the first time to originary finitude, and therefore he led us to what most opposes power: the experience of powerlessness. In "What is Metaphysics," Heidegger says that the feeling of anxiety places us "in utter impotence" (Heidegger 1998: 90). Nevertheless, it seems, he did not free repetition from the being of we who are finite, as if the repetitions out into the future — what Heidegger called "transcendence" — would return us to what we originally or properly were. Heidegger thereby restricted the potencies of repetition to the same. Yet, if it is the case that there is no proper being of us, if in other words the self-relation is open to endless reconfigurations (due to the experience of time being endless[38]), then repetition becomes, not transcendence, but the intransitive, or, as we said above, repetition becomes creative. The difference between transcendence and intransitivity leads us to compose several highly determinate formulas concerning the idea of return, formulas through which we can distinguish Heidegger's thought from that of Foucault and Deleuze. First, we must think of return not as a memory of the origin, and not even as the forgetfulness of the origin, but as "counter-memory," as what effectuates itself against what is remembered, making a difference.[39] Second, we must think of return not as a promise fulfilled, but as amplification, as a kind of "refrain" that endlessly varies itself.[40] And, finally, we must think of return not as a return to being, but as the becoming of the beings. This formula of beings (including the beings called "man") becoming brings us to one more: we must define philosophy not by the feeling of anxiety before the nothing of one's own death which demands of you to become what you properly are – but by the feeling of shame before the intolerable suffering of others which demands of you to become other than how you find yourself. This difference between the feeling of anxiety and shame explains why, it seems, Heidegger, unlike Foucault and Deleuze, never felt the need to speak out for prisoners. Even though he wrote about power, Heidegger never spoke out for the powerless. Thus he never spoke frankly, he never spoke out *as a means so that* the powerless would become other than what they are. Such outspokenness of course would have required courage. Although, as Deleuze (and Guattari) claim (Deleuze and Guattari 1994: 108), Heidegger may have introduced shame into philosophy – he made philosophy compromise with the intolerable – he did not convert shame into courage. And even if this courageous speaking out for the powerless were to be a failure, even if no one were to listen, these utterances, these statements, these works, would still remain. They would remain as a call for a people to come and a land to come; they would call forth a world that is other and a life that is other.[41] In other words, the conversion of shame into courage is the primary genetic condition for philosophy. Only through this conversion to activity is philosophy able to have a reality and a use. Only through this conversion is philosophy able to call us to go beyond or over our existence as human all too human.

## Notes

1 The article on which this chapter is based was co-authored with Andrea Janae Sholtz. "Speaking out for Others: Philosophical Activity in Deleuze and Foucault (and Heidegger)," co-authored with Andrea Janae Sholtz, for *Between Deleuze and Foucault*, ed. Daniel W. Smith, Thomas Nail, and Nicolae Morar (Edinburgh: Edinburgh University Press, 2016).
2 At a more general level, there seem to be three similarities between the way in which Deleuze conceives philosophy at the end of life and the way Foucault conceives philosophy at the end of his life. In his final courses at the Collège de France, Foucault seems to isolate three components of philosophy, as he understands it based on the study of ancient philosophy (that is, Plato, but especially the Stoics and the Cynics). First, philosophy is a way of living based in an *ascesis* or test. Second, philosophy has a linguistic aspect, which consists in frank-speaking or speaking out (*parrēsia*). And finally, philosophy has a complicated relation to political institutions: from a "necessary exteriority" it stands "over and against [*en face de*]" politics and speaks the truth (veridiction) (Foucault 2010: 286). ("Necessary exteriority" is an expression of the Cynical, anti-Platonic relation of philosophy and politics. The cynic Diogenes is not the philosopher-king. Instead, in relation to Alexander the Great, Diogenes calls himself a "dog." But even when Foucault discusses Plato's philosopher-king, he insists on a certain non-coincidence of philosophy and politics.) Similarly, for Deleuze, philosophy involves a conceptual persona who presents a way of life; the persona in particular presents the "pedagogy of the concept." Second, as we can see already (and this is what is best known about *What is Philosophy?*), philosophy involves a linguistic aspect, which is the creation of the concept. And finally, for Deleuze, philosophy has a complicated relation to political institutions: from a "utopia" or more precisely a non-place, it "takes the critique of its own time to its highest point" (Deleuze and Guattari 1994: 99). For both Deleuze and Foucault, this critique from "the outside" is done, as Foucault would say, in the name of a life that is

other and a world that is other, and, as Deleuze would say, in the name of a people to come and a land to come.
3 Michel Foucault, "Theatrum philosophicum," in Foucault 1998: 366 and 364, translation modified.
4 It is well known that in his final interview, Foucault says, "For me, Heidegger has always been the essential philosopher. My whole philosophical development was determined by my reading of Heidegger" (Foucault 1988: 250, translation modified). Less well known but we think equally important is that fact that, when Deleuze in *What is Philosophy?*, speaks of "speaking for" (*parler pour*) the illiterate, the aphasic, and the acephalous, this discussion, which is in effect the climax of Part I, occurs in the context of Deleuze describing how Heidegger brought shame into philosophy (Deleuze and Guattari 1994: 108–9). For Foucault's early studies, see Didier Eribon, *Michel Foucault*, trans. Betsy Wing (Cambridge, MA: Harvard University Press, 1991), pp. 30–1. David Macey, *The Lives of Michel Foucault* (New York: Vintage, 1993), p. 34. The quotation with which I began is often cited. See Alan Milchman and Alan Rosenberg, *Foucault and Heidegger: Critical Encounters* (Minneapolis: University of Minnesota Press, 2003). Béatrice Han's essay in this volume is particularly interesting. Béatrice Han, "Foucault and Heidegger on Kant and Finitude," in *Foucault and Heidegger*, pp. 127–62. See also Jean Zoungrana, *Michel Foucault. Un parcours croisé: Lévi-Strauss, Heidegger* (Paris: L'Harmattan, 1998).
5 In *Nietzsche and Philosophy*, Deleuze says that the Nietzschean overman is defined by a different way of sensing: "The aim of critique is not the ends of man or of reason but finally the Overman, the overcome, overtaken man. The point of critique is not justification, but to feel otherwise [*de sentir autrement*: another sensibility]" (Deleuze 1983: 94).
6 Deleuze cites Heidegger's "Overcoming Metaphysics, in *The End of Philosophy*.
7 See also *The Fold*, where Deleuze late in his career (original French publication 1988) takes up again Heidegger's language of the *Zwiefalt* (Deleuze 1993: 30).
8 Deleuze cites again "Overcoming Metaphysics." But here in the fourth point, he also cites Jean Beaufret's *Introduction to Poème de Parmenide* (Paris: Presses Universitaires de France, 1955), and Beda Alleman, *Hölderlin et Heidegger* (Paris: Presses Universitaires de France, 1954).
9 By focusing on the same (gathering), Deleuze's criticism of Heidegger is virtually identical to that of Foucault and that of Derrida (Foucault 1970: 334; Derrida 1986a: 141–2).

10 Here Deleuze cites Heidegger's interpretation of Nietzsche in *What is Called Thinking?*
11 In *Difference and Repetition*, Deleuze calls what we are calling a "creative repetition" a "clothed" or disguised" repetition (Deleuze 1995: 84). Undoubtedly, with this description of recommencement (creative repetition), Deleuze seems to be very close to Heidegger's own reflections on the artwork, on the *Abgrund* (the foundationless), on the *Ereignis* (the event of propriation), and on another beginning. Indeed, the French word "recommencement" could be rendered in English as "another beginning."
12 Here is the occurrence: "This is why modern thought is devoted, from top to bottom, to its great preoccupation with return, to its concern with recommencement, to that strange, stationary disquietude which forces upon it the duty of repeating repetition. Thus from Hegel to Marx and Spengler we find the developing theme of a thought which, through the movement in which it accomplishes itself . . . , curves over upon itself . . . [and] achieves its circle. In opposition to this return . . . , we find the experience of Hölderlin, Nietzsche, and Heidegger, in which the return is given only in the extreme retreat of the origin" (Foucault 1970: 334).
13 In relation to the finite conditions of knowledge, we can say, using Kantian terminology, that man has no "intellectual intuition."
14 Foucault calls this "originless origin" the "rip" from which, itself having no chronology or history, time has issued forth (Foucault 1970: 332). "Rip" renders "déchirure," which probably is intended to render Heidegger's idea of a "Riss."
15 "Retrieval" renders "répétition" in French, "Wiederholung," in German. "Wiederholung" is a fundamental feature of Heidegger's thinking at the time of *Being and Time* (Heidegger 2010: 316–18, §66). It organizes as well Heidegger's 1929 *Kant and the Problem of Metaphysics* (Heidegger 1997: 143, Introduction to Part IV).
16 In "Ariane s'est pendue," Foucault says that "[To think intensity] is to reject finally the great figure of the Same, which, from Plato to Heidegger, has not stopped locking Western metaphysics into its circle" (my translation). But here too, Foucault provides no explanation (Foucault 2001a: 798).
17 This obvious conception of promise involves the idea of balance or justice, as if it were possible to fulfill the promise, balance it out, and do justice to it. Yet, perhaps it is possible to conceive promising on the basis of a fundamental disjunction, disjointure, or injustice. This unbalanced concept of the promise seems to be the concept Derrida developed in his *Specters of Marx* (Derrida 1994: 24). See also my earlier analysis of the promise in

Derrida in Leonard Lawlor, *Derrida and Husserl* (Bloomington: Indiana University Press, 2002), p. 219, in particular.

18 See François Ewald, "Foucault and the Contemporary Scene," in *Philosophy and Social Criticism*, vol. 25, no. 3: 81–91, especially p. 83: "If there is an ethical line in Foucault – and there is one – it is fundamentally tied to the idea that one must combat this danger of repetition."

19 David Webb has made an important contribution to our understanding of Foucault's archaeology (although it could be argued that he overemphasizes the mathematical and formal in Foucault and does not take account of Foucault's comments on literature). David Webb, *Foucault's Archaeology: Science and Transformation* (Edinburgh: Edinburgh University Press, 2013).

20 Deleuze and Guattari mention and cite Primo Levi's *The Drowned and the Saved*, trans. Raymond Rosenthal (New York: Summit Books, 1986).

21 This distinction between *parrēsia* and the speech act repeats and modifies the distinction between the statement (*l'énoncé*) and the speech act Foucault had made more than ten years earlier (Foucault 1970: 79–87, and 92–6; the second set of pages concern the position of the subject of the statement).

22 Foucault is aware that *parrēsia* might fail. In particular, the history of the concept of frank-speech indicates that it is frequently confused with flattery, the "dangerous double" of *parrēsia* (CF-GSO1, 280/304).

23 See Macey, *The Lives of Michel Foucault*, pp. 257–89; Eribon, pp. 224–37; James Miller, *The Passion of Michel Foucault* (New York: Anchor Books, 1993), pp. 165–207; and Julian Bourg, *From Revolution to Ethics: May 1968 and Contemporary French Thought* (Montreal: McGill-Queen's University Press, 2007), pp. 79–95.

24 In his course on Foucault and power, in 1985–1986, in particular, the lecture of 7 January 1986, Deleuze claims that Foucault sensed that something is going to happen in the prisons. Foucault, according to Deleuze, was aware of what was going on in American prisons. See: http://www.cla.purdue.edu/research/deleuze/documents/Deleuze_FoucaultPower_7Jan1986_2-5.pdf, Accessed on 11 November 2012.

25 See Michel Foucault, "Manifest du G.I.P.," document 86 (Foucault 2001a: 1042). The small summary I just presented is based on the introduction to document 86. For a more detailed and important narrative of the entire GIP movement, see Phillippe Artières, Laurent Quéro, and Michelle Zancarini-Fournel, *Le groupe d'information sur les prisons. Archives d'une lutte, 1970–1972* (Paris: IMEC, 2003), especially Part 1, and pp. 34–6.

26 In his course on Foucault and power, in 1985–1986, in particular, the lecture of 7 January 1986, Deleuze claims that Foucault conceived the GIP in a non-centralized way, and that this lack of centralization was an idea that descended from May 1968. Deleuze uses the Guattarian term "transversal" to describe the GIP network and the type of struggle in which the GIP was engaged. While discussing Foucault's transformations of the basic Kantian questions, Deleuze also describes Foucault not as a "universal intellectual," but as a "specific" or "singular intellectual." See: http://www.cla.purdue.edu/research/deleuze/documents/Deleuze_FoucaultPower_7Jan1986_2-5.pdf, accessed on 11 November 2012.

27 Not based in a universal truth – Foucault of course, like Heidegger, is interested only in the genesis of truth – the GIP leads Foucault to redefine the role of the intellectual. As is well known, Foucault says in "Intellectuals and Power" that "The role of intellectual is no longer to situate himself 'slightly ahead' or 'slightly to one side' [of the oppressed] so he may speak the silent truth of each and all" (Deleuze 2004: 207).

28 The French is: "Il s'agit de laisser la parole à ceux qui ont une expérience de la prison." See also "Intolerable 1," in Artières, Quéro, and Zancarini-Fournel, *Le groupe d'information sur les prisons. Archives d'une lutte, 1970–1972*, p. 80: "The GIP (Prison Information Group) is not aiming to speak for the inmates of the different prisons. On the contrary, it aims to give to the inmates themselves the possibility of speaking, and to say what happens in the prisons. The purpose of the GIP is not reformist. We are not dreaming of the ideal prison. We wish that the prisoners say what is intolerable in the system of penal repression."

29 In his course on Foucault and power, in 1985–1986, in particular, the lecture of 7 January 1986, Deleuze says that the new kind of intellectual that Foucault is (he mentions also Oppenheimer and Genet as this new kind of intellectual) do not speak in "the name of a universal value," but "in the name of his own singular experience." See: http://www.cla.purdue.edu/research/deleuze/documents/Deleuze_FoucaultPower_7Jan1986_2-5.pdf, Accessed on 11 November 2012.

30 In his course on Foucault and power, in 1985–1986, in particular, the lecture of 7 January 1986, Deleuze recounts Foucault's practice of distributing the questionnaire. See: http://www.cla.purdue.edu/research/deleuze/documents/Deleuze_FoucaultPower_7Jan1986_2-5.pdf.

31 The first GIP bulletin, which collected some of the results of the questionnaire, also tells us that one inmate found that what was most intolerable about the visits was the distance established by the double bars in the

meeting room, which forbids any intimacy. Another inmate said that what was most intolerable was not being able to kiss the kids.

32 Foucault uses the word "moyens" constantly in the interviews and statements concerning the GIP. And, even after the GIP had dissolved, Foucault still spoke of "moyen." See document 123, "L'intellectuel sert à rassembler les idées mais son savoir est partiel par rapport au savoir ouvrier," in Foucault 2001a: 1289–91, in particular p. 1289.

33 Beside the audible image of the echo, Foucault also uses the image of "a genuine brush fire" (*un véritable feu de bruyère*) (Foucault 2001a: 1045).

34 Serge Livrozet, *De la prison à la révolte* (Paris: L'esprit frappeur, 1999). In his preface, Foucault speaks of Livrozet not merely recounting his memories of the adventures he had as a thief, but also of Livrozet taking up his right to speak of the law. Foucault describes Livrozet as a thinker.

35 For the "optics" of the GIP, see Michael Welch, "Counterveillance: How Foucault and the Groupe d'information sur les prisons Reversed the Optics," in *Theoretical Criminology*, vol. 15 (2011), no. 3: 301–13.

36 In his course on Foucault and power, in 1985–1986, in particular, the lecture of 7 January 1986, Deleuze reiterates that the GIP did not represent the prisoners. See: http://www.cla.purdue.edu/research/deleuze/documents/Deleuze_FoucaultPower_7Jan1986_2-5.pdf, Accessed on 11 November 2012.

37 Foucault 1977: 194. Here Foucault says, "We must cease once and for all to describe the effects of power in negative terms: it 'excludes,' it 'represses,' it 'pushes down,' it 'censors,' it 'abstracts,' it 'masks,' it 'conceals.' In fact, power produces; it produces reality; it produces domains of objects and rituals of truth. The individual and knowledge that is to be gained of him belong to this production."

38 That time is endless is really what Nietzsche's eternal return doctrine means. It is really what Foucault is trying to show in Chapter 9 of *The Order of Things* and what Deleuze is trying to show in both *Difference and Repetition* and *The Logic of Sense*.

39 Foucault introduces the notion of counter-memory in his 1971 "Nietzsche, Genealogy, History" (Foucault 1998: 369–91, in particular p. 385).

40 Deleuze and Guattari introduce the notion of the refrain (the ritornello) in their 1980 *A Thousand Plateaus* (Deleuze and Guattari 1987: 310–50; also Deleuze and Guattari 1994: 21, where they speak of the concept as a "refrain" [*ritournelle*]).

41 In a famous article, Gayatri Chakravorty Spivak criticizes Deleuze and Foucault's discussion in "Intellectuals and Power." See Gayatri Chakravorty

Spivak, "Can the Subaltern Speak?" in *Colonial Discourse and Post-Colonial Theory: A Reader*, ed. Patrick Williams and Laura Chrisman (New York: Columbia University Press, 1994), pp. 66–111. Spivak claims that Deleuze and Foucault do not recognize how representation works, its "double session" (p. 74). That is, following Derrida, she sees that representation contains an ambiguity between speaking for and presenting as in an artwork (p. 70). So, even if Deleuze and Foucault are trying to allow the inmates to speak on their own account, they cannot because "the subaltern" is always caught in (contaminated by) the ambiguity of representation, and therefore reduced ideologically. As she says at the end of her essay, "the subaltern cannot speak" (p. 104). Yet, if one looks at the GIP documents (in addition to "Intellectuals and Power"), it is clear that Foucault and Deleuze have tried or strategized in a very specific way to allow the inmates to speak on their own account. In particular, as we have tried to show, Foucault made the GIP be independent of any political party and therefore any ideology. In this way, he tried to free the inmates from general concepts that would reduce them so that they might appear as a singularity, as an event. More importantly, both Deleuze and Foucault were aware of the risks involved in the GIP's practice of allowing the inmates to speak on their own account. There is no guarantee of success. What is important about this moment of French thought is the strategy (to speak like Derrida) that increased the possibility of success, while not lapsing into good conscience. Insofar as success (complete liberation from ideology) is impossible, one is required to try to do more. Deleuze in particular is aware that what made GIP a true event is its counter-effectuation in works such as concepts and artworks. The work remains even if no one listened at its inception. Therefore our shame at being human remains too, and just as in Derrida, in Deleuze one is required to do more.

# 8

# "The Dream of an Unusable Friendship": The Temptation of Evil and the Chance for Love in Derrida's *Politics of Friendship*

It is perhaps impossible to overestimate the importance of Heidegger's 1929 *Kant and the Problem of Metaphysics* (Heidegger 1997). Through his interpretation of Kant's First Critique, Heidegger led us to the "hidden art" of the schematism. The core of Heidegger's interpretation consists in showing that the schematism, lying in the middle between the faculties of the sensibility and the understanding, must be understood as a pure form of auto-affection, and that auto-affection must be understood through the flow of time. Heidegger shows us that the temporal movement of auto-affection contains a difference that cannot be closed off from becoming other. Kant, however, as Heidegger shows, tried to close off this difference by interpreting the transcendental foundation in the schematism anthropologically. Even more, Heidegger argues that Kant shrank back from the radicality of this foundation because of his concern for the purity of morality.

Across the twentieth century, many philosophers have grappled with Heidegger's Kant book. However, Derrida seems to be the philosopher who has most appropriated these Heideggerian claims about Kant, about the radical foundation, auto-affection, time, difference, man – and even Heidegger's claims about Kantian morality. We should not forget that Heidegger prepares for his laying out of the schematism as auto-affection by interpreting the power of imagination in practical reason and in particular in the feeling of respect (Heidegger 1997: 111, §30); and that, as early as his 1964 "Violence and Metaphysics," Derrida appropriates the Kantian feeling of respect as part of his defense of phenomenology, including Heidegger's (Derrida 1978: 96). Later in his career, Derrida often discusses Kant, but it seems that one of his most extensive discussions, since it speaks of moral friendship in Kant's *Metaphysics of Morals*, is Derrida's 1994 *Politics of Friendship*.

This chapter is entirely devoted to *Politics of Friendship* and I have three reasons for focusing solely on it. First, at the most fundamental level, it is impossible, I think, to conceive collectivities such as a people without recourse to the concept of friendship. If we want to speak about politics or ethics, we must develop, invent, or create a new concept of friendship. Derrida's *Politics of Friendship* makes a major contribution to this endeavor. Second, at a personal level, I am still baffled by the experience of friendship and love: what is friendship, who is really a friend? What is love and what is love in friendship? These are questions that Derrida asks continuously in *Politics of Friendship*. Third, and lastly, as I have already indicated, while other Derrida texts have considered Kant's writings on art and politics, *Politics of Friendship* is the only book Derrida has ever written that considers Kant's moral philosophy.[1]

Rivalling Derrida's 1974 *Glas* (Derrida 1986), *Politics of Friendship* is a difficult book to understand. Nevertheless, what is most obvious about it is that, within, Derrida questions the Western philosophical tradition's valorization of fraternity as the fundamental model for friendship and thus for politics.[2] While in

*Politics of Friendship* Derrida takes up a large variety of thinkers in the Western philosophical tradition who have spoken of friendship, it is clear that Derrida thinks that Kant, as "the philosopher of the French Revolution"[3] – with its motto of "Liberté, Égalité, Fraternité" – holds a central place in this tradition.[4] In fact, Derrida thinks that Kant represents a kind of "rupture" in this tradition, precisely because the feeling of respect implies distance between friends. Kant's recognition of the necessity of distance looks to be unprecedented in the Western philosophical tradition since the tradition has always seemed to define friendship by proximity. Despite this apparent rupture with the tradition, Kant, when he speaks of friendship, does not depart from the traditional model for friendship in fraternity. Derrida argues, as we shall see, that Kant places the figure of the brother in the middle as the *schematism* between the sensibility, which is love, and the Idea, which is equality. The schematism of fraternity, *on the one hand*, determines the Idea of equality as equality of birth (*isogonia*) and thus as homogeneity. *On the other hand*, it determines the feeling of love as brotherly love (*philadelphia*) and thus as homophilia. For Derrida, the fraternal schematism absolutizes one possibility of friendship – the relation between brothers – over all other possibilities of friendship – over the relation between sisters, between women, and between women and men. In other words, Kant limits friendship. Consequently, for Kant, all the kinds of friendship based in love must become fraternal, and, in particular, women must become brothers – so that all of us, all humanity, can reach the goal of what we think we truly should be. In this Kantian teleology, love has little chance. In order to give a chance to love, we must break through the limit of fraternal friendship.[5]

In order to make this breakthrough, Derrida turns to the other "rupture" in the philosophical tradition of friendship, and that is Nietzsche (Derrida 1997: 312/281).[6] Nietzsche is a kind of rupture for Derrida, because he is the first person to reverse the utterance attributed by Diogenes Laertius to Aristotle (Derrida 1997: 97/79).[7] Of course, Derrida's almost endless repetition of Aristotle's utterance is one of the things best known about *Politics of Friendship*. For Derrida, Nietzsche represents a rupture, because – even though Nietzsche still speaks of brothers, and although he makes, as everyone knows, infamous comments about women – Nietzsche's friendship is a friendship of excessive love, a love so excessive that it lets the friend (or the beloved) be infinitely distant. Through its distancing, this love gives off the appearance of enmity: not "Oh my friends, there is no friend," but "Oh my enemies, there is no enemy." In fact, the enmity that this love gives off implies that it is a love that is excessively respectful. Bound as it is to respect, this love is a passion that is not pathological in Kant's sense of pathology; it is a passion that does not treat other persons merely as means to an end (Derrida 1995a: 16; Derrida 1997: 54). It does not turn them into goods or possessions aiming at utility. Derrida calls it, as the essay's title announces, "an unusable friendship."[8] As he says, "The dream of an unusable friendship survives, a friendship beyond friendship, and invincible before [all] dialectics" (Derrida 1997: 217). This unusable friendship is perhaps what Nietzsche had in mind with the superman, with the going over man. It is also perhaps what Derrida has in mind with democracy to come or even a cosmopolitanism to come.[9]

Therefore, on the basis of *Politics of Friendship*, we are going to go from Kant's fraternal–friendship limitation of love to Nietzsche's breakthrough to a love in friendship. Yet, this movement of breakthrough is complicated; it is not a straight line. If Derrida, in *Politics of Friendship, and we too*, intend to give a chance to love, if we intend to disrupt the fraternal schematism aiming at the Idea of equality, then what we are attempting is fratricide. This attempt is *the* temptation; it is the temptation of evil, hence the subtitle of my essay: "The Temptation of Evil and the Chance for Love." Indeed, if the temptation of evil disrupts the straight path to the Idea, if it then sidetracks humanity's emergence from "childhood," if it detours humanity's progress toward enlightenment, if it veers all of us away from what we have believed we truly should be, then the fraternal temptation amounts to a crime against humanity. But, it is this temptation, and *only this temptation*, that results in Derrida's idea of an unusable and superhuman (or non-anthropological) friendship.

## I. Derrida's Analysis of Kant: The Difficulties with Love; The Friend of Man; and the Cost of Humanization

As the section subtitle indicates, Derrida's analysis of Kant in the final two chapters of *Politics of Friendship* divides into *three parts*.[11] *First*, Derrida analyzes §46 of *The Metaphysics of Morals* (called "On the Intimate Union of Love and Respect in Friendship").[12] He focuses on this paragraph because in it Kant quotes Aristotle's reputed utterance: "oh my friends, there is no friend" because of the "difficulties" of "friendship considered in its perfect form." These difficulties, as we shall see in a moment, concern the role of love in friendship. Love, for Kant, to put this as simply as possible, always tends to be excessive. *Second*, Derrida moves from §46 to §47 of *The Metaphysics of Morals* (called "Moral Friendship"). While §46 had presented perfect friendship as an unattainable Idea, §47 presents "moral friendship," as perfect friendship between two people, as an event that can actually happen in history, rare like a "black swan." The "black swan" is Kant's image. In §47 Kant also speaks of "pragmatic friendship," as another kind of moral friendship. Unlike the friendship between two people, pragmatic friendship, or "the friend of man," as Kant calls this person, is friends with or loves all humanity. Now, Kant seems to imply that "the friend of man" also actualizes moral friendship rarely like a "black swan." As we shall see, the friend of man is able to actualize moral friendship for all of humanity by means of "the anthropological schema of the family" (Derrida 1997: 293/262). Then *third*, following the thread of the anthropological, Derrida analyzes §14 of *The Anthropology from a Pragmatic Point of View* (called "On Permissible Moral Illusions").[13] In this context too, Kant mentions Aristotle's reputed utterance because friendship involves appearances, like common courtesies, that are false. Yet, Kant thinks that these false appearances are like counterfeit money that can come to function like real money and can even become gold; the illusions can become true. The becoming-true of the illusions of friendship is, as the word "anthropological" suggests, the "humanization of man" (Derrida 1997: 272). In the third part of his Kant analysis (in Chapter 10 of *Politics of Friendship*), Derrida notices that Kant claims, without explanation, that the history of humans becoming humanized comes at a high cost; something is lost. Derrida asks simply, "Just what [is lost]?" (*Quoi au juste?*) (Derrida 1997: 275). If we look at the three basic claims of the analyses together, we can see already the high cost. What is lost is this: female friendship, friendship between men and women, and sexual difference in general (Derrida 1997: 253). It is this injustice that leads to Derrida's temptation of fratricide.

In more detail, the first part of the analysis, as we said, concerns §46 of *The Metaphysics of Morals*. Here Kant himself outlines the "difficulties" with perfect friendship, the difficulties that maintain perfect friendship as an unattainable but necessary ideal (as an "Idea in the Kantian sense," as Derrida says). The difficulties stem from the way in which Kant defines perfect friendship. On the one hand, as the title of the section indicates, perfect friendship unifies love and respect. On the other hand, Kant defines it as each friend having "the maximum of good intentions" toward one another, which leads to the first difficulty. If perfect friendship is defined by a maximum of good intentions, it is not clear how we are to measure the equality of feelings. Reciprocity, as Derrida points out (and he makes this point repeatedly in *Politics of Friendship*), is not equality. Love between the friends can be reciprocal, but not equal since one friend can have a more intense love. In other words, there might be "excessive ardor in love." This excessive love brings us to what Kant calls "the major difficulty," which is, in Derrida's words, "the unstable balance of these two feelings which are opposed as fusional 'attraction' (love) and 'repulsion' which keeps at a distance (respect)" (Derrida 1997: 254). Here Kant relies on what he calls "the natural law of attraction and repulsion." From the natural law, in order to regulate the unstable balance, Kant seems to derive a maxim, indeed, an imperative: friends should not love each too closely or be too intimate, too familiar; instead, they should maintain distance between themselves.

It is this necessity of distance in friendship that leads Derrida to claim that Kant produces a rupture in the philosophical canon on friendship, a canon that has always seemed to valorize proximity. However, Kant's rupture with the tradition – he is not Nietzsche, after all – is not so clear-cut since Kant limits the distance to a "proper distance" (in Derrida's French, "une distance convenable") (Derrida 1997: 254 and 154), that is, he limits it to a distance that is suitably familiar. Kant's imperative of suitable or proper distance means that he is always concerned, as Derrida is showing us, with limiting improper, unsuitable, or inconvenient excess. For Kant, we must have neither excessive distance nor excessive proximity, neither excessive respect nor excessive love. Yet, since Kant places the moral imperative of suitable distance on the side of friendship and respect, and not on the side of love and ardor, Derrida concludes that Kant's principal worry is with the excessiveness of love.

For Kant, as we said a moment ago, *love always tends toward excess*. An excess of love introduces into the natural law of attraction-repulsion, as Derrida says, a "catastrophe" (Derrida 1997: 256). This catastrophe in love is well-known from common experience. Too much gentleness and tenderness, too much closeness and attraction leads to a stifling relation, and finally, as we all know, to a rupture in the relationship. In other words, with excessive love, *attraction becomes possession*, and possession motivates repulsion and the disruption of the social bond. What then is to be done with this consequence of repulsion and disruption? According to Derrida, Kant has identified a situation (that of excessive love), in which the principle of repulsion should not be compensated with the principle of attraction. Tending as it does toward excessiveness, attraction inevitably leads to a worse repulsion. Instead, one has to compensate for and limit the repulsion that derives from excessive attraction with repulsion, with "painful respect." Echoing formulas one finds in "Violence and Metaphysics," Derrida says: "repulsion against repulsion" (Derrida 1978: 117). Similarly, we should not compensate the principle of attraction with repulsion; one has to compensate attraction with attraction: "attraction against attraction, a slightly but not too tender friendship." As Derrida concludes, love, for Kant, is the enemy: "in the excessive attraction unleashed by love, love gives way [*donne lieu*] to rupture, enmity, and war. Love bears hatred within itself. Love then is the evil and the remedy for the evil" (Derrida 1997: 256–7). At the conclusion of this first part of the Kant analysis, Derrida calls love "a passion made of dark colors," a black passion. The color black makes the transition to the second part of Derrida's Kant analysis, which concerns the event of "the black swan."

We find the "black swan" in §47 of *The Metaphysics of Morals* (called "Moral Friendship"). Kant's discussion in §47 is obscure and Derrida's analysis of it is equally obscure. In this paragraph, following the philosophical canon, Kant claims that occasionally, rarely, like the black swan in nature, "perfect friendship" occurs in history. Kant uses the "black swan" image only in reference to "perfect friendship" which is a synonym for "moral friendship." Perfect or moral friendship, as we said above, is a friendship between two people alone. Yet, in §47, Kant also speaks of "the friend of man," who is the friend of many more than two people; he is the friend of all humanity. Derrida seems to be arguing that, when Kant speaks of the "friend of man," he is implying that this more friendly friendship also happens in history. Like the rare occurrence of perfect friendship, the friend of man happens rarely: he too is like a "black swan" (even though Kant does not explicitly use this image in reference to the friend of man). For Derrida, the transition to the event of the "black swan" called the friend of man lies in the definition of perfect friendship.

Perfect friendship, for Kant, is between two people who can keep a *secret*. As Derrida notes, Kant calls this friendship between two people "moral" (and not "aesthetic," which would be a friendship based only in feeling or sensibility) because, like all secrecy, this amicable secrecy is based in a promise: each friend has complete and perfect confidence in the other to keep the secret that each has shared with the other. The sharing of the secret seems to be limited to the two friends alone. But, as Derrida stresses (and as he says frequently when he discusses secrecy [Derrida 1989b: 25]), is it possible for anyone, for any finite human being, to know, really and absolutely know, how to keep a secret? Is denying having a secret a better way to keep a secret than disclosing some part of it? No one knows for sure, and, Derrida adds, neither does Kant (Derrida 1997: 259). In short, the secret is not a strict object of knowledge. The problem of knowing how to keep the secret arises because, as Derrida asserts, there is always, necessarily, a third person. If there were no third person, there would be no need for two people to promise to keep the secret. The third person therefore is an essential component of the concept of secrecy.

Because secrecy, for Kant, is the essence of perfect moral friendship, which is limited to two people, and because secrecy always necessarily implies a third person (or more), then perfect moral friendship, Derrida seems to be arguing, always seems possible to extend itself beyond the two to an indeterminate number of people. And indeed, Kant suddenly, and without a clear transition, speaks of "pragmatic friendship," which is the concern with the ends of all humans. As we have already noted, although Kant says that pragmatic friendship remains a "wish" or an ideal (because of its indeterminate range), Kant implies, at least according to Derrida, that pragmatic friendship occurs in history with the rare occurrence of the friend of man. Although pragmatic friendship will always be a limited and insufficient experience (again because of its indeterminate range), when it occurs it is an actual experience of moral friendship.

Since pragmatic friendship, "the friend of man," is an actual experience, conditioned by space and time, Derrida concludes that sensibility must be involved. The limited but actual experience of the friend of man cannot take place except upon "the background" of sensibility. This sensible or aesthetic ground for "the friend of man" must be universal; it must be, as Derrida says, a general or generic condition. It must be, simply, the feeling of love for the entire human race.

Kant, however, insists that the meaning of the expression "the friend of man" is "narrower" ("plus strict," in Derrida's French) than the meaning of the expression "the philanthropist," narrower than "the one who merely loves man." While the philanthropist establishes a community of love and joy for humanity (an aesthetic community of feeling), the friend of man is able to establish not only an aesthetic community but also a rigorous rational community. He is able to do so because he is guided by an Idea. This Idea, as Derrida points out, is the idea of equality among men (Derrida 1997: 226) and allows us to see better how Kant is distinguishing between the philanthropist and the friend of man. The meaning of "the friend of man" is "narrower" than the meaning of "philanthropist" because only the friend of man feels an obligation to the Idea of equality. For the friend of man, equality is not only a representation or a concept but also a feeling of obligation, duty, debt, or gratitude. Through the feeling of duty, sensibility is linked, more narrowly, stricter, closer, the purely rational Idea of equality. The relation between sensibility and the Idea is the condition for the possibility of the existence of the friend of man (Derrida 1997: 261).

Derrida stresses that, although Kant had just given us a strict definition of the friend of man, Kant then tells us how to imagine the friend of man: he must be represented as a "brother under one father, who wills the happiness of all." It seems that Derrida is arguing that Kant (like so many other philosophers before him in the canon) resorts to the figure of the brother and father, in short, to the family, because the image of the family allows one to conceive all humans as bound together. The image of the brothers under *one* father makes *all* humans suitable friends. If all of us are the sons of one father, if all of us are brothers, if all of us are of the same birth, then all of us are kin and included in a social bond. If humans are *already* – here is the background or ground, the condition of possibility, here is the prior and the a priori – if all of us are already bound together as one large family, then it is possible for one human to emerge from within the family, who loves all members of the family: the friend of man, a member of the family already and thereby already bound to them, loves the entire "family," loves all of the "family members." In other words, the friend of man is able to arise as someone who loves all humans since all humans are already brothers and in familial love with each other. Here, Derrida is careful. He recognizes that Kant, despite his "strict" definition of the friend of man (versus the philanthropist), does not confuse *this* fraternity, that is, the "brotherhood" of the human race, with "the fraternity called 'natural,' strict, literal, sensible, genetic, etc." (Derrida 1997: 262). The family is a figure; the representation of the brother is a representation; the image of the brothers is an image. Not being strict and literal, this image belongs to the faculty of the imagination.

We can see immediately where the fraternal image is located. As Derrida says, Kant positions the image of the brother "*in view of* the idea of equality and *in view of* responding to the obligation attached to it" (Derrida 1997: 262, Derrida's emphasis). In other words, Kant positions the image of the brother between "in view of responding to the obligation" and "in view of the idea" – that is, between the feeling of the obligation for equality (the image *responds to* the feeling) and the idea of equality (the image *looks toward* the idea). The Kantian positioning of the image of the brother places the brother or more broadly the family, or still more broadly, *the anthropological*, in the middle between sensibility and the Idea. Through the image of the brother, the Idea of equality is determined as symmetrical (based in one father and the same birth: isogony [Derrida1997: 93]) and the sensibility is determined by this Idea of symmetrical equality as familial (equal and reciprocal) love. As Derrida's constant and deliberate use of the word "schema" throughout *Politics of Friendship* indicates that the Idea is schematized on the sensibility through the image of the brother. The image of the brother, of the family, of the familiar, of the suitable, of the *oikeiotēs*, of the proximate and near, in a word, presence, occupies the place of the schematism in Kant's metaphysics of morals. In a moment, we shall return to this middle place, this place of the a priori or the originary, to the "hidden art" of the schematism. We need to notice now only that, as sensible or imaginal schema, this figurative fraternity, Derrida argues, "remains fastened back into sensible or imaginal fraternity, to the *virility* of the *congeneric*" (Derrida 1997: 262, Derrida emphasis).

Kant's positioning of fraternity in the middle place between sensibility and Idea (between "responding to" and "looking toward") suggests history. Thus, in the third part of Derrida's Kant analysis, which concerns §14 of Kant's *Anthropology from a Pragmatic Point of View* called "On Permissible Moral Illusions" (which is located in a larger discussion of sensibility and then within a smaller discussion of play-acting), Derrida immediately states that Kant's discussion of deceptive appearances or illusions as being morally salutary – decorum and politeness, proper attire and manners command respect – amounts to a story or a history. In fact, Derrida argues that the discussion of deceptive appearances should be seen as part of Kant's Enlightenment story about humanity emerging from childhood (Derrida 1997: 275). The story is a moral subterfuge. We start out with deceptive appearances. We pretend to be polite to one another by saying nice things to one another. But then, as we continue to do the play acting, we come to realize that we should not treat each other as means to an end. We should not treat each other as instruments for the satisfaction of our desires. The truth of the pretense of politeness is that we should treat each other with respect and thus we should treat each other morally. The story begins in non-truth and ends up (or should end up) making non-truth true. As Derrida says, "It is indeed a matter of a history of truth. A matter, more precisely, of a trial of *verification, as* the history of a becoming-true of illusion" (Derrida 1997: 274, Derrida's emphasis).

Now Derrida notes that Kant compares the pretense of politeness, in this "history of a becoming-true of illusion," to "small change," to coins that are not worth much, and as deceptive, the pretense of politeness can be compared in fact to counterfeit money.[14] Therefore, for Derrida, Kant's comparison means that the history of illusion becoming truth is like an *economy* in which the counterfeit coins change into or are made into real money: the coins are given as worthless, but they return as gold. As we anticipated in the Introduction, here Derrida tells us that the changing of the counterfeit coins into gold takes place, according to Kant, at a "considerable loss." Kant does not tell us what is lost. However, in the telling of the story, he of course provides an example of the pretense: women, Kant claims, are disappointed when the male sex does not admire their charms. Although the intention of these "charms" is love – they are "carnal lures" (Derrida 1997: 264) – they are, according to Kant, morally permissible or salutary, if they are presented with constraint and reserve.[15] In short, women must give themselves off as *modest*.[16] The modest appearances of women are salutary, because they save the woman from being mere enjoyment, from being a mere means or instrument to an end. Modesty therefore, as Derrida says, is "eminently moral and fundamentally egalitarian" (Derrida 1997: 274). In other words, modesty changes women into men, which means that the woman becomes a brother. Through modesty the woman ends up participating in universal fraternity, in a word, in humanity (Derrida 1997: 274).

We must understand the consequences of what Derrida is trying to show us with his Kant analysis. Derrida is trying to make us see that, for Kant, we must not let the deceptive appearances be appearances that never completely or ultimately disclose the truth. For Kant, in Derrida's eyes, there must be a revelation; or at least the revelation must be posited as an Idea (as an *arché* or *telos*) (Derrida 1997: 223–4).[17] For Derrida, as we shall see when we turn to Nietzsche, and this point about Derrida's thinking is well-known, appearances necessarily remain so because they are indefinitely iterable, and their indefinite potentiality means that they never fully reveal the truth (Derrida 1997: 216); they never end up in pure presence. For Kant, in contrast, if we let the appearances be what they are (iterable), then we do not ascend to what humanity should *truly* be; we do not elevate ourselves to our moral standing. The appearances should lead us to our autonomy. The economy of changing the counterfeit coins into gold, therefore, is not just a process of verification but also a process of authentification. But, this ascent or sublimation into what humanity should truly be, is an ascent into fraternity. If the history is supposed to end up in truth or if history should end up in morality, in other words, if we must change the fake money into gold, if we must make women modest, if we must make women be brothers and participate in universal fraternity, again if the path to fraternity is the only straight path to morality, if virility is the only right path to virtue, then fratricide, as Derrida stresses, is the general form of im-morality. Derrida is trying to make us see that, for Kant, fratricide is radical evil. As Kant says, in this section of the *Anthropology*, those who disdain small change as small change and do not try to change it into gold commit "high treason against humanity."

## II. "The Dream of an Unusable Friendship": The Temptation of Evil and the Chance for Love

Derrida's analysis shows us that Kant sets up a series of questionable limitations. First, there is no reason to think that respect for the other requires only suitable or convenient distance. Derrida suggests in his analysis that respect might require infinite distance (Derrida 1997: 255). He also wonders if it is necessary to define love as attraction and respect as distance (Derrida 1997: 255). Would it not be possible to conceive love in terms of distance and respect in terms of proximity? The second limitation Kant erects is this: respectful distance, proper or suitable distance, limits excessive or infinite love. As we saw, when excessive love threatens a rupture of the social bond, the suitable repulsion of respect counters the repulsion that result from unsuitable and excessive love. Yet, does excessive love necessarily result in the social bond being ruptured? Does excessive love have to be excessively possessive? But then, third, moving from perfect friendship between two people to the friend of man, Kant limits the love of humanity (philanthropy) with the idea of equality. Yet, might we not wonder whether the love of humanity extends as far as the love of the unequal? Is it not possible that the love of humanity is guided by the idea of what makes every single other different from every single other? But then, fourth, we can wonder about the Kantian concept of equality. Kant limits the idea of equality by means of the image of the brothers under one father. Equality is isogony. Equality limited by birth, by the family, by anthropology limits friendship to the suitable, proper, and appropriate friend. Friendship is limited to the like or fellow-man (*semblable*, in Derrida's French [Derrida 1997: 155]). In other words, friendship is limited to the homo-fraternal (Derrida 1997: 306) and homo-philia (Derrida 1997: 104). As Derrida says, there is not a woman in sight, no sister, no mother, no female friends (Derrida 1997: 262). And if there is a woman in sight, her difference and alterity is already neutralized by using the simulacrum of modesty to determine her as moral: changing counterfeit coins into gold. Through this change of her "charms," her love, which has the potential to be excessive, has been limited. She has become nothing but a brother.

Overall, Derrida has shown us that Kant positions the image of the brother as the schema between the sensibility of love and the idea of equality, thereby limiting both. Yet, we know from Heidegger's Kant book that the middle place – the "between" – is *the* place: it is the place of "originary heterogeneity" (Derrida 1997: 105). As Derrida says, it is "the place of the irreplaceable" (Derrida 1997: 262). He continues, "We must know that the place of the irreplaceable is a really singular place. If it is irreplaceable ... , it is so in order to receive substitutable inscriptions. It is the place of possible substitution. It never confounds itself with what occupies it, with all the figures that come to be inscribed in it and that pass themselves off as copies of a paradigm or as the examples of an irreplaceable exemplar" (Derrida 1997: 263).[18] The anthropological schema of the family – the one father and the brothers – has passed itself off as *the* paradigm and the *exemplar*. Occupying this place, the anthropological schema of the family disfigures or even violates the empty or at least non-figurative middle. In fact, we must recognize that, if the place of the schematism is empty or non-figurative, then any given figure of it disfigures what it is. *Its proper sense is never given as such.* Even more, we must recognize that, if we speak as Kant does of a strict sense of friendship – the friend of man – this strict sense dissimulates the proper sense. The strict, literal, restrained sense of love, that is, love among what we call a "natural family," among "blood relatives," dissimulates the proper sense of love. And even though Derrida admits, as we have seen, that Kant recognizes that human fraternity is a figure, this figure remains linked to virility and thereby to the strict or so-called "natural" sense of the family and birth. As Derrida tells us, *the proper sense of love* always, necessarily, promises more than the strict sense and more than any given figure of love (Derrida 1997: 240).[19] Even as it empties out any given sense, figure, or image of it, even as it seems to reduce itself down to zero, the proper sense of love gives excessively and gives more. We see now what is lost in Kant's demand of us that we make small change turn into gold. What is lost is the potency, the virtuality, the "perhaps-ness" of love; this is a potency that is worth more than gold. We must break with fraternity, if we want to recover all the potencies of love, if we want to recover the hyperbolic sense of love. Love must be given its chance, but, as we know, such a chance risks evil. Violence must be done to brotherly love, or, more precisely, violence must be done against the violence of brotherly love.

For Derrida, one condition is required for the rupture with the fraternal model of friendship, and thus for the chance for a love beyond brotherly love. The condition is expressed in the following quotation, which we presented already above. Derrida says, "Beyond all the dialectics whose ineluctable experiences we multiply, beyond the fatal syntheses or reconciliations of opposites, *the dream of an unusable friendship* survives, a friendship beyond friendship, and invincible before these dialectics" (Derrida 1997: 217, my emphasis). This quotation means that, in order to break with the fraternal model of friendship, we must "dream," indeed, think or conceive "an unusable friendship" that unifies, as Kant would say, love with respect, but in a union that is not synthesized and reconciled, a union that remains invincible in relation to all dialectics. What is an unusable friendship?

For Derrida, an unusable friendship is a friendship beyond all utility, beyond all means-ends relation, beyond all market pricing, in short, beyond all economy. Clearly then, the idea of an unusable friendship is based on the Kantian moral demand *never* to treat other persons as mere means to an end. Nevertheless, to truly break with utility, with mutuality, and with the return on one's investment, the idea of an unusable friendship must break with what we could call the root of Kantian moral philosophy. As is well-known, Kant's moral philosophy remains close to Christian thought: the one father who is in heaven commands us to love our enemies in order for us to receive the profit of a heavenly afterlife (Derrida 1997: 285–6, and 65, 59). Similarly, as we just saw in Derrida's Kant analysis, Kant advocates that we change small change into gold. Kant advices that we use behaviors like decorum and politeness, which are false (again, "Oh my friends, there is no friend") to gain the "heaven" of moral truth – and happiness. In effect, Kant advises us, in his pragmatic anthropology, to instrumentalize ourselves in order to gain a profit. Derrida's point is clear: under the influence of Christianity, Kant's pragmatic anthropology violates his own categorical imperative. When he advocates the "ruse" of modest dress for women, which saves them from being used by the desires of the ones they attract, Kant is, nevertheless, advocating a sublime kind of utility. They are pieces of property used in the moral subterfuge of the humanization of man. In contrast, Derrida advocates that we break with this story, with this sublime economy. But, he is not advocating that we abandon all ruse, lures, and appearances. After all, phenomenology has shown that our only relation to others is mediated by such ruses, appearances, and indications (Derrida 1997: 54), and it is this phenomenological insight into the absence, irreducible in the experience of others, that ups the ante on the Kantian imperative of respect for persons (Derrida 1978: 123). Departing therefore from Kant, Derrida follows Nietzsche.[20]

## III. Derrida's Analysis of Nietzsche: Salutary Deceptive Appearances; the Loving Call; and Generosity

Like Derrida's Kant analysis, his Nietzsche analysis contains obscurities, which, undoubtedly, come as much from Nietzsche's strange texts as from Derrida's counter-intuitive argumentation. Derrida's analysis, as we anticipated in the Introduction, focuses on Nietzsche's reversal of Aristotle's reputed statement. Instead of "Oh my friends, there is no friend," we read in *Human, all too Human* (Book I, §376, called "Of Friends"): Perhaps to each of us there will come the more joyful hour when we exclaim: 'Friends, there are no friends!' thus said the dying sage; 'Foes, there are no foes!' say I, the living fool."

In reference to this statement, Derrida *generally* is claiming that the living fool is in fact the dying sage in disguise (Derrida 1997: 59). The dying sage, who was calling for friends, is pretending to be the living fool, calling for enemies. Nietzsche, of course, is aware that, in the Western philosophical tradition, a higher wisdom, true wisdom, is sometimes presented as a kind of foolishness: "Behind the mask [of the living fool], a sage wiser than the sage" (Derrida 1997: 59).[21] And, here, Derrida speaks of "a new political wisdom" (Derrida 1997: 60).[22] However, for Derrida, the new wisdom is connected to way in which the dying sage conceals the secret of his love through his *pretending and feigning, through his passing himself off or giving himself off as* something else — we shall speak of generosity in a moment.

Thus, although Derrida does not make this point in his Nietzsche analysis, we can notice that the dying sage resembles both the modest woman of Kant's *Anthropology* and the perfect friendship of his *Metaphysics of Morals*. Like the modest woman, the dying sage, out of love, pretends to be not in love with the ones called.[23] The pretense of non-attraction distances the ones called from him. Through the distance established, the dying sage saves the others from the violence involved in love. Recall that "love is the enemy." Saving them from this evil internal to love, the dying sage's deceptive appearances, like the modest woman's appearances, are salutary. And, like perfect friendship, the dying sage shares his secret with the ones called; his secret is the enmity of his love, which he presents *as enmity*, truthfully, to the ones called. Yet, unlike Kant's modest woman, the dying sage passes himself off, not as a friend or brother, but as an enemy; and unlike Kantian perfect friendship – and earlier, of course, we had wondered, in Derrida's Kant analysis, how best to keep a secret – it seems that the dying sage shares his secret, or a part of it, in order to conceal it better. Or, we could even say that he declares his enmity *out loud*, while keeping his true enmity, which is the violence of love, *silent*. The final conclusion Derrida seems to be drawing from the analysis of Nietzsche's *Human, all too Human*'s reversal of Aristotle's reputed utterance, therefore, is twofold. On the one hand, the dying sage, unlike the modest woman, distances the others from him infinitely because he passes himself off not as a friend, but as an enemy. On the other hand, unlike perfect friendship and unlike Kant's story of moral subterfuge, the truth is never revealed, because the ones called are too far away to see the dying sage for what he is. The truth is never revealed as such because the feigned enmity – "don't love me, do be my enemies" – never makes the distance suitable, narrow, and strict.

This truth, if we can call it a truth, takes us to the heart of the black passion called love. We need to recall again, as Kant knew (and as so many other sages knew), that love *is* indeed the enemy. The concept of love implies that there is no stable distinction between friend and enemy (Derrida 1997: 59). The concept, if we can call it a concept, is always inadequate to itself (Derrida 1997: 66); its proper sense is always improper, and never like itself (Derrida 1997: 159). In order to understand the instability of love, we must, once again, turn to "Violence and Metaphysics." There, Derrida had shown that *the other must appear* – so that, *on the one hand*, we are able to perceive the other as such. Only through this appearance are we able to speak *to* the other. Yet, *on the other hand*, when the other appears as such in a phenomenon, and *the other must appear* – this appearing is an essential necessity – the other is captured within the general sense of other. Only through this appearance are we able to speak *of* the other. In other words, although we have access to the other only through a phenomenon, the phenomenalization of the other eliminates the other's alterity within a general concept, which turns all others into the same (Derrida 1978: 128–9). Similarly, and more simply, in *Politics of Friendship*, Derrida claims *at once* that there is no love without the declaration of love *to* the other (Derrida 1997: 9) and that "speech [*of* the other] ruins friendship" (Derrida 1997: 54). This "at once" claim means, *on the one hand*, that, if I want you to be my friend, I must tell you – declare out loud and call to you – that "I love you." And, this declaration indeed means that I love you. I want you to be close to me: "Come over, I am your friend." Nevertheless, *on the other hand*, when I declare my love to you, when I call you "my love," I make you *of* me: *my* love, the same as me. I bring you so close to me that you pull back from me and rupture the intimacy. As we saw in the Kant analysis, love as excessive attraction always ends up breaking the social bond. Therefore, in my love for you, at the same time I am your friend and your enemy. Therefore the structure of the declaration, or better, of the call lies in the heart of the black passion of love.[24] The structure of the call is indeed contradictory, as we just saw, but it contains within itself a possibility. *Here is the chance for love*. The chance for love appears when we pay attention to what one says "out loud" and what one "keeps silent" ("à haute voix" [Derrida 1997: 9] and "se taire" [Derrida 1997: 54] in Derrida's French) in any call. In other words, to find the chance for love, one must pay attention to what is explicit and what is implicit, what is posited and what is presupposed in any call – whether it is a declaration of love or hatred (hatred too has to be declared).

This is how the silently presupposed and the explicitly posited seem to work in the call. As soon as I call you to me *out loud*, it is as if I am saying *silently and not out loud* "I love you, listen" (Derrida 1997: 218). By means of the very words I use (regardless of their content), a bond has to exist between us so that you are able to understand the words in the call. The use of language implies that a kind of agreement, consent, or promise has already been established between you and me. Friendship must have already been established. Regardless of whether they call for friends or enemies, every call therefore is implicitly love. Yet, *at the same time*, and inseparable from the silent presupposition of the amicable calling into agreement and proximity, my call to you "must always ask or presuppose [*not out loud, but silently*] the question, 'are you there?'" (Derrida 1997: 173). Just as the structure of the call necessarily presupposes that you are present in agreement with me, the structure of the call also necessarily presupposes that you, the one called, *not be there*. In other words, there would be no reason for me to call you if you were already present before me. Every call, necessarily, and regardless of who or what is called or posited, requires distance. *The chance for love appears in the call's necessary distance.* The structure of the call therefore includes necessarily as silent presuppositions *at once* intimacy, closeness, and proximity – community – *and* separation, being away, and distance – solitude. In other words, the structure of the call necessarily brings the ones called into proximity and sameness and it necessarily puts them at a distance and guards their difference. The *loving call* violently possesses the ones called and at the same time it frees them from this very violence.

With this chance in mind, let us return to Nietzsche's dying sage who is passing himself off as a living fool. We can now see his wisdom. The dying sage does not declare *out loud, with a loud voice, openly*, his love. Instead, the dying sage *explicitly, out loud, and with a loud voice* declares his hatred, and yet, implicitly, *silently, to himself, secretly*, he is saying that he loves the ones called. Because of the very structure of the call, his explicit call to enmity still necessarily presupposes love. It is as if the dying sage is saying out loud, "Stay away, I am your enemy"; but, silently, he is saying "I need you, be close to me! I love you, my enemies." Therefore, out of love, the dying sage, through his explicit call to enmity, pushes those called farther out than the distance required by the essential structure of the call, farther out than proper, suitable, or convenient distance. By pretending to be the living fool calling for enemies, the dying sage explicitly repels the others away from him; he distances the others, let us say, *he distances her*, from him – even as he implicitly calls her in love. Consequently, she is too distant for fusion and identification; she is too distant to be changed into the proximate, the familiar, and the fraternal; she is too distant to be changed into the beloved or the brother. She can no longer be a possession that can be used. Most importantly, she is too distant for his actions to be deadly and violent. The distance means that he keeps his hands off her.

To make the point as clearly as possible, we must say that the dying sage in his explicit call for enmity still loves the ones called. He loves them and wants them to be near. This love is still, up to this point, the desire for possession. This is why the dying sage is malicious and wicked, even evil (Derrida 1997: 60). He wants to violently possess them; he wants to count them among his goods (Derrida 1997: 17). Yet, the dying sage's love goes further than the point of possession. The dying sage pretending to be a living fool does not utter his declaration of love *out loud* because he wants to *dispossess* the ones he is calling.

He renounces his love *out loud* without renouncing it *silently*. In doing so, the dying sage's secret love is more than the desire for possession, more than avarice, more than lust, more than self-love (Derrida 1997: 174 and 213). As Derrida says, "[The dying sage pretending to be a living fool] loves them enough not to want to do them all the evil he wants for them. He loves them too much for that" (Derrida 1997: 60, Derrida italicizes both sentences in their entirety). Here indeed, love tends to be excessive, but it is excessive in its desire to free the ones called from possession. Therefore, the explicit declaration of enmity ("Oh, my enemies") seems to be more loving than love. We are tempted to name this excessive desire to free the ones called from possession "true love" ("the maximum of good intentions"); or at least, it must be called "hyperbolic love" (Derrida 1997: 60). And, this hyperbolic love is, as Derrida calls it, "philanthropy" because the secret, as we saw, always necessarily goes beyond two people; it always implies, at the least, the third (Derrida 1997: 60). *This* philanthropy, not Kant's friend of man, is what Derrida means with unusable friendship. Unusable friendship is excessive love that excessively distances the ones loved.

How are we to imagine an unusable friendship? What figure or figures?[25] Derrida appropriates two images, one from Nietzsche and one from Aristotle, to help us think about unusable friendship. They are two images of generosity. They are relevant to dying sage's pretense of enmity because, as we recall, the dying sage *gives himself off* as the living fool. The *first image* comes from one of Nietzsche's most infamous statements about women, from Book I of *Zarathustra*, the speech called "On the Friend": "Woman is not yet capable of friendship: women are still cats or birds. Or at best, cows." Yes, this is an infamous comment, but, at the least, it provides a figure different from that of the brother; the cow is not a fellow-man. As Derrida stresses, we must recall the cow comment's context. Immediately before making this comment about women, Zarathustra had complained that women were not yet capable of friendship because they only know how to love, that is, to possess or be possessed. But then immediately after the cow comment, Zarathustra addresses men and tells them they, like the women, are not yet capable of friendship because of their avarice. In other words, they are no better than women because they too know only possession. But at least, we have to say, the women, like the cow – and this point seems to make women "better" than men who are "worse" – at least women give and are not consumed by their desire to possess. Cows basically do not demand a return on their investment of milk. Derrida therefore recalls this infamous comment about women because cows give sustenance without, apparently, any desire for reciprocation. The *second image* Derrida gives us comes from Aristotle's *Eudemian Ethics* (1239a35). It is undoubtedly a better figure of generosity than Nietzsche's cow figure, although it also involves women and milk. Mentioning Antiphon's *Andromache*, Aristotle speaks of mothers who allow other women to adopt their children in order to nurse them. Aristotle points us to this case because he thinks that this story allows us to see that in friendship we should always prefer loving over being loved. As always, Aristotle valorizes activity over passivity. But, for Derrida, the story allows us to see mothers who love their children so much that they do not wish to receive the pleasure and love that comes back to them through suckling. They are so generous that they do not want reciprocal love.

Derrida, of course, quickly connects this renunciation of maternal enjoyment to the death of the beloved, since, if one continues to love a person even after her death, that love given can never be reciprocated (Derrida 1997: 11–12). Although Derrida does not draw this conclusion, we must say that it is this excessive love of someone beyond death that brings the other excessively close to the lover, closer than any corporeal proximity and closer than any material contact. Here we would have to introduce Derrida's discourse of spectrality. The distance of the deceased beloved haunts the lover inside him as a specter. Perhaps, one has to say that if one truly loves the other and therefore truly renounces reciprocation and return, then as a true lover, one should want the other to die. What a disturbing conclusion! But it seems to follow from Derrida's idea of an unusable friendship. A perhaps less frightening conclusion would be this: one has to mourn the passing of the lover even before he or she has died. If it is true love, one's relation to the friend or beloved must be spectral, even while the friend or the beloved is alive. This love, at once so close and so very distant, is indeed a black passion.

Thanks to these figures – are they the images of a superhuman love (Derrida 1997: 287)[26] – we can say that the sage's generosity is great, his pretense (or, should we say, *her* pretense?) is so filled with love for the other (not with self-love) that she does not expect anything in return from those she calls to herself. In fact, the pretending sage's respect is so excessive that the distance of the others is so far away that they do not have to reciprocate her love for them. No equality that can be measured is established here. Unlike the modest woman who feigns fraternal friendship in order to sublimate her love into the truth of human moral goodness, the sage feigns not to be friendly and fraternal, in order to hide the malicious, loving truth about herself and in order to let the others be equally other to one another in their inequality (Derrida 1997: 22).[27] The distance that she establishes through her feigned enmity forbids any profit, salary, or gold. The distance forbids any reconciliation, any synthesis, any union, and any equalization. Here we have a generosity that is dissymmetrical and disproportionate, non-reciprocal and non-equivalent. With unusable friendship, love and respect are unified while they remain "out of joint." Here we have a schematism, the hidden art" of the imagination, which does not pay off any profit, salary, or gold.

## IV. Conclusion: Crimes against Life?

We started with Heidegger's Kant book, *Kant and the Problem of Metaphysics*, which pointed us toward the "hidden art" of the schematism. The "between" of the schematism, as the form of time, turns out to be originary heterogeneity: time is out of joint. In his career, Derrida gives many names to the disjointure of time, the most famous of which being "différance" (Derrida 1982: 1–28)[28] In *Politics of Friendship*, he settles on the name "contretemps" (Derrida 1997: 14–16).[29] "Contretemps" is the name of disjoined time – it is the structure of the call – because, on the one hand, "contretemps" refers to that which happens against or counter to the continuous flow of time: an event happens by chance, unforeseen, like the black swan; and yet, on the other hand, "contretemps" refers to that which happens against or counter to the discontinuous flow of time: an ideality is omnitemporal, like the species bird. For Derrida, the relation between the event of the black swan and essence of birds is one of "perhaps." Perhaps the essence of birds will effectuate, or better, counter-effectuate, a black swan; perhaps the event of the black swan will counter-effectuate an essence of birds. No one knows for sure what will come about through the "perhaps" of the "contretemps."

In *Politics of Friendship*, Derrida shows that the difference between Kant and Nietzsche is the difference between teleology and something like an a-teleology (Derrida 1997: 221–2). For Derrida, Nietzsche's statements or utterances (*ses énoncés*) are teleiopoetic: they aim at making (*poesis*) something happen at a distance (*tele*), but this distance is never closed (Derrida 1997: 31). Although this is a clumsy way to speak, we must say that teleiopoetic statements exhibit a kind of teleology. The example Derrida gives us comes from §2 of *Beyond Good and Evil*. Speaking of the "dangerous perhaps," Nietzsche says, "Alas! If only you knew how soon, how very soon, things will be – different!" This sentence, like any other sentence (even if it is only reporting) affects and changes its addressee. In this case, by the time you get to the end of the sentence, this "if only you knew how soon, how very soon, something else is coming" changes you. It gives you a gift of knowledge. However, the sentence does not report the knowledge; the content of knowledge which the sentence has given you remains indeterminate. By the time you reach the end of the sentence, you still do not yet know what else is coming. Will it be good or will it be bad? The sentence aims at something out in the universe or out in the world, but we just don't know how big this world, universe, or cosmos is.[30] The figure for the adverb that lies in the middle of the sentence between the non-knowledge of the beginning and the knowledge of the end, the image for the "how soon, how very soon" is an arrow. The teleiopoetic statement is like an arrow that hits its mark immediately. The "how soon, how very soon" travels at breakneck speeds across the distance – and then withdraws back into its bow in order to be launched across the distance again. This is the arrow of the dying sage disguised as a living fool calling for enemies. It is at once the arrow of war against Cupid's arrow.

These images of the "between" – the disguised dying sage and the arrow – are very different from that of the brother. The figure of the brother gives us a different kind of utterance. In *Politics of Friendship*, Derrida mentions several times the motto (*le devise*) of the French Revolution (Derrida 1997: 284): "Liberté, Égalité, Fraternité." Derrida tells us that the revolutionaries debated about whether to include the word "fraternity" in the motto because they worried that its Christian resonances would betray the revolution. Of course, they decided to include it at the end of the motto (Derrida 1997: 268n10). However, Derrida also tells us that some revolutionaries wanted to place the word "fraternité" in the middle, transforming the motto into "Liberté, Fraternité, Égalité." Fraternity would then be the "affective term linking freedom and equality" (Derrida 1997: 268n10). By providing the affective link, brotherhood mediates between the singularity of freedom and the universality of equality. The goal of this motto is only and alone the equality of all men who are, as it were, brothers before one father. Again, we can imagine this "device" as an arrow. Fraternity is an arrow that crosses the distance slowly. Of course, the humanization of man takes time. It takes time to for humanity to emerge from its "childhood." And yet, nevertheless, the arrow hits its mark. All of us, including women, become or should become – the arrow is still traveling – brothers. Or, the better image for the motto of the French Revolution is the straight path with no detours: fraternity marches straight over from freedom to equality, achieving the *telos* of autonomy. Before the moral law, we are all brothers. Yet, this teleological determination closes off the distance; it closes off the potencies of love. These potencies must be reopened. We reopen this power only through what Austin called a speech act (Austin 1962). As we shall see now, each of the "three ways of speaking," effects a change in the one to whom they are addressed.

## Notes

1 Derrida has of course written on Kant's Third Critique (Derrida 1987a: 17–147, especially p. 138, where Derrida speaks of the sublime and comparison). Derrida's discussion of Verlässlichkeit ("utility"; "reliability"; "thanks to which"; "by the force of which") in Heidegger's "Origin of the Work of Art" is also relevant to *Politics of Friendship* (Derrida 1987a: 344–57). Of course, Kant's political writings on cosmopolitanism and hospitality are a constant theme in Derrida's late writings (Derrida 2000a). A lecture dating from 1993 discusses Kant's definition of the lie (Derrida 2002: 28–70). And there is Derrida's 1980 address on Kant's "The Conflict of the Faculties" (Derrida 2004: 83–112).
2 The following texts have been consulted in the writing of this essay. The most helpful for thinking about Derrida's *Politics of Friendship* is Samir Haddad, *Derrida and the Inheritance of Democracy* (Bloomington: Indiana University Press, 2013). Haddad's book is one of the few that has an illuminating chapter on *Politics of Friendship* (pp. 100–18). Here are the sources in alphabetical order. Geoffrey Bennington, *Interrupting Derrida* (New York: Routledge, 2000); Martin Hägglund, *Radical Atheism: Derrida and the Time of Life* (Stanford: Stanford University Press, 2008); David Farrell Krell, *Derrida and our Animal Others* (Bloomington: Indiana University Press, 2013); Michael Naas, *Derrida from Now on* (Bronx: Fordham University Press, 2008); Jacob Rogozinski, *Faire Part. Cryptes de Derrida* (Paris: Linges, 2005); Kas Saghafi, *Apparitions – Of Derrida's Other* (Bronx: Fordham University Press, 2010); Alex Thompson, *Deconstruction and Democracy* (London: Continuum, 2005).
3 For instance, in "The Philosophical Manifesto of the Historical School of Law," Marx says that "Kant's philosophy is rightly to be regarded as the *German theory* of the French Revolution" (Marx 1967: 100, Marx's emphasis).
4 My focus on Kant and Nietzsche was partially guided by Derrida's essay

called "The Politics of Friendship" (Derrida 1988a). Here Derrida basically extracts discussions from *Politics of Friendship*, Chapter 10, the last chapter, which concerns Kant and Nietzsche.

5 Derrida continues his discussion of fraternity (and refers to *Politics of Friendship* frequently) in his 2002 *Rogues*, in particular, in Part I, Chapter 5, which is called "Liberty, Equality, Fraternity, or How Not to Speak in Mottos" (Derrida 2005a: 56–62).

6 Derrida refers to Nietzsche's *Human, all too Human*, Book I, §376 ("Of the Friend"), Epilogue to Book I ("Among Friends"), Book II, §246 ("The Wiseman Pretending to be a Fool") (Nietzsche 1986); *Beyond Good and Evil*, § 2 and §214 (Nietzsche 1966); and *Thus Spoke Zarathustra*, Book I, §14 ("On the Friend") (Nietzsche 1968). Derrida uses the French translations of Nietzsche found in *Œuvres philosophiques complètes* (Paris: NRF Presses Universitaires de France, 1971). John D. Caputo's essay on *Politics of Friendship* is helpful in regard to Derrida's reading of Nietzsche. John D. Caputo, "Who is Derrida's Zarathustra? Of Fraternity, Friendship, and a Democracy to Come," in *Research in Phenomenology*, 29 (1) (1999): 184–98.

7 Derrida acknowledges late in *Politics of Friendship* (Chapter 8) that the utterance attributed to Aristotle is translated sometimes in the philosophical canon as "Oh my friends, there is no friend" – this translation is the one Derrida favors – and at other times as "He who has many friends has none [or, has no true friend]" – Derrida calls this translation the "recoil" (*repli*) version. If Aristotle actually said this sentence, it seems to have been inspired by the ending of Plato's dialogue, *Lysis*.

8 In addition to "unusable friendship," Derrida speaks of "love in friendship" (*aimer d'amitié*), which is the title of Chapter 2, and the more well-known "lovence" (*aimance*) (Derrida 1997: 35).

9 Fred Evans, "Cosmopolitanism to Come: Derrida's Response to Globalization," in *A Companion to Derrida* (Oxford: Blackwell Publishing, 2014), pp. 550–64. While Evans' essay does not explicitly discuss *Politics of Friendship*, it lays out the basis structure of Derrida's thought in relation to politics so well that one cannot avoid citing Evans' "Cosmopolitanism to Come" constantly.

10 Derrida refers to Kant's *Metaphysics of Morals*, "The Doctrine of Virtue," the final pages of "The Ethical Doctrine of Elements," "On the Intimate Union of Love and Respect in Friendship" (§46) (Kant 1996); *Anthropology from a Pragmatic Point of View*, "The Anthropological Didactic," "On the Cognitive Faculty," "On the Appearances that are allowed in Morality" (§14) (Kant 2007). Lara Denis has written an interesting article on

marriage and friendship in Kant. Denis criticizes Kant for not taking love seriously enough. Lara Denis, "Friendship to Marriage: Revising Kant," in *Philosophy and Phenomenological Research*, vol. 63, no. 1 (July 2001): 1–28.
11 See Derrida 1997: 252–7 (Chapter 9); (2) 257–63 (Chapter 9); (3) 273–5 (Chapter 10).
12 Derrida uses the French Philonenko translation of Kant's *Metaphysics of Morals*. Immanuel Kant, *Métaphysique des mœurs*, trans. A. Philonenko (Paris: Vrin, 1985).
13 Derrida uses Foucault's translation of *The Anthropology*. Immanuel Kant, *Anthropologie du point de vue pragmatique*, trans. Michel Foucault (Paris: Vrin, 1970). I have used The Cambridge Edition of the Works of Immanuel Kant. Immanuel Kant, *Anthropology from a Pragmatic Point of View*, trans. Robert B. Louden, in *Anthropology, History, and Education*, ed. Gunter Zöller and Robert B. Louden (New York: Cambridge University Press, 2007), pp. 227–429.
14 For more on counterfeit money and generosity, see Derrida 1992b.
15 Much of what Derrida says here about ruse in Kant resembles what Foucault says in his *Introduction to Kant's Anthropology* about *Kunst* (art) (Foucault 2008: 90–1).
16 As always, Kant adds the strict or proper Latin term to modesty: "pudicitia" (Derrida 1997: 273). Here Derrida uses the French term derived from the Latin: "pudeur."
17 For the problem of revelation versus revealability, see Derrida 1997: 18–19.
18 Here Derrida mentions the *khôra*, of which he has often written. Derrida 1995b: 89–127.
19 Although Derrida here and throughout his career has criticized propriety (see especially "White Mythology" in *Margins of Philosophy*), he seems to make this criticism in the name of an improper propriety, in the name of an impure purity (Derrida 1982: 207–72). Derrida's most important discussion of the proper and the pure is in his *Monologualism of the Other* (Derrida 1998: 47).
20 Derrida warns us that he is not following Nietzsche completely (Derrida 1997: 33).
21 Derrida does not mention Foucault's *History of Madness*, which of course lays out the interactions between madness or folly and reason or wisdom (Foucault 2006: 23–4).
22 Here Derrida turns to a different paragraph in *Human, all Too Human*, Book II, §246.
23 On modesty, see Derrida 1998a: 49–51.

24 Derrida's idea of the call seems to be based in what Heidegger says about the call in *On the Way to Language*. See Heidegger 2001: 196.
25 It might seem up to this point that the image Derrida is seeking, through the Nietzsche analysis, is the figure of the enemy. However, as his analysis of Schmitt shows, the figure of the enemy can be that of a suitable or appropriate enemy, my brother as an enemy (whom I truly love and love more through the expression of my enmity) (Derrida 1997: 163). We need only think of Cain and Abel in order to see how the figure of the enemy betrays the proper sense of love.
26 Deleuze had already spoken of the superman having a different sensibility (Deleuze 1983: 163).
27 As Derrida says here, "tout autre est tout autre." See Chapter 4 above for the analysis of this sentence.
28 Later in his career, Derrida utilizes the word "anachronism." See Derrida 1993: 65.
29 The question of priority and origin is remarkably difficult in Derrida's thought generally. Probably, the most important discussion of origin is in *Of Spirit* (Derrida 1989a: 107–8). The discussion of origin in *Of Spirit* is clear that the origin must be heterogeneous; it must be divided. Thus the concept of "contretemps" is *Politics of Friendship* fits well with the discussion of "origin-heterogeneous" in *Of Spirit*. However, in *Politics of Friendship*, it seems that potentiality, which Derrida calls "the perhaps" ("le peut-être"), is most prior, and perhaps prior to the "contretemps." It is prior to the fundamental agreement and acquiescence that we find in Heidegger, which itself is prior to the question. Nevertheless, the idea of responding to the other, which implies that the other puts me in question, and which implies a call to me, seems to be almost as originary as "the perhaps." See Derrida 1997: 38–9 (the "perhaps," question, and acquiescence); Derrida 1997: 228–9 (responsibility); and Derrida 1997: 250–2 (responsibility).
30 In *Philosophy in a Time of Terror*, Derrida says, "What I call 'democracy to come' would go beyond the limits of cosmopolitanism, that is, of a world citizenship. It would be more in line with what lets singular being (anyone) 'live together,' where they are not yet defined by citizenship, that is, by their condition as lawful 'subject' in a state or legitimate members of a nation-state or even of a confederation or world state. It would involve, in short, an alliance that goes beyond the 'political' as it has been commonly defined . . . This does not, however, lead to a depoliticization – quite the contrary. Yet it does require another thought another putting into practice of the concept of the 'political' and the concept 'world'" (Derrida 2003: 130–1).

# 9

# Three Ways of Speaking, or "Let Others be Free": On Foucault's "Speaking-Freely"; Derrida's "Speaking-Distantly"; and Deleuze's "Speaking in Tongues"

Foucault, Derrida, and Deleuze have recognized the originality of the idea of the performative (Austin 1962).[1] Chronologically, Foucault comes first. In his 1969 *The Archaeology of Knowledge*, he turns to the "speech act" as "one last possibility, and the most probable of all, of defining the statement [*l'énoncé*]" (Foucault 1972: 82).[2] After describing the performative, Foucault concludes that a "bi-univocal relation" between the statement and the performative cannot exist (Foucault 1972: 83). There is one primary reason, according to Foucault, why the performative cannot define the statement. Even if one says that an illocutionary act is complete, one has to admit that the act is complete only if several statements have already been made, prior to the act. The illocutionary act is made possible by the juxtaposition of statements. Foucault concludes that the statement is "indispensable"; it is that "on the basis of which" we can determine speech acts. A statement then is a prior or even an a priori "verbal performance."[3] The statement is a "place of emergence," an "irruption"; it is an event (Foucault 1972: 121). In his 1971 "Nietzsche, Genealogy, History," Foucault will define an event as "the irruption of forces" (Foucault 1998: 376). Nevertheless, despite the irruption of forces, a statement, Foucault tells us, is in principle "remanent," that is, repeatable (Foucault 1972: 124).

Similarly, in 1971, Derrida, in "Signature Event Context" (Derrida 1982: 309–30), turns to the "problematic of the performative" because he thinks that speech act theory has transformed the concept of communication (Derrida 1982: 322). Derrida stresses, however, that the "infelicities" that Austin encounters with the performative arise from what Derrida calls "a common root." These linguistic "impurities," "parasites," or "abnormalities," for instance, non-serious speech and citations, are rooted in the linguistic codes. As Derrida claims, no "performative statement [*un énoncé performatif*]" would succeed if it "did not repeat a coded … statement" (Derrida 1982: 326). In other words, Derrida is claiming that a performative statement is able to function, only if the statement conforms to a code, whose forms are "repeatable" or "iterable." Therefore, iterability is necessarily prior to all utterances or statements, a necessary or structural possibility of all speech acts, whether serious or non-serious, of all success and all failure in communicating, in short, for any event. Because of the priority of iterability, all linguistic utterances are in reality "marks" (Derrida 1982: 326). Nevertheless, while formally prior to events, iterability, for Derrida, is also and necessarily "emergence," "a force of rupture" (Derrida 1982: 317). And finally, like Foucault in 1971, Derrida mentions Nietzsche as the philosopher who initiates the thought of force (Derrida 1982: 322).[4]

Finally, we come to Deleuze and Guattari's 1980 *A Thousand Plateaus*. Like Foucault and Derrida, they recognize the importance of "Austin's famous theses." Speech act theory is important for them because it requires that language be defined through a "pragmatics," or even "a politics of language" (Deleuze and

Guattari 1987: 82). Even though speech act theory leads Deleuze and Guattari to a pragmatics, they ultimately reject it because it relies on a concept of intersubjectivity. For Deleuze and Guattari, we must be more "abstract" than linguistic systems of information and intersubjective acts of communication, more abstract than *langue* and *parole*. We must abstract linguistic utterances so much that we see how they rely on what Deleuze and Guattari call the "order-word" (*mot d'ordre*). Order-words, statements like "you are no longer a child," are the a priori of language. Order-words change your subjective status: you must now act as an adult. Order-words are events but despite being so, are repeatable. It opens up a variation, which is bound neither to constants nor variables (Deleuze and Guattari 1987: 93). Of course, in *A Thousand Plateaus*, whenever Deleuze and Guattari speak of continuous variation, they refer to Nietzsche's eternal return doctrine. In his 1962 *Nietzsche and Philosophy*, Deleuze had already described the eternal return doctrine in terms of forces and "the power of transformation" (Deleuze 1983: 47 and 42).

For Foucault, the force of the statement requires us to "restore discourse's event character" (Foucault 1972: 229). For Derrida, the force of iterability requires us to rethink "the eventhood of an event" (Derrida 1982: 326). And, for Deleuze (and Guattari), the force of the order-word requires us to express "the pure event" (Deleuze and Guattari 1987: 263). Despite the similarity, if not identity between Foucault, Derrida, and Deleuze in regard to the task of rethinking, restoring, and expressing the event, the very wording of the task discloses a difference. The "event character" (*caractère d'événement*), for Foucault, leads to discourse's existence or reality. In contrast, for Derrida, "the eventhood of an event" (*l'événementalité d'un événement*) leads to language's essence or ideality. And for Deleuze, "the pure event" (*l'événement pur*) leads language's becoming. In *The Archaeology of Knowledge*, Foucault defines the statement, which must be coded in order to be "remanent," as "repeatable materiality" (Foucault 1972: 105). For Derrida, because he develops the idea of iterability from the materiality of language (writing), we can say that a coded statement is "material repeatability" (Derrida 1981: 50–1, 64). We find no parallel expression in Deleuze (and Guattari); however, they speak of "tensors," in which one cannot decide whether the particle-sign is "repeatable materiality" or "material repeatability." In other words, for Foucault, it is the *material* of the repeatable that produces emergence, while, for Derrida, it is the *repeatability* of the material that produces emergence; and for Deleuze, it is pure variation, or more precisely, a variation that is *no longer relative* to either matter or repetition that produces emergence. In still other words, for Foucault, it is the verbal performance or act (of speaking) that makes something emerge, while, for Derrida, it is the mark or form (of speaking); and for Deleuze, it is the particle-sign. These precise differences derive from Foucault interrogating the *act* itself that makes an event happen, while Derrida interrogates the *form* itself; and Deleuze interrogates a "*neither form nor matter.*" The most basic question that Foucault, Derrida, and Deleuze seem to be asking is: how, in what manner or way, does an event take place?[5] What sort of act *and* what sort of form *and* what sort of matter-form produces a change in us, in our thinking and behaving, in our way of living? As the subtitle of this chapter states, the answer lies in speaking-freely, speaking-distantly, and speaking-in-tongues. It is the question of the *act* that leads Foucault, in his final courses at the Collège de France, to the investigation of the ancient practice of "speaking freely" (*parrēsia*). In these investigations,

## THREE WAYS OF SPEAKING, OR "LET OTHERS BE FREE"

Foucault constructs what he calls an "ethics of speech." It is the question of the *form* that leads Derrida, in the courses from which he writes *Politics of Friendship*, to the investigation of "speaking distantly" (*teleiopoesis*). And it is the question of the matter or act and form that leads Deleuze (and Guattari) to investigate "speaking in tongues" (*glossolalia*) in *A Thousand Plateaus*.

In this chapter, I plan to examine the practice of speaking in Foucault, Derrida, and Deleuze. Without ignoring the complexity of each one's thought, I have placed emphasis on the "ethics of speech" in Foucault, the "logic of speech" in Derrida, and the "pragmatics of speech" in Deleuze (and Guattari). The accentuation will allow us to see the divergence between them in regard to speech acts. But it will also allow us to see their convergence, which allows us to place them under the general category of speaking out. The three specific ways of speaking share one conceptual feature – the *dissymmetry* of the relation between the one speaking, and the one to whom the speaking is addressed. However, in Foucault, Derrida, and Deleuze, the dissymmetry is presented in different ways. In Foucault, it is through the idea that speaking-freely (as opposed to flattery) aims at making the listener to whom the speaking-freely is addressed be sovereign and independent of the speaker (Foucault 2005: 379 and 385). In Derrida, the dissymmetry is presented through the literal meaning of the word "teleiopoetics": a teleiopoetic statement makes something happen in proximity and soon (*telos*) and at a distance and in the future (*tele*) (Derrida 1997: 31).[6] In Deleuze (and Guattari), glossolalia, which is at the center of their idea of a minor language, makes something happen that is so extreme that the whole world goes into becoming. Dissymmetry means placing others in a non-economic, non-relative, and unmeasurable relation. Therefore, speaking-frankly (*parrēsia*), speaking-distantly (*teleiopoeisis*), and speaking-in-tongues (*glossolalia*) — all "three ways of speaking" aim at *liberating* the addressee. However, the root of the convergence between Foucault's *parrēsia*, Derrida's *teleiopoesis*, and Deleuze's *glossolalia* is Kant's categorical imperative. In fact, the root is the categorical imperative in this form: one should never treat the person in oneself or in others as a mere means to an end, but always as an end in itself.[7] Even though this formula of Kant's categorical imperative seems obvious, I think it is the only way into a solution to the problem of how to speak out against violence. We have to say, "Enough with utility and economy!" Even if it is impossible to completely eradicate violence, these three ways of speaking aim at letting others be free.

## I. Three Ways of Speaking

### A. "Ethics of Speech": Speaking-Freely (Parrēsia) in Foucault's Final Lecture Courses at the Collège de France

Taking up themes found in his earliest writings like *The History of Madness*, in particular, the theme of freedom,[8] Foucault's late studies of ancient and medieval thought move from the care of the self, that is, from the conversion of the self into being a subject of truth, to spiritual exercises, to the need for spiritual guidance, and therefore to the need for someone who can guide. After locating it within ancient Greek democratic practices, *parrēsia* appears in the context of the late Greek and early Roman idea of a spiritual director (Foucault 2005: 137). In order for the practices of the self to "save" someone, someone else — the spiritual director — is "indispensable" (Foucault 2005: 127). Besides calling the spiritual director by the traditional names of "master," "sage," "philosopher," or "priest," Foucault calls him "an effective agency for producing effects [*un opérateur*] within the individual's reform and formation as a subject" (Foucault 2005: 130). The word "opérateur" suggests that the spiritual director is someone who makes something function. In *parrēsia*, the spiritual director "operates" speech (the *logos*). *Parrēsia* is a "verbal activity" or a "speech activity," a "doing" (Foucault 2001: 13). It is wisdom or philosophy considered in "its allocutionary force" (Foucault 2010: 350), that is, in its effects on the listener. *Parrēsia* is always an address to an other, on whom it produces effects. And insofar as it produces effects on an other, *parrēsia*, like the statement in *The Archaeology of Knowledge*, is an event. Left unanswered in *The Archaeology*, the question of how statements come into existence is answered by *parrēsia*.

In the final courses, Foucault distinguishes *parrēsia* from the performative, just as he had distinguished the statement from the performative in *The Archaeology of Knowledge*. In the course, *The Government of Self and Others*, Foucault outlines three characteristics, through which he isolates *parrēsia* from the performative (Foucault 2010: 61–6). First, a performative utterance, as is well-known, requires an institutionalized or coded context or a well-defined situation, because of which the effect of the performative utterance is known in advance. Therefore, the performative utterance takes place in a world that guarantees that the saying effectuates the content of the utterance. In contrast, *parrēsia* opens the situation to effects that are not known. While the performative is "a completely determined event as a function of the general code and institutional field in which the utterance is made," *parrēsia* is an "irruptive event." *Parrēsia* does not produce a coded effect; it produces "an unspecified risk," the worst of which is the death of the speaker. *Parrēsia* is dangerous. This danger, Foucault says, is "the crux of *parrēsia*" (Foucault 2010: 56). As we shall see in a moment, the "crux" of speaking-freely involves a dynamic of friend and enemy.

Second, in performative utterances, the subject's status is indispensable for the performative utterance to have its effects. The person who performs a wedding must have the authority to do so. He (or she) must be a priest, minister, or judge. However, the performative utterance does not require something like a "personal relation between the person who utters and the statement." In contrast, *parrēsia* formulates the truth at "two levels." The first level is the statement of the truth itself, the content. The second level is that of the parresiastic act itself. Here one authentically thinks that what is said is genuinely true. The parresiastic statement is the affirmation of the affirmation. With *parrēsia*, there is a "pact of the speaking subject with himself." The subject "binds" himself to the statement he has made and to the act of making it: this is the truth and I am the person saying it. This intensification, or even "exaggeration," as Derrida would say, of the statement of truth, Foucault says, is "essential to the parresiastic act."[9]

Third, while the performative utterance assumes that the person speaking has the status required for the intended effect, it does *not* require the person speaking to exercise his (or her) own freedom as an individual speaker. According to Foucault, *parrēsia* is "the exact opposite." What makes the parresiastic act different from the performative utterance is that, despite the status that the subject might have, the individual who speaks in *parrēsia* asserts "his own freedom" (Foucault 2010: 66). The exercise of one's own freedom is why we find "courage in the heart of *parrēsia*." It is why the Romans translated "parrēsia" as "libertas":

speaking-freely (Foucault 2010: 46). Thus with these three characteristics we have "the crux," "the essence," and "the heart of *parrēsia*": the danger of speaking the truth; the intense binding of oneself to the stated truth; and the assertion of one's own freedom, in a word, courage. These three characteristics define, for Foucault, "the ethics of speech" (Foucault 2005: 137).[10]

The ethics of speech distinguishes *parrēsia* not only from performative utterances, but also, and equally importantly, from flattery and rhetoric.[11] According to Foucault, and this is well-known, flattery and rhetoric are connected. The basis of rhetoric, as a technique of persuasion, is flattery, while the instrument of flattery is rhetoric, especially, its "tricks" (*ruses*) (Foucault 2005: 373). Flattery is the moral adversary of *parrēsia*, while rhetoric is its technical adversary. More strongly, flattery is the enemy and *parrēsia* must get rid of it, because flattery is false discourse. Of course, in contrast, *parrēsia*'s "ethics" consists in telling the truth. For Foucault, what is most important, as in Kant, is telling the truth. More specifically, while we just saw that flattery is connected with rhetoric, flattery is also coupled with anger. The anger and consequent abuse of power by a superior causes the inferior to engage in flattery (for instance, a tyrant over his subjects or a master over his slaves). In the general schema of flattery, we have a ruler who cannot control his temper (Foucault 2005: 374). The tyrant has not been able to form himself so as to have self-control and independence. Lacking self-control, the ruler "exceeds the real function of his power over others" (Foucault 2005: 377). Complementary to and opposite from the superior's angry exercise of power, the inferior has only one instrument to use in order to manipulate the superior's power: speech. Here is where the flatterer uses the art of rhetoric (Foucault 2005: 383–6).[12] The inferior "praises";

he tells the tyrant what he wants to hear. And by addressing the superior in this way, the flatterer "boosts" and "reinforces" the superior's excessive power. However, being "mendacious," "lying," and "duplicitous," the discourse blinds the superior. In fact, because of his insufficient relation to himself, the flattered ruler finds himself dependent on the flatterer and his discourse. In his dependency, the ruler's self-relation is mediated by the other (the flatterer) and as such finds himself subject to the flatterer's wickedness. Thus, the "dialectic" of flatterer and flattered reverses the relation of inferior and superior (Foucault 2005: 376). The flatterer's discourse allows him to make use of the superior's power, leaving the flattered ruler "impotent" (Foucault 2005: 375–8). In short, the flatterer gets what he wants.

*Parrēsia*, therefore, is anti-flattery and speaks to an other in such a way so that the other "will be able to form an autonomous, independent, full and satisfying relation to himself" (Foucault 2005: 379). Because the parresiastic speech is true, the addressee is able to internalize and subjectivize this true discourse, allowing the other to do without the speaker. In effect, in *parrēsia*, there is no dialectic. After the internalization and subjectivation of the truth, the other does not become the same as the one who spoke freely to him. The other addressed is able to become free of the speaker, move away, and become distant. *Parrēsia* is also anti-rhetoric. In contrast to rhetorical flourishes, images, and ruses used to persuade the addressee, *parrēsia* tells the truth nakedly and without adornment. Several times, Foucault reminds us that the literal meaning of "parrēsia" is "telling all" (Foucault 2005: 372; Foucault 2001: 12). Moreover, unlike rhetoric, which is an art for which the subject-matter determines the "how" of speaking, *parrēsia* is defined by the prudence and skill for saying truth at this very moment (the *kairos*). Finally, in contrast to rhetoric whose aim is the advantage of the speaker, *parrēsia* aims to establish the other's autonomy. *Parrēsia* "acts on others, but always to the greatest advantage [*pour le plus grand profit*]" of the other (Foucault 2005: 385).

Nevertheless, *parrēsia*'s relation to rhetoric is more complicated than its relation to flattery. While Foucault claims that *parrēsia* is not an art and therefore not rhetoric, he also claims that *parrēsia* has certain practices and even tactics (Foucault 2005: 385). The tactics of *parrēsia* explain why the ancients compare *parrēsia* to navigation and medicine (Foucault 2005: 388). In other words, in order to obtain the intended effect of speaking freely, it may be "necessary" to make use of rhetoric; to take it up "obliquely, and use it only if need be" (Foucault 2005: 386). When needed (the *kairos*), *parrēsia* might use rhetoric, including its images and ruses. The tactical use of rhetorical devices means that, when Foucault reminds us of *parrēsia*'s literal meaning as "telling all," he is not implying that "telling all" is *parrēsia*'s primary meaning. In fact, Foucault locates the literal sense of telling all only within Christian confessional practices. In regard to *parrēsia* in the ancients (in Plutarch, for example), Foucault speaks of there being a "pejorative sense" to *parrēsia*, a "bad" *parrēsia*, which consists in being a "chatterbox" (Foucault 2005: 342). When needed, *parrēsia*, in order to be "good," does not tell all. While Foucault speaks of "the automatism of the work of the *logos*," he also notes that true discourse's automatic effects on the hearer do not always occur. There are always those who hear the discourse, but who do not listen (Foucault 2005: 337). It might then be necessary to speak in a way that is "rough, violent, and abrupt." It might be necessary "to tell the truth as quickly, loudly, and clearly as possible" (Foucault 2010: 55). Therefore, *parrēsia* is "a particular way of telling the truth"

(Foucault 2010: 52), a way that, he states, even includes the aphoristic form (Foucault 2010: 56). With this particular way of telling the truth, we see that, for Foucault, *parrēsia* is not always completely naked. As Derrida would say, the truth is not always and in fact cannot be wholly revealed.

*Parrēsia* also includes the form of "irony."[13] Of course, Socratic irony (and critique), for Foucault, is the model of *parrēsia* (Foucault 2010: 233). Yet, he says that the "matrix scene of *parrēsia* [*scène matricielle*]" is the drama between Plato and Dionysus (Foucault 2010: 50 and 65). In fact, "the birth of *parrēsia*" really occurs from this maternal scene, when (according to Plutarch) Dionysus asks Plato why he came to Sicily. Plato responds with the statement: "I came to Sicily in search of a good man." Through this statement, Plato "lets it be understood" (*laissant entendre*) that Dionysus is not a good man. In other words, somewhere "below" (*sous*) what the statement gives explicitly to be "heard" (*entendu*), like a "subtext" (*sous-entendu*), is the truth about Dionysus. The effects of this statement with its implicit or indirect truth are well-known. Dionysus's reaction is violent, angry power exercised against Plato (Foucault 2010: 67) and he becomes Plato's enemy.

Therefore, the parresiastic statement or utterance might fail (with the effect of animosity) – or it might succeed. When it succeeds, Foucault tells us, *parrēsia* increases the benevolence of the hearers toward one another. In short, it increases friendship (Foucault 2005: 389). *Parrēsia* is the "opening of the heart" (Foucault 2005: 137). Importantly, Foucault says that, "The exercise of *parrēsia* must be dictated by generosity. Generosity towards the other is at the very heart of the moral obligation of *parrēsia*" (Foucault 2005: 385). It is only by *giving* the truth to the other in a particular way, through this linguistic act of generosity, that one may increase the other's freedom. Through its tactics, *parrēsia* aims to "intensify" freedom; it is "the highest exercise of freedom" (Foucault 2010: 67).

### B. *"Logic of Speech": Speaking-Distantly (teleiopoesis) in Derrida's Politics of Friendship*

Just as Foucault's lectures on *parrēsia* extend his earliest reflections on freedom, Derrida's concept of *teleiopoesis* extends his earliest reflections on language.[14] We have already spoken of the fundamental role of Derrida's iterability. In *Politics of Friendship* and in other later works (Derrida 1992: 15), iterability becomes the call (or the address or the declaration) (Derrida 1997: 215–16). It calls someone to presence (the one called is the intentional pole of my utterance); and yet, it calls someone to presence because the one called is not present (the intentional pole of my utterance has not yet been reached). The one called is at once present and absent; he (or she) comes near without coming near. The structure of the call, therefore, consists in an unstable balance of presence and absence which is the "crux" of *teleiopoesis*. *Teleiopoesis*, for Derrida, "makes" (*poesis*) speech so that it hits its goal immediately thereby bringing the goal nearby (*telos*), and so that speech opens a distance thereby delaying the hitting of the goal (*tele*).

We can see the unstable balance of presence and absence in Aristotle's statement, reported by Diogenes Laertius: "oh my friends, there is no friend." Derrida's analysis focuses on the opening omega (ω) (in Diogenes' Greek) of Aristotle's alleged statement which could be interpreted as either a vocative interjection ("*Oh* friends") or the dative of a pronoun ("he *for whom* there are friends") (Derrida 1997: 209). The ambiguity of the opening omega has led to two different ways of rendering Diogenes' Greek: either as "Oh my friends, there are no friends" or "he for whom there are [a multitude] of friends has no friend." According to Derrida, the ambiguity of the opening omega refers to the difference between the performative and the constative. *Either* we have a call that does something (the call out to absence) *or* we have an assertion that reports something (the call into presence). The contradiction between the performative and the constative internal to the opening omega shows us the structure of every teleiopoetic statement, and also what is implicit in *every utterance*, whether it be constative or performative. We have a "logic of language" functioning here, which the "oh my friends, there is no friend" makes explicit. This one statement makes the structure of all utterances explicit.

The teleiopoetic logic works in this way. *Explicitly*, as we just saw, the "oh my friends, there is no friend" is at once a performative and a constative: at once, it is a call *to* friends *and* a report *about* the lack of friends. *Implicit to every assertion or report* is the fact that it must be addressed to someone. Implicitly, every assertion, even one about the lack of friends, *calls out to friends*, who are not present, not yet reached, and who might not be friends, but enemies. The call implicit to every utterance implies necessarily what is stated explicitly in Aristotle's statement: "there is *no* friend," hence the need to call out to absent friends. Here is the *negation* essential to all teleiopoetic statements. Similarly, *implicit to every call or performative* is the fact that it must report. Implicitly, every call, even one addressed to an enemy, reports *that there are friends*. The negation (the call to someone not present) implicit to every assertion is always coupled necessarily to a position or affirmation, made explicit in Aristotle's address: "Oh my *friends*," that is, in the call, is the statement that "there *are* friends present." Therefore, due to the negation, the teleiopoetic logic, for Derrida, is *not synthetic*.[15] Nevertheless, even if the negation separates to the point of a contradiction, then the teleiopoetic logic is *not analytic*. It also essentially affirms or asserts. In other words, the teleiopoetic logic is neither an analytic logic that separates into opposites nor a synthetic (or dialectical) logic that unifies the opposites into a synthesis. The teleiopoetic logic is neither a logic of non-contradiction nor a logic of contradiction overcome. This dis-unity of negation and affirmation is the "essence" of *teleiopoesis*.

Derrida uses the image of the chiasm (the "crux") to define this unstable balance between the "enveloped constative assertion" in every performative and the "silent interjection" in every assertion (Derrida 1997: 213–14). Where the chiasm crosses, there is a presupposition about consensus. The consensus is even more fundamental than linguistic codes. For language to function at all (either well or badly), there must have been a consensus established about the codes (constative), and yet for language to function, again at all, there must be a consensus to be called forth (performative). In other words, for me to say anything to you, you must minimally understand the meaning of the words I utter. Silently, it must assert that a consensus has already been established about the meanings and forms of my words for there to be the beginning of understanding. And yet, for me to say anything to you, I must minimally call to you about whether you understand what I'm saying. Silently, I call to you to fulfill the consensus about the meanings and forms of my words. An agreement must have already been struck (friendship) and yet, at the same time, an agreement is still to be struck (enmity). The force of *teleiopoesis* to bring forth a possible friendship or a possible enmity is based in a prior friendship and a prior enmity. Derrida expresses the chiasm of friendship within the teleiopoetic statement with the phrase "real possibility" (Derrida 1997: 131). It's *real*: the event of friendship has already happened; and it remains *possible*: the event of friendship is still to come. Like *parrēsia* in Foucault, *teleiopoesis* in Derrida answers the question of how an event takes place.

With teleiopoetic logic we have been speaking of a general structure that underlies all linguistic utterances: every utterance is at least implicitly, at once and necessarily, undecidably, constative and performative. However, the teleiopoetic statement as such (and as differentiated from every kind of utterance) is defined by the undecidability being made explicit enough for the statement to be recognized as paradoxical or aporetical. In fact, and this requirement cannot be underestimated in Derrida: the undecidability must be intensified and exaggerated. It must even be shouted out in the loudest voice possible. Through its exaggerated paradox, *teleiopoesis* brings about not just the experience of friendship, but also what lies beyond friendship: love. Love is precisely the exaggeration of the structure of the call. Love is the very "heart" of speaking-distantly.

The instability of love lies in the fact that there is no love without the declaration of love *to* the other (Derrida 1997: 9) and that "speech [*of* the other] ruins friendship" (Derrida 1997: 54). In other words, love means that, on the one hand, that if I want you to be my friend, I must tell you that "I love you." With this explicit declaration, we have the call into absence and into distance – the distance of *teleiopoesis* explains why we are calling it "speaking-distantly" – we have the call to establish a consensus. Not yet are you my friend and lover. Therefore you might be my enemy. This distance and enmity is what lies in the

## THREE WAYS OF SPEAKING, OR "LET OTHERS BE FREE"

"subtext" (*sous-entendu*) of the explicit call to love. What grows out of this concealed distance and enmity is violence. When I declare my love to you, when I call you "my love," I make you *of* me: *my* love, the same as me. I try to bring you as close to me as possible so that you are my possession. We do not need to appeal to the countless stories of jealousy in order to recognize that love is usually possession. We also know from common experience the outcome of this kind of love: when I attempt to possess you, you pull back from me and rupture the intimacy. Love ends.

The excessive friendship that is love usually exaggerates the constative side of the call. It simply asserts, "you are *mine*." Love usually simplifies the complication of love into possession. In love, at the same time, I am your friend and your enemy. The truth of love is that love wants to establish a bond of intimacy, which means that it wants to possess the beloved; and then, when possession becomes excessive, it breaks the bond and produces enmity. But, this enmity is usually not said out load. In love, I always say "I love you," while silently I think "I hate you." We can see already that there are possibilities, real possibilities in love. The possibility of saving the other from possession, and letting the other be free, appears when one reverses what is said out load and what is said silently, what is implicit and what is explicit, what is posited and what is presupposed (Derrida 1997: 9 and 54). Derrida finds this reversal in Nietzsche when Nietzsche's "living fool" reverses the Aristotle statement into "oh my enemies, there are no enemies." Therefore, through his reading of Nietzsche in *Politics of Friendship*, Derrida shows us how, through what form, to truly love the other.[16] This form is *teleiopoesis* itself, its crux, essence, and heart.

Instead of declaring one's love explicitly, out loud, or with a loud voice, "the living fool" declares his hatred explicitly, out loud, and with a loud voice. The statement of enmity is true because, as we saw, love is implicitly violent. The statement is a veridiction, but it is formed in such a way that truth-telling of enmity is still love. Implicitly, *silently, to oneself, secretly*, one says to oneself that one loves the ones called "enemies." It is as if one is saying out loud, "Stay away, I am your enemy"; but, silently, one is saying "I need you, be close to me! I love you, my enemies." Therefore, out of love, this statement – "oh my enemies, there is no enemy" – in its explicit call to enmity, pushes those called farther out than the distance required by the essential structure of the call. In other word, this enmity is an extreme form of Kantian respect. By pretending to be or giving oneself off as the enemy, through a "ruse," one explicitly repels the others away from oneself; you distance the beloved from yourself – even as you implicitly call the beloved in love. Consequently, the beloved is too distant for fusion and identification; she is too distant to be *of me*. She can no longer be a possession that can be used. Most importantly, she is too distant for one's loving actions to be deadly and violent. This distancing "operates" an excessive act of love. With an "open heart," the exaggeration of friendship into explicit enmity drives the beloved away in order to save her (him, or it).

To make this point as clear as possible: when you speak this statement of enmity, you implicitly love the ones called. Even as you call them "enemies," you love them and want them to be near. But this love is still, up to this point, the desire for possession, which explains why your speaking is always malicious and wicked, even evil (Derrida 1997: 60). You want to speak of them as your very own beloved; you want to assert that the other is a possession or a good (Derrida 1997: 17). Here however, the implicit love goes further. The teleiopoetic statement renounces love out loud (negation) without renouncing it silently (affirmation). Renouncing the love out loud, the secret love is more than the desire for possession, more than avarice, more than lust, more than self-love (Derrida 1997: 174 and 213). This love loves the others too much to do the evil one wants to do (Derrida 1997: 60). This love is hyperbolic, but it is excessive in its desire to free the ones called from possession (Derrida 1997: 60). Therefore, the explicit declaration of enmity ("Oh, my enemies") seems to be more loving than love. The teleiopoetic statement gives to the other the gift of freedom without any desire for reciprocation. Its generosity aims to never use the other as a means to an end. As Derrida says (and we stressed this quotation in the last chapter), "The dream of an *unusable* friendship survives, a friendship beyond friendship" (Derrida 1997: 217, my emphasis). Although the wisdom is never to reveal the hyperbolic love as such, as such the hyperbolic love of dispossession is "the highest exercise of freedom"; it intensifies the freedom of the other.

### C. "Pragmatics of Speech": Speaking-in-Tongues in *Deleuze and Guattari's A Thousand Plateaus*

Deleuze and Guattari's reflections on language in *A Thousand Plateaus* extend Deleuze's idea of a "loquendum" in *Difference and Repetition* (Deleuze 1995: 143), and in particular Deleuze and Guattari's determination of a minor literature in their 1974 Kafka book (Deleuze and Guattari 1986). We have already stressed Deleuze and Guattari's valorization of the performative, which opens the way for their "pragmatics of speech." However, the pragmatics of speech leads them to consider indirect discourse, the discourse behind or below explicit utterances and writings. For them, indirect discourse is unconscious. It refers to a collective enunciation in the background, which is rooted in formations of political power (Deleuze and Guattari 1987: 78). Therefore, the collective enunciations are always "order words," "mot d'ordre," a term to which we shall return at the end of this section.

Appropriating Stoic logic, Deleuze and Guattari say that order-words express "incorporeal transformation." For Deleuze and Guattari, order-words answer the question of how an event takes place. For example, when someone says to you that "you are no longer a child," the act of making this statement transforms you, "instantaneously," as they say, into an adult and it commands you to stop acting like a child. The purpose of order-words lies in ordering "words and things," expression and content, or minds and bodies. And in relation to the mind, expression, or language side of these conjunctions, the order-words set up standards, constants, and universals that make a language system (*une langue*) be major, representing the statistical averages of a population of speakers. In contrast, and most generally then, what Deleuze and Guattari aim to do in the "Postulates of Linguistics" plateau, in *A Thousand Plateaus*, is unearth the indirect discourse – this is the real purpose of their "pragmatics of speech" – and find a treatment that will *un-regiment* a major language. The question is: how is it is possible to unmake these "abominable" order-words, which always order death, so that they give way to something like a password, which commands flight (or freedom)? To answer this question, they must describe a different "treatment" of language, that is, "minorization," which is a treatment that is not based in constants, not based in forms of expression that are separated from "extrinsic factors," and finally

## THREE WAYS OF SPEAKING, OR "LET OTHERS BE FREE"

one that does not aim at information and communication. There are three components to the minor treatment through which we are able to "un-regiment" a major language: (1) writing; (2) tensors; and (3) the very treatment itself that turn a major language into a minor one. It is within this context of criticizing linguistic standards, constants, and universals that Deleuze and Guattari, famously, speak of stammerings (*bégaiments*); mutterings (*rumeurs*); and cries (*cris*); and of course speaking-in-tongues (*glossalalie*) (Deleuze and Guattari 1987: 98, 77, and 96). We shall see the role of speaking-in-tongues immediately, when we turn to the first un-regimenting component: writing (Deleuze and Guattari 1987: 83–4).

Although in general writing plays a minimal role in Deleuze and in Deleuze and Guattari's texts, writing is the very "heart" of a minor discourse. The "mass" of whisperings, stammerings, mutterings, stutterings, and tongues that constitute indirect discourse are only a whisper. As they say, the "faculty" from which indirect discourse emerges is twofold: the whisperer and the one to whom it is whispered (*le souffleur et le soufflé*) (Deleuze and Guattari 1987: 84). As the whispering indicates, for the most part, the whispering tongues (*langues*) remain implicit, and nearly silent. The near silence affects the one to whom these words are whispered since we follow the orders given to us. However, the presence of the whispering remains at the level of the unconscious. Thus, Deleuze and Guattari say that "to write is perhaps to lead this [structure] of the unconscious to the light of day, to select the whispering voices." Through writing alone or through deliberate composition taken in its widest sense (to include art but also philosophical concept formation), the whispering voices become more than a silent presence. They are literally given voice. To write, for Deleuze and Guattari, as it is for Derrida, is to make the unconscious pass into consciousness, or even into an "I think," that expresses it, that publishes it, that screams it out load and directly – like *parrēsia*.[17]

But, how are the whispering voices actually spoken? This question brings us to the second component, which is "essential" to speaking-in-tongues. Just as the folksong, as the material, must be deterritorialized from its territory, and then formed into an opera, the unconscious whispers must be deterritorialized from the constants within which they are caught, and then transformed into what Deleuze and Guattari call "tensors" (Deleuze and Guattari 1987: 99).[18] Tensors are words whose phonic material and expressive form are so tightly woven together that one cannot decide whether one should call the abstract machine of language "repeatable materiality" or "material repeatability." In a tensor, the form of expression and the form of content become indiscernible, to the point that we are confronted with a kind of sign that is neither simply repeatable nor simply material. Here again, we must think of stuttering or stammering. The *formation* of tensors explains why Deleuze and Guattari distinguish between *speaking* a foreign language and *making* a foreign language within one's own language (Deleuze and Guattari 1987: 98). You must connect the sense of foreignness of the foreign language to your native language. Just as there is a distinction between speaking a foreign language and making your own language foreign, there is also a distinction between *stuttering* while speaking and *making* your own language stutter. Like the sense of the foreign, you must connect the sense of stuttering to your own speech. More precisely, in order to *make* your own language stutter, the actual stuttering must pass into a stuttering formed within your own language, making the familiar language sound like a foreign language.[19]

## THREE WAYS OF SPEAKING, OR "LET OTHERS BE FREE"

The transformation of the actual stuttering into formed stuttering might take place in this way. One remembers, perhaps painfully, listening to a person who, when he came to the end of a clause, "stalls," so to speak, at "and," saying "and, and, and, and." One then withdraws from the actual stuttering of the word "and" latent or virtual possibilities of the word "and." These latent possibilities are based in the fact that the word "and," as a syncategoreme, that is, as a conjunction and not a noun, has no meaning in itself. One is not able to determine strictly whether the "and" is synthetic or analytic (or un-synthetic).[20] The latent or "foreign" possibilities might also come from etymologies or from implications of the word.[21] Within the word "and," there is the possibility of saying (or writing) the word "and" repeatedly but each time it is varied by connecting it with the etymological meaning of the word "answer." Literally, the English word "answer" means "and another word." *And then*, one connects the English word with the German word, "Antwort," which translates the French word "réponse." *And then*, one goes from "réponse" to responsibility, which makes the word "and" be penetrated with issues in the social field. (We shall return to the question of responsibility below in the conclusion.[22]) Each time a possibility is written, the word "and" becomes more intense, making the reader ask what happened and what is going to happen. Deleuze and Guattari describe the effects of the tensor in this way: "the tensor effectuates a kind of transitivation of the sentence, causing the last term to react upon the preceding term, back through the entire chain." The "transitivation" ends up making the tensor and the discourse that develops it tend toward self-contradiction. Self-contradiction is how intense the discourse becomes. The tensor is that which makes language, a word, a phrase, a sentence, a cliché, a slogan, or a watchword intense. The tensor, therefore, should actually be called "the intensive" (Deleuze and Guattari 1994: 22). Yet, it is only through this intensive form tending toward self-contradiction, as in *teleiopoesis*, that one is able to *make* a language itself stutter.

We can see already that a tensor is formed by means of a certain kind of treatment of a natural language like English, French, or German. The "treatment" is the third component for making a minor language (Deleuze and Guattari 1987: 104–6). The minor treatment is the "crux" of speaking-in-tongues and provides us with a more precise sense of deterritorialization. In its most general form, the minor treatment is *abstraction*: you must abs-tract, ex-tract, or sub-tract. In other words, just as you must deterritorialize the folksong from its territory in order to form an opera (Deleuze and Guattari 1987: 311–12), and just as you "draw out" a sense "from a sentence or its equivalent" in order to form a concept (Deleuze and Guattari 1994: 24), you must "with-draw" a variable from a constant in order to form a variation. Abstraction is the only way one is able to form a tensor. More specifically, the treatment consists in a "single operation" with two sides.[23] On one side, abstraction is understood through the procedure of "impoverishment." Impoverishment, according to Deleuze and Guattari, allows you to bypass a constant by "narrowing [it] down" (*resserrer*) or by "restricting" (*restriction*) it so that the constant no longer appears as a universal.[24] However, the models erected by linguistics for speaking (and writing) are not eliminated. In impoverishment, they have been *reduced* to a statistical aggregate so that they no longer have the value of being the essential forms of a language. In short, impoverishment de-standardizes the majoritarian standards of language. On the other side and simultaneous with impoverishment, abstraction is understood through the procedure of "proliferation." The procedure of "proliferation" extends and expands the variables. It "overloads" and "supercharges" the variables but does not, however, turn them into rhetorical figures and metaphors. Because of the un-closeable ellipsis produced by impoverishment, the supercharged variables do not refer to a literal or primary meaning. Without a primary meaning, "paraphrasing" then becomes possible, and there is nothing to stop the expansion of the paraphrasing. Deleuze and Guattari conclude that both from the side of impoverishment and from the side of proliferation, "there is a rejection of reference points and a dissolution of constant form – in order to favor dynamic differences." The minor treatment, therefore, constructs a continuum of variation. And, as we saw with the "crux" in Foucault and Derrida, the "crux" of speaking-in-tongues involves a dynamic friend and enemy.

If we now return to the first component, writing, we see that composing a minor language, either in writing or speech, aims to make the unconscious voices whispering conscious in us. Through writing, the whispering voices are intensified enough so that we actually hear them. Writing even shows us that composing a minor language aims to constitute a kind of self-consciousness, an "I think" that "bears witness to the dispersed, quiet voices" (Deleuze and Guattari 1987: 104), turning those voices into the expressed of explicit statements or utterances. However, not only does the formation of a minor language aim to make us conscious (really conscious) of the dispersed and quiet voices, it aims to make all of us, everyone and the whole world, be conscious of the voices. Lying deep within the unregimenting component of writing, the aim making everybody and the whole world become is really the "heart" of speaking-in-tongues. Therefore, near the end of "The Postulates of Linguistics" chapter, we find Deleuze and Guattari speaking of "everybody-becoming" (*devenir tout le monde*). Through impoverishment, tensors have a variation – and, and, and, and, etc. – whose amplitude constantly undermines the threshold of the majoritarian standard. In other words, the tensor's amplitude resists the social collectivity governed by capitalism. In addition, through proliferation, it contains the power to constitute the becoming-minoritarian of everybody and the whole world. Once heard, the expressed voices open the whole world, this whole world, to the *possibilities* of "other worlds and other planets." Therefore, the aim of forming a minor discourse lies in giving everyone these possibilities. As Deleuze and Guattari say, "Becoming-minoritarian as the universal figure of consciousness is called *autonomy*" (Deleuze and Guattari 1987: 106, my emphasis).

In order to better understand the "heart" of speaking-in-tongues, we must return to the order-word. We have been using the accepted English translation for the French "mot d'ordre." The transliteration to "order-word" captures the ordering or commanding nuance of the French phrase. However, "mot d'ordre" could also be rendered in English as "watchword." Watchword not only refers to the key word of an organization but also to the word spoken to the soldier on watch to gain entrance. In other words, through "watchword," we can understand the "mot d'ordre" as a password (Deleuze and Guattari 1987: 110).[25] In fact, the password nuance of "mot d'ordre" is essential. These order words, so quiet within us, must be transformed into tensors; or, more precisely, they must be treated with abstraction so that they become passwords.

As mentioned above, Deleuze and Guattari claim that all "mots d'ordres" are death sentences. When you are commanded to act like an adult, disobeying this command carries certain

## THREE WAYS OF SPEAKING, OR "LET OTHERS BE FREE"

penalties, the worst of which is death. However, Deleuze and Guattari immediately claim that flight is "inseparably connected" to the death sentence, that is, flight is "included in it," and "fused" with the death sentence. The question is: how does one unearth the watchword within the order-word? To help us understand this conversion from death to flight, Deleuze and Guattari introduce two "conceptual persona" (Deleuze and Guattari 1994: 81): "the invariant, hieratic king" and "the teacher of metamorphosis" (*maître de métamorphoses*) (Deleuze and Guattari 1987: 109). We can see immediately what the priestly king does: he imposes order, oppositions, and rigid segments, in a word, invariants that forbid metamorphosis. But what does the teacher of metamorphosis do? Most generally, the teacher of metamorphosis rings the alarm bell warning the one to whom the death sentence is being applied that she should flee. The teacher tries to suspend the death sentence, delay it, he postpones and procrastinates so that the one to whom the death sentence applies remains alive (Deleuze and Guattari 1987: 123). There is no freedom, of course, without remaining alive. More specifically, the teacher of metamorphosis "abstracts" death from its constant. In contrast to the priestly king who stabilizes death as the ideal, uncrossable limit, the teacher makes death proliferate. Now death becomes micrological. Like Seneca, the teacher of metamorphosis engages in a "meditation on death."[26] Or, the teacher of metamorphosis is like "the living fool."

The passage from death to flight then appears in this way. The teacher of metamorphosis hears within the death sentence the voice of the judgment: "You have been sentenced to death, *because you are not good*." But then, unlike the priestly king, she abstracts the idea of goodness from what appears to be its constant. She does not suppress goodness; she only impoverishes goodness. The teacher takes up "goodness" as a minimal form, perhaps nothing more than the form of the word: goodness worthy of its name. Minimized, goodness proliferates. The teacher proliferates more goodness, because she hears more voices of goodness that have remained present but silent. She shouts them out loudly; she makes all the tongues be heard. The teacher of metamorphosis speaks in this way: "goodness *is* this, *and* that, *and* that, *and* even that, *etc.*" Through "speaking in tongues," she makes goodness pass to the limit (Deleuze and Guattari 1987: 108 and 367), which places it on an absolute horizon that always recedes (Deleuze and Guattari 1994: 44). Passing through each conjunction, which asserts that goodness *is* this (*ceci e(s)t cela*), goodness passes through "little deaths" that make differences proliferate. At the limit, like the relation of a circle and a tangent, goodness approximates something entirely different from the good, perhaps, something closer to evil. Consequently, evil comes to be connected, perhaps necessarily connected, to goodness so that no separation between them can be established. Through the proliferations of conjunctions, goodness ends up contradicting itself. How can the death sentence be applied in the name of goodness when every idea of goodness we have is contaminated by evil? Even more, through the extreme proliferation of goodness, autonomy too stops being a constant. The figure of autonomy becomes vague as it passes into variation. It becomes a "universal" that is never able to judge completely good from evil. If its voice could be amplified, "autonomy" would only ever say: "You are not autonomous enough. Keep going! Don't stop!" Thus the addressees of the order-word are not just fleeing; they are following "the witch's flight" (Deleuze and Guattari 1994: 41). In conclusion, we must realize that, although the teacher of metamorphosis speaks "for" (*pour*) others, she proliferates goodness only "so that" (*pour que*) others benefit, only so that everyone and the whole world benefits, or, as one would say in French, "au profit des autres": she speaks only so that others profit. This "so that" is not utility. It treats others as ends in themselves. It is based in an act of love.

## II. Conclusion: "Let Others be Ends in Themselves"

Through the analysis of these three ways of speaking, we have seen a convergence among the three appear. Using terms found in Foucault's lecture, we were able to identify, in each way of speaking, a "crux," an "essence," and a "heart." In speaking-freely, the crux lies in the danger and risk that come along with telling the truth. As in Plato's confrontation with Dionysus, telling the truth could result either in friendship or enmity. In speaking-distantly, the crux lies in the inseparability between the constative and the performative in all utterances, an undecidability based in the presence and absence in the call's structure. As we saw clearly, speaking-distantly always involves a dynamic of friendship and enmity. Finally, in speaking-in-tongues, the crux lies in the abstracting treatment of language, and, in particular, in the treatment's two sides. Impoverishment produces enmity, while proliferation intensifies friendship. Intensification brings us to the *essence*. In speaking-freely, the essence is the intensification of the affirmation of the truth. There is no speaking-freely without the personal relation to the truth. One not only asserts the truth, one really believes in that truth, and therefore one is able to make the other be independent. In speaking-distantly, the essence is the exaggeration of the dis-unified affirmation and negation in the structure of the call. There is no speaking-distantly without the exaggerated affirmation of friendship and the exaggerated negation of friendship. The double exaggeration makes one's love for the other so great that one makes the other be distant. In speaking-in-tongues, the essence is the proliferation of a tensor. There is no speaking-in-tongues without the "stuttering" of the "and." The "stuttering" or proliferation of the "and" keeps adding others in to the truth or to goodness to infinity. The "stuttering" goes so far that it ends up including the whole world. The inclusion of the whole world brings us to the *heart*. The heart beating in speaking-freely is courage. One must be fearless in asserting one's freedom in speech. The heart beating in speaking-distantly is love. One must love the other so much that one lets the other be free. The heart beating in speaking-in-tongues is writing. This heart is only apparently different from the other two. One must write the whispering voices so "loudly" that the whole world and everyone goes into becoming, or more precisely, has the potential to become otherwise than how they are today. One must express the voices so clearly that everyone will be fearless in the expression of their freedom. This way of expressing is an act of love. Because speaking-in-tongues seems to have the most allocutionary force, we are tempted to conclude that speaking-in-tongues is the "best" way of speaking. However, we need all three in order to let others be independent, distant, and free – in order for there to be a chance for love.

Of course, the title of this section alludes to Kant's moral theory. As I said in the book's Introduction, I know that placing Kant's moral theory in the background of Foucault, Derrida, and Deleuze's reflection on ethics and politics is controversial. Nevertheless, it seems to me that speaking-freely, speaking-distantly, and speaking-in-tongues strive to obey what Kant calls "the highest practical vocation" for humans: never to treat the

# THREE WAYS OF SPEAKING, OR "LET OTHERS BE FREE"

person in oneself or in others merely as a means, but always as an end in itself. As Derrida says (and I must state this quotation again because it is so important), "The dream of an *unusable* friendship survives, a friendship beyond friendship." An unusable friendship aims never to use the other within an economy that increases my power; it only ever strives to increase the freedom of the other. Then we have Foucault saying (and I also quoted this comment above): "*Generosity towards the other* is at the very heart of the moral obligation of *parrēsia*." Finally, we have Deleuze (and Guattari) saying: "Becoming-minoritarian as the universal figure of consciousness is called *autonomy*." What is most clear in *parrēsia*, *teleiopoesis*, and *glossolalia* is that these ways of speaking aim never to make the hearer of the speaking be dependent on the speaker. This truth-telling aims always for the advantage of the other.

I have just used verbs like "to aim" and "to strive." I used these words of incompleteness because the intensification of the freedom of others encounters a problem that is perhaps irresolvable. The problem can be expressed in this question: through action taken in the broadest sense to include speaking, how are we able to make others be independent? As we saw, starting from the idea of allocutionary force, the three ways of speaking we have been considering have effects on the hearer. However, like all speaking, this effect is violent. When I speak *to* the other, I always speak *of* the other because I presuppose as an assertion that he or she is my friend, a member of my community, in consensus with me, and thus the same as me. More precisely, speaking is always violent because I capture the singularity of the other (its interior life) under a general concept. In this case, I capture alterity itself. Thus the problem has to be expressed in this question: how is it possible to speak to the other without doing violence to the other, or at least to reduce the violence done to its lowest level? With this question we are really trying to find a solution to the problem of the worst violence.

With this question we move from ethics to logic. The logic of both *parrēsia* and *teleiopoesis* is a specific way of formalizing speech. With this formalization, we are far from Kantian logic. The fundamental form for speaking-distantly is that the phrase includes *undecidably* both a negation and an affirmation. Then one exaggerates the undecidability itself. One exaggerates and makes explicit the absence, distance, negation, and enmity concealed in every utterance. One exaggerates and says out loud the negation and the enmity in order to open as wide a distance and as dark an absence as possible. But the phrase negates proximity and presence, not out of hatred. There is no hatred here because the affirmation of friendship into love is also exaggerated. Silently, your love for your apostle is so excessive that you want the apostle to be so independent that she is able to survive without you. You say to yourself, "I love you more than you can imagine."

Here too, with the logic of *teleiopoesis*, we encounter a problem. At least, at the most superficial level, speaking distantly seems to strive to free the other. Put simply, it seems to aim at one other, the friend or the beloved. Derrida, of course, would contest this superficial reading of this idea of speaking-distantly. After all, throughout all of his writings, he has stressed our inability to know (in the strong sense) the interior life of another, making that other person be more than what he appears to be, and therefore more than just one person. Consequently, when I call to you, "my friend," I am calling to a multiplicity hidden beneath your face. Nevertheless, the impression remains that *teleiopoesis* seems individualistic, an event between me and you. Indeed, Foucault's speaking-freely is explicitly ethical, and not political. The question therefore becomes: is it possible to aim at the whole world and everyone? This question brings us to the pragmatics of speech.

The pragmatics of speech not only intensifies and exaggerates freedom, it also absolutizes freedom. Or more, precisely, it absolutizes potentiality (*puissance*, not *pouvoir*, not the power to oppress). Here, absolutization means that the potential for freedom is neither relative to expression nor to content, neither to any particular regime of signs nor to any particular regime of power (to oppress and control). This idea approaches a kind of utopian thinking, as Deleuze and Guattari admit (Deleuze and Guattari 1994: 99–100, and 110–12). Nevertheless, as they also assert, utopian thinking provides resistance to the present (Deleuze and Guattari 1994: 110). How? Recall the teacher of metamorphosis (or the spiritual director, or the living fool). The proliferation of the "and" in her discourse has the potential (*et cetera*) to go to the horizon, and to produce something that is the opposite of all the ideas conjoined by the "and." Because of its indeterminacy, the "and" even has the power to produce the impossible. This enormous power of transformation goes beyond any particular people and any particular territory. It is this extreme power of transformation that the teacher of metamorphosis is trying to teach to the whole world and to all peoples. The inclusion of all the others in the openness of potentiality, absolute freedom, is that for which the teacher of metamorphosis, the living fool, and the spiritual director are striving. It is that for which all three speak. As Foucault, Derrida, and Deleuze knew, and as we know, all three ways of speaking are dangerous. Speaking-out requires courage. It requires courage because speaking-out, we hope, will produce an event: "let all the others be ends in themselves!"

## Notes

1 Paul Ricœur's *Interpretation Theory* provides a useful summary of Austin's idea of the speech act (Ricœur 1976: 14–15). Speech acts refer to what happens by means of speech. The classical examples are well-known: "I now pronounce you man and wife."
2 On the statement, see "Statement" by Richard A. Lynch in *The Cambridge Foucault Lexicon*, ed. Leonard Lawlor and John Nale (New York: Cambridge University Press, 2014), pp. 482–5.
3 For an excellent study of *The Archaeology of Knowledge*, see David Webb, *Foucault's Archaeology* (Edinburgh: Edinburgh University Press, 2013).
4 In *Force de loi*, Derrida says, "What we have to think is the exercise of force in language itself, in language's most intimate essence, as in the movement by which it would disarm itself absolutely from itself" (Derrida 1994a: 26–7, my translation). This sentence does not appear in the English translation. It is probably a later addition Derrida made for the French publication.
5 The question of the event (the *Ereignis*) was already Heidegger's question. It is still the question that animates much contemporary philosophy. Deleuze's *Logic of Sense* is devoted to transforming the traditional concept of essence into one of event (Deleuze 1990). Of course, there is Badiou's *Being and Event*, trans. Olivier Feldham (London: Continuum, 2005) and the work by Claude Romano, *Event and Time*, trans. Stephen E. Lewis (Bronx: Fordham University Press, 2014) and *Event and World*, trans. Shane Mackinlay (Bronx: Fordham University Press, 2009). Finally, François Raffoul is in the process of completing an important book on the event to be called *Thinking the Event*.
6 The Nietzsche quotation comes from *Beyond Good and Evil*, paragraph 214: "Our Virtues."
7 We introduced the role of Kant's moral philosophy in the last chapter.
8 See the discussion of libertinage in *The History of Madness* (Foucault 2006: 96–101).
9 Foucault had anticipated this intensification of the truth in *Lectures on the Will to Know*, when he speaks of sophism. Late in the course, he describes the intensification of truth as "truthful truth" (*la vérité veritable*). See Foucault 2014: 62 and 219.
10 See Edward McGushin, *Foucault's Askēsis* (Evanston: Northwestern University Press, 2007), especially Part 1, for an extensive treatment of *parrēsia*. See also Frédéric Gros and Carlos Lévy, *Foucault et las philosophie antique*

(Paris: Kimé, 2003), for several essays that examine Foucault's relation to Stoicism. For a sympathetic yet critical reading of Foucault's late ethics, see Karen Vintges, "Must we Burn Foucault," in *Continental Philosophy Review*, vol. 34, issue 2: 165–81.

11 The three characteristics also distinguish *parrēsia* from strategies of demonstration and teaching (Foucault 2010: 52–5).

12 Foucault presents a shorter version of the definition of rhetoric (in relation to *parrēsia*) in *The Government of Self and Others* (Foucault 2010: 53).

13 Despite the fact that the lectures *The Government of Self and Others* (I) and *The Courage of Truth* (*The Government of Self and Others II*) occur in consecutive years, Foucault seems to change his mind about the relation of *parrēsia* and irony, or he implicitly is distinguishing a bad irony from a good irony. See Foucault 2010: 54, and Foucault 2011: 233.

14 Although hardly noticed, in the 1967 *Voice and Phenomenon*, Derrida had spoken of *parrēsia*: "[intuitive knowledge] does not oppress what we could call the freedom of language, *the speaking-freely [franc-parler] of a discourse, even if it is false and contradictory.* One is able to speak without knowing" (Derrida 2011: 76; my emphasis).

15 In *Politics of Friendship*, Derrida frequently mentions Plato's dialogue on friendship, the *Lysis*, a name that literally means "to unbind," as in the word "ana-*lysis*" (Derrida 1997: 153).

16 The quotation is from Nietzsche in *Human, all too Human* (Book I, §376, called "Of Friends"): "Perhaps to each of us there will come the more joyful hour when we exclaim: 'Friends, there are no friends!' thus said the dying sage; 'Foes, there are no foes!' say I, the living fool" (Derrida 1997: 59).

17 For Deleuze and Guattari, conceptual personae originate in indirect discourse, as the "true agents" of the philosophical enunciation (Deleuze and Guattari 1994: 64–5).

18 For more on tensors, see Lyotard 1993: 19, 46, and 55.

19 As an example of a tensor, Deleuze and Guattari refer to the French word "et," which, as they say, has always been in a struggle with the verb "etre." Of course, their description of this struggle leads us reformulate the idea of a judgment ("this is (*est* or *et*) that").

20 For this analysis of the word "and," see Derrida 2000.

21 It seems clear that unearthing etymologies, but also drawing out unimagined implications from the word's etymologies make the language in which one speaks sound strange. But we still need something like the form of the judgment to see (or hear) the struggle.

22 A noticeable shortcoming of this book is the absence of any reflection on Levinas, in particular, on his conception of responsibility. See Levinas 1969: 178–9, and 244.
23 Deleuze had described these "two sides" already in "Coldness and Cruelty" (Deleuze 1997a: 28–31).
24 Impoverishment also strips away the lexical and syntactical forms of the language. The two procedures to form a minor language are based in the two procedures of vice-diction in regard to ideas as laid out in *Difference and Repetition*: specification of adjunct fields and condensation of singularities. Like abstraction, a procedure of "depotentialization," which liberates the idea from variables and variation as the approximation of an endpoint, seems to be required prior to the procedures of specification and condensation. See Deleuze 1990: 190 and 174.
25 In "Coldness and Cruelty," Deleuze speaks of "mots d'ordres," being overcome in a higher function of language (Deleuze 1997a: 20; the word "mot d'ordre" is rendered as "imperative").
26 Foucault 2005: 357–8.

# Conclusion:
# Speaking Out Against Violence

The spiritual director (the figure of Plato), the living fool, and the teacher of metamorphosis provide us with images of life that must be contrasted with or even opposed to those of the hate criminal and the suicide bomber. Unlike the hate criminal who wants to reduce the speech of others to silence (complete and final silence), the teacher of metamorphosis wants to speak out, and loudly for the freedom of others: "Let others be ends in themselves!" As we saw with our investigation of the GIP, the teacher even wants to let others speak for themselves. Recall that "speaking for" (*parler pour*) happens "so that" (*pour que*) others may become different from what they are today. This speaking-for is really speaking-out. It speaks out in the least violent way and in the name of the least, not the worst, violence. We must understand more precisely what the least violence is and, of course, this final investigation will require a further specification of the worst violence. If the worst violence amounts to the extreme exercise of power to violate others, then the least violence must amount to the extreme exercise of powerlessness. When we really understand the experience of powerlessness, then we will be able to see that the activity of using the violence of speaking, in a form that is the least violent, against the worst violence – "violence against violence" – so that others may be free results in a new kind of poverty, one that has nothing to do with the false and indeed bizarre claim of globalization that "capitalism has brought more people out of poverty than any other economic system."[1] Before we see this new kind of poverty, we need to summarize the ideas we have seen so far.

## I. Summary of the Ideas

The complex ideas that we have presented here can be simplified into three claims. *First*, if one wants to philosophize well, then one must not deviate from the phenomenological starting point: the epoché. The epoché suspends all belief in a world that exists independently of experience. It reduces all being "in itself" to subjective experience, to "phenomena," to "immanence." Based in Descartes' idea of methodical doubt, the reduction of all external things to immanence takes us back to the cogito, that is, it takes us back to thinking, which, since Plato, has been conceived as interior monologue. In a word, the epoché takes us back to *auto-affection*. As countless phenomenological and Bergsonian investigations have shown, interior monologue, like every kind of speaking, indeed, like every kind of auto-affection, and, even more, like every kind of experience, is conditioned by the movement of time. Moreover, the phenomenological and Bergsonian investigations have shown that temporalization or the duration, while maintaining a continuity, connection, or contamination, always divides itself between what comes back from the past and what comes in from the future, between the singular and intense difference of the now or the new and the memory or the writing that can be repeated indefinitely or universally into the future. The disjointure between "writing and difference" or between "difference and repetition" implies there is always "a minuscule hiatus" in experience, a hiatus that implies that, despite interior monologue's appearance of immediacy and sameness, auto-affection is always and necessarily, in reality or in truth, hetero-affection. In fact, the hiatus implies that the mediated experience of the other must be generalized to all experience, even to the experience of oneself. The word "hiatus," however, must be understood through the word "disjointure." The relation between the difference of the now and the repetition of memory is not just a hiatus or gap, but really, as a relation of disjointure, the hiatus implies that all experience is unjust. We must recognize that at the most fundamental or transcendental level of experience, despite all appearances of peaceful dialogue, there is violence.

And yet – we turn now to the *second* claim – the disjointed hiatus gives us the only possibility for genuine change, development, or *becoming*. The disjointed hiatus implies that there is no purely determinate origin of time and that there is no purely determinate endpoint of time. In other words, due to the disjointed hiatus, we must think of the world as one created by an imperfect god. It is as if this god created the world by means of an inexact calculation. It is as if this god, not being omniscient, did not know how to balance the relation between all the categories of the world such as mind and matter, time and space, and quality and quantity. It is as if this god could think only in terms of a ratio that could not be equalized. Therefore it is as if the world originated in an irrational number, and that, of course, produces a series that extends infinitely, like the anexact essence of roundness (not circularity). Thus, despite the appearances of sameness and identity, the repetition based in an irrational number is a creative repetition; it is "a repetition that makes a difference." In other words, "the potencies of repetition" cannot be restricted. Within repetition, there is a "virtuality" or a "perhaps," which goes beyond all the rational possibilities that might be realized. The virtuality or the "perhaps" of repetition necessarily dis-adequates and dis-identifies what is repeated. In other words, repetition liberates what is repeated from the genera and species that homogenize, restrict, and capture; it liberates what is repeated from the categories and concepts that subsume, take up, and appropriate. The unbalanced or even deranged ratio opens repetition up. It breaks free of the strict prison of meaning. This mad reason therefore gives us the only chance for freedom from violence.

We now see the paradox of the first two claims: the very disjointure that necessitates violence is at the same time the only chance for non-violence. This paradox implies one last claim, the *third*. As we know, all irrational numbers, like pi for instance, can be rounded up (or down) into a whole number. What does rounding up to a whole number actually do? Rounding up to a whole number in fact amounts to the attempt to rationalize the irrational series by absolutizing one possibility of the series. It attempts to make all the potencies of repetition present so that the virtual no longer remains. To be as clear as possible, we must say that rounding the irrational number up into an integer is equivalent to absolutizing a genus or a species, a category or a concept; it absolutizes a value. Consequently, rounding up strives to close off the openness of repetition, to halt becoming at a stopping point, and to finish off all change. This attempt, striving, or even will – the will to extreme power – to finish off, to bring to an end, and to close everything down has to be conceived as the complete end of the world. To put this claim as simply as possible, this will aims at the worst violence. But this superlative claim, I think, implies that the transcendental violence discovered within the movement of time is "better" than the worst violence. At the least (another superlative claim), with transcendental violence *something always remains*.

We can schematize even more briefly the three claims. First, all auto-affection is hetero-affection and therefore the necessity of violence. Second, the openness to alterity is becoming and therefore the chance for non-violence. Finally and third, the attempt to eliminate the necessity of violence and the chance of non-violence – the will to absolutize, to finish off, to bring to an end, and to close down, that is, the will to the end of the world – is the worst violence. What then is required from us in order to retreat from the will to the worst violence? It seems certain that we need a new way of thinking that is not based in determinate genera and species, categories and concepts. In other words, what we need is a new way of speaking (and writing) that is adequate to the fundamental dis-adequation, dis-identification, in-exactitude and injustice that we have outlined in the premises. As I have tried to show, we can begin to think about this new way of speaking through Foucault's idea of speaking-freely, Derrida's idea of speaking-distantly, and Deleuze (and Guattari's) idea of speaking-in-tongues.

## II. Violence against Violence, or a New Kind of Poverty

As we can see from the summary, we are able to start to solve the problem of the worst violence from the very seed of transcendental violence. The seed is temporalization. As Aristotle and then Kant showed, time belongs to the soul or to inner sense. A step in the reversal of Platonism is the return to inner experience and we must not underestimate the philosophical importance of this. There is no way to comprehend immanence without this return. What does Deleuze mean, in *Difference and Repetition*, with "repetition for itself" unless he means inner experience? And when Deleuze speaks of the Kantian crack in the self he is transforming auto-affection into hetero-affection. Deleuze learned this transformation of course from Heidegger. To say this again, it is Heidegger's Kant book that demonstrated the foundational importance of auto-affection. As we have seen, the phenomenology of auto-affection shows that, negatively, there is no immediate self-presence; there is no "own-ness"; and even the voice with which I speak to myself is not my own. To think there is a sphere of own-ness is to suffer from an illusion. This illusion must be dispelled. As Antitheses says, we must learn how "to converse with oneself" (Diogenes Laertius 2005: 9). In other words, we must unlearn how to hear badly, hearing only oneself, and learn to hear better, so that we hear those others inside of us. The essential fact that the sphere of interior life is not strictly my own implies, positively, that there are others within me. The claim that there are others in me may seem irrational, like irrational numbers. Perhaps it is. But we need this kind of "unreason." Freud has shown better than anyone else that we do not control our interior life. Think of the crucial psychoanalytic example of dreams. Like ghosts, dreams haunt our interior life. In addition to the dreamy specters of the night, there are memories. Even the memories of myself as a child speak to me with a voice that is not my own. Clearly, I am no longer a child. But, the memories that most remain are the painful ones. These memories cry out to me. They cry out for justice. And when we hear these cries from the past, we can only feel shame, a shame that forces us to respond to them.

## CONCLUSION: SPEAKING OUT AGAINST VIOLENCE

Although we hinted at it above (Chapter 9), the concept of responsibility has been absent from this book. However, clearly, responsibility is an essential component of the network of ideas we are developing. The fact that, when I hear well (superior hearing), I hear other voices in me, crying out for justice, implies, as we just indicated, that it is necessary to respond to them. This "it is necessary" (*il faut*) is an essential and absolute necessity. It is necessary because, as we saw (Chapter 2), thanks to an eidetic variation, it is not possible to imagine a present moment or a now-point that does not come after a previous point and that does not remember a past moment. No matter what now-point I think of, there is always a prior retention. The essential insight showed us that we are not really, truly able to distinguish and separate interior monologue from external dialogue. When I speak in general, that is, with or without the intention of communication, some moment always comes prior to the speaking. It could be silence or noise, but something like a context precedes all speaking. All speaking therefore is essentially a responding to the past.

But now, if we add to this essential insight, the necessity of it being impossible to have direct or immediate access to the interior life of another (see the Introduction), then we must conclude that the others in me, like the Freudian unconscious, are never fully present. As we saw in the Introduction, based on this phenomenological insight into the experience of alterity, the Kantian imperative to treat others never as a means to an end must be exaggerated. Whatever value we assign to others, this value is not enough. The others inside of me or outside of me call but we never know (here knowledge meaning complete intuitive presence and evidence) exactly that for which they are calling to us. Yes, they are crying for justice, but we cannot know, in the strict sense, how to fulfil the demand. Even though we might be hearing well, we can never hear well enough. We can only have faith that we are responding well. Our inability to know that for which others, either inside me or outside of me, are calling to us transforms the normal, finite concept of responsibility into a, so to speak, abnormal and infinite concept of responsibility. While the normal concept of responsibility includes the idea that one is able to complete that for which and to which one is responsible, this "abnormal" or new concept implies that one is never able to complete the responsibility; responsibility is structurally incomplete. No matter how well I respond, that response is not good enough. There can be no good conscience. The others in me, or outside of me, to whom I am responding and before whom I am, so to speak, on trial, always demand more. This responsibility is so infinite, that I find myself responsible even after or beyond the death of the others. Like the past "me" that I am no longer, the others cry out for justice even from the grave.

Because temporalization functions at the absolute foundational level of experience (see Chapter 3), infinite responsibility to others, for others, and before others, is prior to every other sort of relation, especially those whose mediation attempt to reduce infinite responsibility to finite responsibility. Recall that Derrida says that unusable friendship is beyond all dialectics. The resistance of infinite responsibility to all forms of mediation has an extreme consequence. When I bring the unconscious whispers to consciousness and really hear them, when I hear well the cries of others (either in me or outside of me), when I undergo the experience of infinite responsibility, then even the mediating role of the world comes to an end. As Derrida says, "Each time, the end of the world," and Derrida adds that this claim is no hyperbole (Derrida 2005: 140, also pp. 158–60). We can see why he says so. Infinite responsibility precedes the world as its absolute foundation, and because the foundation can never resemble what it founds, infinite responsibility resists all mundane mediations that might arise from all of us being in the world. In the experience of infinite responsibility essentially the world does not exist. If we can speak of something like existence or being here, we would have to say that only the non-mediating relation to others exists. We must not be confused. This "end of the world" is not the worst violence. It is violence – the others invade my consciousness and I try to make them the same as me – but it is violence with a remainder: the relationship to others for whom I am responsible remains. The remainder opens the possibility for the world to be rethought on the basis of infinite responsibility. This rethinking of the world from its true foundation would aim to make the whole world and everyone pass into becoming. No, this "end of the world" does not aim at the worst violence. It aims at the least violence.

What then is the worst violence? Although I have defined the worst violence as the end of the world without remainder, as the apocalypse without revelation, and finally as suicide without life, the idea of the worst violence remains perplexing. It is perplexing because of the superlative "worst." At first glance, the word "the worst" seems to connote the most violence, which would imply that the worst violence is a numerical violence against many people or living beings. If we defined the worst violence by means of quantity, then we would be confronted with a more difficult question of how many deaths or violations makes violence the worst. If we were, however, to continue to define the worst by quantity, we would be tempted to say that the worst violence happens even when there is violence only against *one* living being: "*each time*, that is, each one, the end of the world." But the worst violence must not be defined by quantity. We must see clearly that the word "worst" connotes a quality of violence. The quality that defines the worst violence is expressed by the clauses: "without remainder"; "without revelation"; and "without life." The worst violence is the kind of violence with nothing left over. It is the *complete* silencing of the voices, the whispers, the murmurs, even the rustling of the wind, inside of me or outside of me. Although the hate criminal may make utterances of prejudice and although the suicide bomber may make utterances of God's glory, these figures actually aim to speak no more. The complete silence is not the silence of the differences between meanings and phonemes. This silencing wills the silence of the very difference and distance between same and other that makes hearing and seeing, and life itself possible. The worst violence strives to close off the voice that is memory, without which it is impossible to dream about a future. The worst violence is *the Event in the worst sense of the word*. As we have shown (Chapter 2), this idea of a complete Event is an illusion (end-heterogeneous). However, as we tried to show in the opening chapters, the expansion of global capitalism, with its "war without war" – that is, with its homogenization of all cultures and therefore all voices, silencing them so that if they are able to speak at all they only speak in the economic genre – seems to approximate the complete Event. We must fight against "the war without war" with "the peace against peace," which is least violence.

What then is the least violence? In common usage, the word "least" connotes quantity. It means the smallest number or the lowest degree of something, in this case, of violence. We must never reject this quantitative definition of the least violence. All of the ideas presented in this book aim at reducing violence of all kinds to the lowest degree. Not war without war, but peace without peace. However, to be precise, the least violence is a qualitative term. The quality is expressed in the phrase "without peace." The quality that defines the least violence is potency. If we recall the discussion above about irrational numbers, we see that the least violence *never* rounds the series up or down into a whole number. The attempt to reduce violence down to its lowest degree goes down only far enough to the disjointed and unjust ratio that generates the series. The least violence goes down only far enough to the source of potency below the numerical instances generated. Transcendental violence remains. The attempt to reduce violence to its lowest degree never reduces it far enough to eliminate the violence that is life itself. The voice of memory, no matter how painful, is never silenced. The potencies of these voices are never exhausted and fulfilled. These voices always call out for more, which means that we are able to dream about a future. We are able to dream about an event whose potencies go further than we could ever imagine – but *never* about an Event.

More concretely, the least violence is defined by the three ways of speaking that we presented in Chapter 9: speaking-freely; speaking-distantly; and speaking-in-tongues. As we saw, these three ways, which I have categorized as ways of speaking-out, evolve from the idea of the performative, and in particular from the idea of allocutionary force.[2] These three ways of speaking-out do something; they produce an event (and again, never the Event). The centrality of the event-character of speaking-out led me to propose that perhaps the pragmatics of speech provides the best way of speaking-out. Nevertheless, we need all three ways, or we need to synthesize them.

The *essence* of speaking-out lies in the form of the utterance. There can be no speaking-out that does not have the form of a self-contradiction. It must include a negation and an affirmation. The form of self-contradiction is based in the fundamental unit of language which is the call. It is important to understand the negation that is essential to the structure of the call or address. Every assertion, including when it is not explicitly addressed to anyone, is implicitly a call. As we commonly say, we always write for some audience, and even when we seemingly speak to ourselves, we speak indeed *to* ourselves. As a call, every assertion and every utterance, every speech act calls out into absence. If the addressee were fully and completely present to me, I would have no need to call to him. Indeed, if the addressee were completely unified with me, there would be no need to speak at all. Yet, this unification is impossible. We never have direct access to the interior life of another living being. This fact bears repeating because we must never underestimate this phenomenological insight. The fact that I cannot think your thought means that even when I assert that you are near to me, as near as possible, you are still and always, necessarily, distant. With the irreducible distance between us, you are *not* and never can be my friend. Therefore, the negation involved in the form of speaking-out cannot be resolved into an affirmation. It cannot be dialecticized and finished off. As we have seen, this irreducible negation can be exaggerated and it must be exaggerated. In order that the address is truly an act of friendship, it must violently drive the others away – so that they may become, so that their potency remains. The exaggeration must go so far as to drive all the others away so that the whole world and everyone may become free. This becoming-free is really what the living fool is telling us. Like the teacher of metamorphosis who stutters the word "and" up to the

## CONCLUSION: SPEAKING OUT AGAINST VIOLENCE

point of a contradiction, the living fool says out loud, from love, "Do *not* be my friend." The living fool's utterance, which exaggerates the negation found in every address, is an act of violence. But from love, the act of violence aims to save the beloved; from love, it aims to achieve the least violence. In other words, the exaggerated negation is "violence against violence."

The exaggeration of the negation in the form of speaking-out brings us to the *crux* and *heart* of speaking-out. The literal meaning of the word "crux" means cross. It means cross both in the sense of the central point at which ideas intersect resulting in a difficulty that cannot be understood, and the Cross, the place of suffering and pain. The crux of speaking-out is precisely the point that cannot be understood. When we speak out, we take a chance and risk our security and even our lives. The consequences of speaking out, of course, might place us up on the cross of suffering and pain. Speaking-out might result in friendship or enmity. When we speak out, we can never know for certain what is going to happen. The unknowable consequences of speaking-out distinguish it from traditional speech acts, whose outcomes are guaranteed by societal rules, and by the fact that speech acts are always safe, while speaking-out is always dangerous. It is this danger that requires the intensification of the affirmation. We must not be afraid of this intensification of freedom. We must not be afraid of saying: "This is the truth – and I am the one speaking it." We know that it is fear that motivates the worst violence. Instead, as Foucault has shown us, what is required is courage in one's heart, the courage to speak out – even though speaking out is dangerous.

As the danger of speaking-out indicates, what really defines the crux of speaking-out is the experience of powerlessness. In order to understand this powerlessness, we must return to the experience of time. As we have claimed, following Derrida, time is fundamentally ana-chronic. It is "out of joint" because time temporalizes or endures by means of two forces, the force of repetition and the force of singularization, the force of universality and the force of particularity. Again, the disjointed hiatus of the two forces is a structure that cannot be imagined otherwise. Every eidetic variation of the experience of time will discover the relation of the two forces. The structure therefore includes necessities that cannot be reduced. These are absolute necessities that are prior to the distinction between theory and practice. These necessities are at once essential and ethical, at once requirements and commandments (or categorical imperatives). In order that time be what it is, it is necessary that there be – and there should be – universalization and continuity; it is necessary that there be – and there should be – singularization and discontinuity. The necessity of these two temporal forces is so strong that we are powerless *not* to obey their command. But, we have enough power to reverse the powerlessness. If we are unable not to obey, *then we are able*. If we are unable to stop repetition and if we are unable to stop singularization, we are able to be unable. Unable to stop repetition, we are able to let it happen; unable to stop singularization, we are able to let it happen. If the worst violence consists in the reaction of repressing all the others down to the point where there is no more becoming, then the least violence would be the reaction of letting all the others *become other that what they are today*. While we have invoked the Heideggerian idea of *Gelassenheit* through the verb "to let," this least violent reaction would be anything but tranquil. It would have to have the courage to speak out and say: "Let others, all of them, be ends in themselves, no matter what!" Here is the crux: the ability to be unable is a kind of power. Perhaps like the reaction of the worst violence, the ability to be unable looks to an extreme exercise of power. After all, to let go of the power to disobey these commandments requires the most strength possible. Letting be, letting go, and doing without the power to dominate even demands a kind of super-human strength. One has to be able to say: "Go! Go ahead! Keep going! Never stop! I can endure the pain." The strength required for this speech, however, is really not the exercise of power. It is the extreme exercise of powerlessness. The ability to be unable is given to us by the very necessities themselves. As we exercise the gift of the powerless ability to let go of the power to dominate others, we pass into a new kind of poverty. The teacher of metamorphosis (whose proper name is perhaps "Bergson") understood this poverty better than anyone else.

## Notes

1 One should add to this claim the claims that Steven Pinker makes in his *The Better Angels of our Nature* (Pinker 2011). Not only does Pinker claim that statistically violence has declined over the course of human history, but also that the reasons for it are processes of pacification (also, processes of civilization, and humanitarianism). Pinker's argument is convincing given the massive amount of statistical data he musters. However, it is possible to question whether these processes of pacification are themselves a form of violence, a form more "insidious" (Pinker 2011: 58) than measurable violence. This question of insidious violence is one of the questions that has motivated this book and my next book, *Violence against Violence*.
2 For an important study of linguistic violence see Butler 1997.

# Bibliography

Alliez, Eric (ed.), *Gilles Deleuze. Une vie philosophique* (Le Plessis-Robinson: Institut Synthélabo Pour le Progrès de la Connaissance, 1998).
Arendt, Hannah, *On Violence* (New York: Harcourt, 1969).
Aristotle, *Nicomachean Ethics, Loeb Classical Library no. 73*, trans. H. Rackham (Cambridge, MA: Harvard University Press, 1982).
Aristotle, "Posterior Analytics," in *The Complete Works of Aristotle: The Revised Oxford Translation*, ed. Jonathan Barnes (Princeton: Princeton University Press, 1984), pp. 114–66.
Artières, Phillippe, Laurent Quéro, and Michelle Zancarini-Fournel, *Le groupe d'information sur les prisons. Archives d'une lutte, 1970–1972* (Paris: IMEC, 2003).
Austin, J. L., *How to do Things with Words* (Cambridge, MA: Harvard University Press, 1962).
Badiou, Alain, *Deleuze. La clameur de l'Être* (Paris: Hachette, 1997).
Badiou, Alain, *Being and Event*, trans. Olivier Feldham (London: Continuum, 2005).
Barbaras, Renaud, *Introduction à la phénoménologie de la vie* (Paris: Vrin, 2008).
Beistegui, Miguel de, *Truth and Genesis: Philosophy as Differential Ontology* (Bloomington: Indiana University Press, 2004).
Benjamin, Walter, *Illuminations: Essays and Reflections*, trans. Harry Zohn (New York: Schocken Books, 1969).
Bennington, Geoffrey, *Interrupting Derrida* (New York: Routledge, 2000).
Bergen, Véronique, *L'ontologie de Deleuze* (Paris: L'Harmattan, 2001).
Bergson, Henri, *Introduction to Metaphysics*, trans. T. E. Hulme (New York: Palgrave MacMillan, 2007).
Bergson, Henri, *Matter and Memory*, trans. N. M. Paul and W. S. Palmer (New York: Zone Books, 1994).
Bergson, Henri, *Time and Free Will: An Essay on the Immediate Data of Consciousness*, trans. F. L. Pogson (Mineola, NY: Dover Publications, 2001).

# BIBLIOGRAPHY

Bergson, Henri, *The Two Sources of Morality and Religion*, trans. R. Ashley Audra and Cloudsley Brereton with the assistance of W. Horsfall Carter (Notre Dame: University of Notre Dame Press, 1977).

Blanchot, Maurice, "Death of the Last Writer," in *The Book to Come*, trans. Charlotte Mandell (Stanford: Stanford University Press, 2003).

Blanchot, Maurice, *The Space of Literature*, trans. Ann Smock (Lincoln: University of Nebraska Press, 1982).

Bogue, Ronald, *Deleuze on Cinema* (London: Routledge, 2003).

Bogue, Ronald, *Deleuze on Literature* (London: Routledge, 2003).

Bogue, Ronald, *Deleuze on Music, Painting, and the Arts* (London: Routledge, 2003).

Bonta, Mark, and John Protevi, *Deleuze and Geophilosophy: A Guide and Glossary* (Edinburgh: Edinburgh University Press, 2004).

Boundas, Constantin V., and Dorothea Olkowski (eds.), *Gilles Deleuze and the Theater of Philosophy* (London: Routledge, 1994).

Bourg, Julian, *From Revolution to Ethics: May 1968 and Contemporary French Thought* (Montreal: McGill-Queen's University Press, 2007).

Bryden, Mary (ed.), *Deleuze and Religion* (London: Routledge, 2001).

Buchanan, Ian (ed.), *A Deleuzian Century* (Durham: Duke University Press, 1999).

Caputo, John D., "Who is Derrida's Zarathustra? Of Fraternity, Friendship, and a Democracy to Come," in *Research in Phenomenology*, 29 (1) (1999): 184–98.

Coetzee, J. M., *Elizabeth Costello* (New York: Penguin Books, 2003), pp. 227–30.

Colebrook, Claire, *Gilles Deleuze* (London: Routledge, 2002).

DeLanda, Manual, *Intensive Science and Virtual Philosophy* (London: Continuum, 2002).

Deleuze, Gilles, *Cinema 2: The Time-Image*, trans. Hugh Tomlinson and Robert Galeta (Minneapolis: University of Minnesota Press, 1989).

Deleuze, Gilles, "Coldness and Cruelty," in *Masochism* (New York: Zone Books, 1997).

Deleuze, Gilles, *Desert Islands and other Texts 1953–1974* (New York: Semiotext(e), 2004).

Deleuze, Gilles, *Difference and Repetition* (New York: Columbia University Press, 1995).

Deleuze, Gilles, *Essays Critical and Clinical*, trans. Daniel W. Smith (Minneapolis: University of Minnesota Press, 1997).

Deleuze, Gilles, *The Fold: Leibniz and the Baroque*, trans. Tom Conley (Minneapolis: University of Minnesota Press, 1993).

Deleuze, Gilles, *Foucault* (Minneapolis: University of Minnesota Press, 1988).

Deleuze, Gilles, *Kant's Critical Philosophy*, trans. Hugh Tomlinson and Barbara Habberjam (Minneapolis: University of Minnesota Press, 1984).

## BIBLIOGRAPHY

Deleuze, Gilles, *Logic of Sense*, trans. Mark Lester with Charles Stivale, ed. Constantin Boundas (New York: Columbia University Press, 1990).

Deleuze, Gilles, *Negotiations*, trans. Martin Joghin (New York: Columbia University Press, 1995).

Deleuze, Gilles, *Nietzsche and Philosophy*, trans. Hugh Tomlinson (New York: Columbia University Press, 1983).

Deleuze, Gilles, *Proust and Signs: The Complete Text* (Minneapolis: University of Minnesota Press, 2000).

Deleuze, Gilles, *Two Regimes of Madness* (New York: Semiotext(e), 2006).

Deleuze, Gilles, and Félix Guattari, *Kafka: Toward a Minor Literature* (Minneapolis: University of Minnesota Press, 1986).

Deleuze, Gilles, and Félix Guattari, *A Thousand Plateaus*, trans. Brian Massumi (Minneapolis: University of Minnesota Press, 1987).

Deleuze, Gilles, and Félix Guattari, *What is Philosophy?*, trans. Hugh Tomlinson and Graham Burchell (New York: Columbia University Press, 1994).

Deleuze, Gilles, and Claire Parnet, *Dialogues II*, trans. Hugh Tomlinson and Barbara Habberjam (New York: Columbia University Press, 2007).

Denis, Lara, "Friendship to Marriage: Revising Kant," in *Philosophy and Phenomenological Research*, vol. 63, no. 1 (July 2001): 1–28.

Derrida, Jacques, *The Animal that therefore I am*, trans. David Wills (New York: Fordham University Press, 2008).

Derrida, Jacques, *Aporias*, trans. Thomas Dutoit (Stanford: Stanford University Press, 1993).

Derrida, Jacques, "Eating Well,' or the Calculation of the Subject," in *Points ... Interviews, 1974–1994*, ed. Elizabeth Weber (Stanford: Stanford University Press, 1995), pp. 255–87.

Derrida, Jacques, *Edmund Husserl's Origin of Geometry: An Introduction*, trans. John P. Leavey, Jr. (Lincoln: University of Nebraska Press, 1989).

Derrida, Jacques, "Et Cetera," in *Deconstructions: a User's Guide*, ed. Nicholas Royle (New York: Palgrave, 2000), pp. 282–303.

Derrida, Jacques, *Eyes of the University*, trans. Richard Rand and Amy Smith (Stanford: Stanford University Press, 2004).

Derrida, Jacques, "Faith and Knowledge," in *Religion*, ed. Jacques Derrida and Gianni Vattimo (Stanford: Stanford University Press, 1998), pp. 49–51.

Derrida, Jacques, *For What Tomorrow*, trans. Jeff Fort (Stanford: Stanford University Press, 2004).

Derrida, Jacques, "Force of Law: The 'Mystical Foundation of Authority'," in *Deconstruction and the Possibility of Justice* (London: Routledge, 1992), pp. 3–67.

Derrida, Jacques, *Force de loi* (Paris: Galilée, 1994).

Derrida, Jacques, "On Forgiveness: A Roundtable Discussion with Jacques Derrida," in *Questioning God*, ed. John D. Caputo, Mark Dooley, and Michael J. Scanlon (Bloomington: Indiana University Press, 2001), pp. 52–72.

# BIBLIOGRAPHY

Derrida, Jacques, *The Gift of Death, Second Edition, and Literature in Secret*, trans. David Wills (Chicago: University of Chicago Press, 2008).

Derrida, Jacques, *Given Time*, trans. Peggy Kamuf (Chicago: University of Chicago Press, 1992).

Derrida, Jacques, *Glas*, trans. John P. Laevey, Jr. (Lincoln: University of Nebraska Press, 1986).

Derrida, Jacques, *Of Hospitality*: *Anne Dufourmantelle invites Jacques Derrida to Respond* (Stanford: Stanford University Press, 2000).

Derrida, Jacques, "How to Avoid Speaking: Denials," trans. Ken Frieden, in *Languages of the Unsayable*, ed. Sanford Budick and Wolfgang Iser (New York: Columbia University Press, 1989).

Derrida, Jacques. *Learning to Live Finally*, trans. Pascale-Anne Brault and Michael Naas (Hoboken: Melville House Publishing, 2007).

Derrida, Jacques, *Limited Inc.*, trans. Samuel Weber (Evanston: Northwestern University Press, 1988).

Derrida, Jacques, *Margins of Philosophy*, trans. Alan Bass (Chicago: University of Chicago Press, 1982).

Derrida, Jacques, *Memoires for Paul de Man*, trans. Cecile Lindsay, Jonathan Culler, and Eduardo Cadava (New York: Columbia University Press, 1986).

Derrida, Jacques, *Monolingualism of the Other or the Prosthetic of Origin*, trans. Patrick Mensah (Stanford: Stanford University Press, 1998).

Derrida, Jacques, *On the Name*, trans. Thomas Dutoit (Stanford: Stanford University Press, 1995).

Derrida, Jacques, *The Other Heading*, trans. Pascale-Anne Brault and Michael Naas (Bloomington: Indiana University Press, 1992).

Derrida, Jacques, *Passions*, trans. Thomas Dutoit (Stanford: Stanford University Press, 1995).

Derrida, Jacques, *Philosophy in the Time of Terror: Dialogues with Jürgen Habermas and Jacques Derrida* (Chicago: University of Chicago Press, 2003).

Derrida, Jacques, "The Politics of Friendship," in *The Journal of Philosophy*, vol. 85, no. 11 (November 1988): 632–44.

Derrida, Jacques, *Politics of Friendship*, trans. George Collins (London: Verso, 1997).

Derrida, Jacques, *Positions*, trans. Alan Bass (Chicago: University of Chicago Press, 1981).

Derrida, Jacques, *Rogues*, trans. Pascale-Anne Brault and Michael Naas (Stanford: Stanford University Press, 2005).

Derrida, Jacques, *Sovereignties in Question: The Poetics of Paul Celan* (New York: Fordham University Press, 2005).

Derrida, Jacques, *Specters of Marx*, trans. Peggy Kamuf (New York: Routledge, 1994).

Derrida, Jacques, *Of Spirit*, trans. Geoff Bennington (Chicago: University of Chicago Press, 1989).

Derrida, Jacques, *The Truth in Painting*, trans. Geoff Bennington and Ian McLeod (Chicago: University of Chicago Press, 1987).

Derrida, Jacques, *Voice and Phenomenon*, trans. Leonard Lawlor (Evanston: Northwestern University Press, 2011).

Derrida, Jacques, *Without Alibi*, trans. Peggy Kamuf (Stanford: Stanford University Press, 2002).

Derrida, Jacques, "Women in the Beehive: A Seminar with Jacques Derrida," in *Men in Feminism*, ed. Alice Jardin and Paul Smith (New York: Methuen, 1987).

Derrida, Jacques, *Writing and Difference*, trans. Alan Bass (Chicago: University of Chicago Press, 1978) (Bloomington: Indiana University Press, 1992).

Diogenes Laertius, *Diogenes Laertius. Lives of the Eminent Philosophers. Books VI-X*, trans. R. D. Hicks (Cambridge: Harvard University Press, 2005).

Djaballah, Marc, *Kant, Foucault, and the Forms of Experience* (London: Routledge, 2008).

Dodd, James, *Violence and Phenomenology* (London: Routledge, 2009).

Eckstrand, Nathan, and Christopher Yates, *Philosophy and the Return of Violence: Studies from the Widening Gyre* (New York: Continuum, 2011).

Eribon, Didier, *Michel Foucault*, trans. Betsy Wing (Cambridge, MA: Harvard University Press, 1991).

Evans, Fred, *The Multivoiced Body: Society and Communication in the Age of Diversity* (New York: Columbia University Press, 2008).

Evans, Fred, "Cosmopolitanism to Come: Derrida's Response to Globalization," in *A Companion to Derrida* (Oxford: Blackwell Publishing, 2014), pp. 550–64.

Ewald, François, "Foucault and the Contemporary Scene," in *Philosophy and Social Criticism*, vol. 25, no. 3: 81–91

Foucault, Michel, *Aesthetics, Method, and Epistemology. Essential Works of Foucault, 1954–1984*, ed. James D. Faubion (New York: The New Press, 1998).

Foucault, Michel, *The Archaeology of Knowledge and the Discourse on Language*, trans. A. M. Sheridan Smith (New York: Pantheon, 1972).

Foucault, Michel, *The Birth of the Clinic*, trans. A. M. Sheridan Smith (New York: Vintage, 1994).

Foucault, Michel, *The Care of the Self*, trans. Robert Hurley (New York: Vintage Books, 1986).

Foucault, Michel, *The Courage of Truth. The Government of Self and Others II. Lectures at the Collège de France 1983–1984*, trans. Graham Burchell (New York: Palgrave Macmillan, 2011).

Foucault, Michel, *Discipline and Punish*, trans. Alan Sheridan (New York: Vintage, 1977).

Foucault, Michel, *Dits et écrits I, 1954–1975* (Paris: Gallimard Quatro, 2001).

Foucault, Michel, *Ethics, Subjectivity, and Truth*, *Essential Works of Foucault, 1954–1984*, ed. Paul Rabinow (New York: The New Press, 1997).

## BIBLIOGRAPHY

Foucault, Michel, *Fearless Speech*, ed. Joseph Pearson (Los Angeles: Semiotext(e), 2001).

Foucault, Michel, *The Foucault Reader*, ed. Paul Rabinow (New York: Pantheon, 1984).

Foucault, Michel, *The Government of Self and Others. Lectures at the Collège de France 1982–1983*, trans. Graham Burchell (New York: Palgrave Macmillan, 2010).

Foucault, Michel, *The Hermeneutics of the Subject: Lectures at the Collège de France, 1981–1982,* trans. Graham Burchell (New York: Palgrave Macmillan, 2005).

Foucault, Michel, *History of Madness*, trans. Jonathan Murphy and Jean Khalfa (London: Routledge, 2006).

Foucault, Michel, *Introduction to Kant's Anthropology*, trans. Roberto Negro and Kate Briggs (Los Angeles: Semiotext(e), 2008).

Foucault, Michel, *Lectures on the Will to Know. Lectures at the Collège de France. 1970–1971* (New York: Palgrave MacMillan, 2004).

Foucault, Michel, *The Order of Things*, anonymous translation (New York: Random House, 1970).

Foucault, Michel, *Psychiatric Power. Lectures at the Collége de France 1973–1974*, trans. Graham Burchell (London: Palgrave MacMillan, 2006).

Foucault, Michel, "The Return of Morality," in *Michel Foucault. Politics, Philosophy, Culture: Interviews and other Writings, 1977–1984*, ed. Lawrence D. Kritzman (New York: Routledge, 1988), pp. 242–54.

Freud, Sigmund, "The Unconscious," in *The Standard Edition of the Complete Psychological Works of Sigmund Freud, Volume XIV (1914–1916)*, trans. James Strachey (London: The Hogarth Press, 1957), pp. 159–204.

Gilson, Erinn, "Review of Ann Murphy, *Violence and the Philosophical Imaginary*," in *Journal of French and Francophone Philosophy*, vol. XXI, no. 1 (2013): 173–82.

Gros, Frédéric, *Foucault et la folie* (Paris: Presses Universitaire de France, 1997).

Gros, Frédéric, and Carlos Lévy. *Foucault et la philosophie antique* (Paris: Kimé, 2003).

Grosz, Elizabeth, "A Thousand Tiny Sexes: Feminism and Rhizomatics," in *Gilles Deleuze and the Theater of Philosophy*, ed. Constantin V. Boundas and Dorothea Olkowski (London: Routledge, 1994), pp. 187–211.

Haddad, Samir, "A Genealogy of Violence, from Light to the Autoimmune," in *Diacritics* 4.2 (2011): 173–93.

Haddad, Samir, *Derrida and the Inheritance of Democracy* (Bloomington: Indiana University Press, 2013).

Hägglund, Martin, *Radical Atheism: Derrida and the Time of Life* (Stanford: Stanford University Press, 2008).

Han, Béatrice, "Foucault and Heidegger on Kant and Finitude," in *Foucault and Heidegger*, pp. 127–62.

Haraway, Donna, *When Species Meet* (Minneapolis: University of Minnesota Press, 2008),

Hardt, Michael, *Gilles Deleuze: An Apprenticeship in Philosophy* (Minneapolis: University of Minnesota Press, 1993).

Heidegger, Martin. *Being and Time*, trans. Joan Stambaugh, rev. Dennis J. Schmidt (Albany: The SUNY Press, 2010).

Heidegger, Martin. *Kant and the Problem of Metaphysics, Fifth Edition, Enlarged* (Bloomington: Indiana University Press, 1977).

Heidegger, Martin. *Pathmarks*, trans. William McNeil (New York: Cambridge University Press, 1998).

Heidegger, Martin, *Poetry, Language, Thought*, trans. Albert Hofstadter (New York: Harper Collins, 2011).

Hoffmanstahl, Hugo von, *The Lord Chandos Letter and Other Writings*, selected and translated from the German by Joel Rotenberg (New York: New York Review Books, 2005).

Holland, Eugene V., *Deleuze and Guattari's Anti-Oedipus: Introduction to Schizo-Analysis* (London: Routledge, 1999).

Husserl, Edmund, *Cartesian Meditations*, trans. Dorian Cairns (The Hague: Nijhoff, 1977).

Husserl, Edmund, *The Crisis of European Sciences and Transcendental Phenomenology*, trans. David Carr (Evanston: Northwestern University Press, 1970).

Husserl, Edmund, *Ideas: General Introduction to Pure Phenomenology*, trans. W. R. Boyce Gibson, with a Forward by Dermot Moran (London: Routledge, 2002).

Husserl, Edmund, "Phenomenology" "Draft D" (the Encyclopedia Britannica essay), in *Psychological and Transcendental Phenomenology and the Confrontation with Heidegger* (1927–1931), trans. and ed. Thomas Sheehan and Richard E. Palmer (Dordrecht: Kluwer Academic Publishers, 1997), pp. 159–80.

Husserl, Edmund, *The Phenomenology of Internal Time-Consciousness*, trans. James Churchill (The Hague: Martinus Nijhoff Publishers, 1964).

Hyppolite, Jean, *Genesis and Structure of Hegel's Phenomenology of Spirit*, trans. Samuel Cherniak and John Heckman (Evanston: Northwestern University Press, 1971).

Kant, Immanuel, *Anthropologie du point de vue pragmatique*, trans. Michel Foucault (Paris: Vrin, 1970).

Kant, Immanuel, *Anthropology, History, and Education*, ed. Gunter Zöller and Robert B. Louden (New York: Cambridge University Press, 2007).

Kant, Immanuel, *Critique of Pure Reason*, trans. Paul Guyer and Allen W. Wood (New York: Cambridge University Press, 1998).

Kant, Immanuel, *Logic*, trans. Robert S. Hartman and Wolfgang Schwartz (New York: Dover, 1974).

Kant, Immanuel, *Métaphysique des mœurs*, trans. A. Philonenko (Paris: Vrin, 1985).

Kant, Immanuel, *Practical Philosophy*, trans. Mary J. Gregor (New York: Cambridge University Press, 1996).
Kockelmans, Joseph J., *Edmund Husserl's Phenomenology* (West Lafayette: Purdue University Press, 1994).
Krell, David Farrell, *Derrida and our Animal Others* (Bloomington: Indiana University Press, 2013).
Lampert, Jay, *Deleuze and Guattari's Philosophy of History* (London: Continuum, 2006).
Lawlor, Leonard, "Becoming and Auto-Affection (Part II): Who are We?" in *Graduate Faculty Philosophy Journal*, vol. 30, no. 2 (2010): 219–37.
Lawlor, Leonard, *Derrida and Husserl* (Bloomington: Indiana University Press, 2002).
Lawlor, Leonard, *Early Twentieth Century Philosophy* (Bloomington: Indiana University Press, 2011).
Lawlor, Leonard, "Heidegger and Foucault," in *The Bloomsbury Companion to Heidegger*, ed. François Raffoul and Eric Nelson (London: Bloomsbury, 2013), pp. 409–16.
Lawlor, Leonard, *The Implication of Immanence* (Bronx: Fordham University Press, 2006).
Lawlor, Leonard "Phenomenology and Metaphysics, and Chaos," in *The Cambridge Companion to Deleuze*, ed. Daniel W. Smith and Henry Somers-Hall (New York: Cambridge University Press, 2012), pp. 103–25.
Lawlor, Leonard, "The Postmodern Self: An Essay on Anachronism and Powerlessness," for *The Oxford Handbook to the Self*, ed. Shaun Gallagher (Oxford: Oxford University Press, 2011), pp. 696–714.
Lawlor, Leonard, *Thinking Through French Philosophy* (Bloomington: Indiana University Press, 2003).
Lawlor, Leonard, *This is not Sufficient* (New York: Columbia University Press, 2007).
Lawlor, Leonard, and John Nale, *The Cambridge Foucault Lexicon* (New York: Cambridge University Press, 2014).
Lawlor, Leonard, and Janae Sholtz, "Speaking out for Others: Philosophical Activity in Deleuze and Foucault (and Heidegger)," *Between Deleuze and Foucault*, ed. Daniel W. Smith, Thomas Nail, and Nicolae Morar (Edinburgh: Edinburgh University Press, 2016).
Levinas, Emmanual, *Otherwise than Being or Beyond Essence*, trans. Alphonso Lingis (The Hague: Nijhoff, 1981).
Levinas, Emmanuel, *Totality and Infinity*, trans. Alphonso Lingis (Pittsburgh: Duquesne University Press, 1969).
Livrozet, Serge, *De la prison à la révolte* (Paris: L'esprit frappeur, 1999).
Lorraine, Tamsin, *Irigaray and Deleuze: Experiments in Visceral Philosophy* (Ithaca: Cornell University Press, 1999).

Lyotard, Jean-François, *The Differend: Phrases in Dispute*, trans. Georges van der Abbeele (Minneapolis: University of Minnesota Press, 1988).
Lyotard, Jean-François, *Libidinal Economy*, trans. Iain Hamilton Grant (Bloomington: Indiana University Press, 1993).
Macey, David, *The Lives of Michel Foucault* (New York: Vintage, 1993).
McGushin, Edward, *Foucault's Askesis: An Introduction to the Philosophical Life* (Evanston: Northwestern University Press, 2007).
Marrati, Paoloa, *Gilles Deleuze. Cinéma et philosophie* (Paris: Presses Universitaires de France, 2003).
Martin, Jean-Clet, *La philosophie de Gilles Deleuze* (Paris: Payot et Rivages, 1993).
Marx, Karl, *Writings of Young Marx on Philosophy and Society*, trans. Lloyd D. Easton and Kurt H. Guddat (New York: Anchor Books, 1967).
Massey, Heath, *The Origin of Time: Heidegger and Bergson* (Albany, NY: The SUNY Press, 2013).
May, Todd, *Giles Deleuze: An Introduction* (New York: Cambridge University Press, 2006).
Mengue, Phillipe, *Deleuze et la question de la démocratie* (Paris: L'Harmattan, 2003).
Merleau-Ponty, Maurice, *Phenomenology of Perception*, trans. Donald A. Landes (London: Routledge, 2012).
Merleau-Ponty, Maurice, *The Visible and the Invisible*, trans. Alphonso Lingis (Evanston: Northwestern University Press, 1968).
Milchman, Alan, and Alan Rosenberg, *Foucault and Heidegger: Critical Encounters* (Minneapolis: University of Minnesota Press, 2003).
Miller, Eddis N., *Kantian Transpositions: Derrida and the Philosophy of Religion* (Evanston: Northwestern University Press, 2014).
Miller, James, *The Passion of Michel Foucault* (New York: Anchor Books, 1993), pp. 165–207.
Murphy, Ann V., *Violence and the Philosophical Imaginary* (Albany, NY: The SUNY Press, 2012).
Naas, Michael, *Derrida from Now on* (Bronx: Fordham University Press, 2008).
Naas, Michael, *Taking on the Tradition: Jacques Derrida and the Legacies of Deconstruction* (Stanford: Stanford University Press).
Nietzsche, Friedrich, *Beyond Good and Evil*, trans. Walter Kaufmann (New York: Vintage, 1966).
Nietzsche, Friedrich, *Human, All too Human*, trans. R. J. Hollingdale (New York: Cambridge University Press, 1986).
Nietzsche, Friedrich, *On the Genealogy of Morals*, trans. Carol Diethe (New York: Cambridge University Press, 1997).
Nietzsche, Friedrich, in *Œuvres philosophiques complètes* (Paris: NRF Presses Universitaires de France, 1971).
Nietzsche, Friedrich, "Thus Spoke Zarathustra," in *The Portable Nietzsche*, ed. Walter Kaufmann (New York: Viking, 1968), pp. 112–439.

Oksala, Johanna, *Foucault, Politics, and Violence* (Evanston: Northwestern University Press, 2012)
Parr, Adrian, *The Deleuze Dictionary* (New York: Columbia University Press, 2005).
Patton, Paul, *Deleuze and the Political* (London: Routledge, 2000).
Patton, Paul, "Deleuze and Democracy," in *Contemporary Political Theory*, 2005, 4: 400–13.
Patton, Paul (ed.), *Deleuze: A Critical Reader* (London: Blackwell, 1996).
Pinker, Steven, *The Better Angels of our Nature: Why Violence has Declined* (New York: Penguin, 2011).
Plato, *The Collected Dialogues of Plato*, ed. Edith Hamilton and Huntington Cairns (Princeton: Princeton University Press, 1961).
Plato, *Cratylus, Parmenides, Greater Hippias, Lesser Hippias*, trans. Harold North Fowler (Cambridge, MA: Harvard University Press, 1939).
Plato, *Euthyphro, Apology, Crito, Phaedo, Phaedrus*, trans. H. N. Fowler (Cambridge, MA: Harvard University Press, 1982).
Plato, *The Republic of Plato*, trans. Alan Bloom (New York: Basic Books, 1968).
Plato, *Theaetetus, Sophist*, trans. Harold North Fowler (Cambridge: Harvard University Press, 2006).
Protevi, John, *Political Physics* (London: The Athlone Press, 2001).
Protevi, John, "Love," in *Between Deleuze and Derrida*, ed. Paul Patton and John Protevi (New York: Continuum, 2003), pp. 183–94.
Putnam, Hilary. "Naturalism, Realism, and Normativity," in *Journal of the American Philosophical Society*, vol. 1, issue 2 (summer 2015): 312–28.
Ricœur, Paul, *Interpretation Theory* (Fort Worth: The Texas Christian University Press, 1976).
Rogozinski, Jacob, *Faire Part. Cryptes de Derrida* (Paris: Linges, 2005).
Romano, Claude, *Event and Time*, trans. Stephen E. Lewis (Bronx: Fordham University Press, 2014).
Romano, Claude, *Event and World*, trans. Shane Mackinlay (Bronx: Fordham University Press, 2009).
Saghafi, Kas, *Apparitions – Of Derrida's Other* (Bronx: Fordham University Press, 2010).
Sallis, John, *Being and Logos: The Way of Platonic Dialogue* (Atlantic Highlands, NJ: Humanities Press International, 1986).
Sholtz, Andrea, J., *The Invention of a People: Heidegger and Deleuze on Art and the Political* (Edinburgh: Edinburgh University Press, 2015).
Smith, Daniel W. "Preface" to the English translation of Gilles Deleuze, *Essays Critique et Clinique* (Deleuze 1997).
Sorel, George, *Reflections on Violence* (New York: Cambridge University Press, 1999).
Spinoza, Baruch, *Spinoza: Complete Works*, trans. Samuel Shirley, ed. Michael L. Morgan (Indianapolis: Hackett Publishing, 2002).

Spivak, Gayatri Chakravorty, "Can the Subaltern Speak?," in *Colonial Discourse and Post-Colonial Theory: A Reader*, ed. Patrick Williams and Laura Chrisman (New York: Columbia University Press, 1994), pp. 66–111.

Steiner, Gary, *Animals and the Limits of Postmodernism* (New York: Columbia University Press, 2013).

Stivale, Charles, *The Two-Fold Thought of Deleuze and Guattari* (New York: Guilford Press, 1998).

Thompson, Alex, *Deconstruction and Democracy* (London: Continuum, 2005).

Vintges, Karen, "Must we Burn Foucault," in *Continental Philosophy Review*, vol. 34, issue 2: 165–81.

Webb, David, *Foucault's Archeology: Science and Transformation* (Edinburgh: Edinburgh University Press, 2013).

Welch, Michael, "Counterveillance : How Foucault and the Groupe d'information sur les prisons Reversed the Optics," in *Theoretical Criminology*, vol. 15 (2011), no. 3: 301–13.

Williams, James, *Gilles Deleuze's Difference and Repetition: A Critical Introduction and Guide* (Edinburgh: Edinburgh University Press, 2003).

Zoungrana, Jean, *Michel Foucault. Un parcours croisé: Lévi-Strauss, Heidegger* (Paris: L'Harmattan, 1998).

Zourabichvili, François, "Deleuze et le possible" in *Gilles Deleuze, une vie philosophique*, sous la direction de Eric Alliez (Le Plessis-Robinson: Institut Synthélabo, 1998).

# Index

the absolute, 22, 25, 63, 77, 167–8, 171
affects, 80, 82, 117, 122, 124, 130–3, 140n12, 186, 235–6
age, 46, 81, 117, 121, 123, 124, 130, 133, 136, 139n5
alcoholism, 35, 58, 119–20, 129
anachronism, 11n2, 75, 240n28
anarchy, 95, 97
anger, 92, 191, 249
animals, 116–19, 124, 128, 131–8, 139n3, 149–50, 152, 154, 187
anthropology, 156–60, 206, 210–11, 218, 223, 225
anxiety, 82, 197–8
apocalypse, 2–3, 9, 11n3, 20, 22, 62, 64, 70, 76, 82, 147, 280, 284–5
apparatus (*dispositif*), 144, 172n4, 174
archaeology, 146, 161–2, 202n19
Arendt, *On Violence*, 90, 103, 110n7
Aristotle, 66n3, 81–2, 86n7, 209, 227, 232, 238n7, 253–4
art, 46, 60, 65, 185, 201n11, 251, 261
auto-affection, 48–52, 54, 58, 64–5, 68, 74, 115–16, 135–7, 206, 278–82

autonomy, 4, 115, 220, 236, 250–1, 266, 268, 271

becoming, 10, 20, 39, 46, 58, 61, 66, 67n7, 70, 82–4, 116–38, 175, 181, 187–8, 196, 198, 206, 244, 250, 265–6, 270, 277, 279–81, 285, 290
Benjamin, 43n13
Bergson, 15, 23, 25–6, 69, 76, 142n20, 278
  *Introduction to Metaphysics*, 25
  *Matter and Memory*, 25
  *Time and Free Will*, 26
blindness, 15–16, 24, 27, 38, 67n12, 73
body without organs, 20, 120
Butler, xi, 291n2

the call, 228–30, 234, 240n24, 253–8, 269, 288
capitalism, 1, 37, 174, 266, 278, 286
care, x, 6
Cartesianism, 47, 56, 72, 115
categorical imperative, 8, 89, 91, 105–6, 108, 246, 290
chaos, 59, 73–4
chiasm, 127, 255–6
Clausewitz, 37, 38

# INDEX

*cogito*, 47, 115, 182, 278
concept, 130, 133, 178–9, 195, 197, 199n2, 261, 264
conceptual personae, 19, 35, 199n2, 267, 275n17
contretemps, 234
counter-effectuation, 61, 65
courage, 5, 83–4, 170–1, 175–8, 187–8, 198, 248, 270, 273, 290
creativity, 8, 35, 98–9, 101, 103, 142n20, 177–8, 182, 185, 197, 199n2, 201n11, 279–80

death, 22, 29, 35, 39, 41n4, 46, 59–61, 66–7n7, 73, 75–7, 102, 134, 170–1, 232–3, 248, 266–8, 284
Deleuze, 4, 7, 17–22, 25, 29, 30, 37, 39, 40n2, 41n4, 45–7, 57–61, 63, 70, 98, 104–6, 116–38, 161, 174, 178–82, 185, 189–95, 198, 199n2, 202n24, 203n26, 243–5, 269
  *Difference and Repetition*, 45, 116, 126, 177–82, 185–6, 201n11, 204n38, 259, 282
  "Foucault and Prison", 189, 193–4, 196–7
  *Kafka: Toward a Minor Literature*, 133, 259
  *Kant's Critical Philosophy*, 11n7, 173n16
  *The Logic of Sense*, 45, 104, 186, 204n38, 274n5
  *Nietzsche and Philosophy*, 181, 200n5, 243
  *A Thousand Plateaus*, 29–37, 41, 42n6, 42n7, 42–3n13, 117–38, 204n40, 242–3, 245, 259–68
  *What is Philosophy?*, 81, 127–8, 130, 139n5, 141n12, 174–5, 177, 186, 200n4

Derrida, 3, 17–19, 24, 25, 39, 40n3, 46, 54–5, 63, 75, 86n5, 106–7, 111n14, 116, 137, 143, 200n9, 206–7, 243–5, 269
  *Aporias*, 40n2
  *Negotiations*, 12n9
  *Politics of Friendship*, 7, 207–37, 245, 253, 257
  *Rogues*, 25, 42n13
  "Signature, Event, Context", 242
  *Specters of Marx*, 107, 201n17
  "Violence and Metaphysics", xi, 2, 6, 11n7, 87, 96, 102, 105, 111n15, 207, 213, 227
  *Voice and Phenomenon*, 24, 116
  *Writing and Difference*, 107
destruction, 30–2, 34–7, 42n7, 62, 120–1, 129, 131
desubjectivation, 117, 121, 129–30
dialectic, 68, 161–2, 179, 224, 250, 284, 288
difference, 4, 10, 68, 95, 98–9, 157, 161, 178–82, 198, 206, 243, 286
differend, 53
dissymmetry, 7, 87, 161, 234, 245
drugs, 58, 119–20
duration, 22–3, 25–6, 278

the earth, 1, 20, 64, 115, 135
economy, 8, 106–7, 219, 224–5, 271
eidetic variation, 54, 62, 66–7n7, 76, 290
end in itself, 6, 8
enemy, 209, 226–7, 230, 240n25, 254, 257–9, 269
Enlightenment, 210, 219
epoché, 5, 47–50, 55–6, 72, 278
eternal return, 69, 90, 94–5, 162, 175, 181, 204n38, 243
eternity, 46, 61–3, 95

# INDEX

ethics, ix, 11n7, 169, 207, 249, 272, 290
  care ethics, x, 11n8
event, 5, 10, 20, 22, 24–8, 39, 41n4, 45–7, 50–1, 58–61, 65, 66n1, 71, 75, 82–3, 85, 98–100, 102, 119–20, 148, 162, 170–1, 175, 177, 181–2, 186, 188, 196, 201n11, 211, 214, 234, 241–4, 247, 256, 260, 272–3, 274n5, 286–7

faith, 42n8, 67n12, 284
fascism, xii, 29–34, 37
fear, 4–5, 26, 31–2, 82–4, 175, 187, 270
finitude, 158, 160, 182, 197, 215, 284
flattery, 7, 202n22, 245, 249–51
flight, 18–19, 28–31, 34–5, 38, 84, 109, 120, 132, 138, 267
the fold (*Zwiefalt*), 179, 200n7
Foucault, 5, 7, 22, 41n4, 174, 178, 182, 185–93, 198, 199n2, 200n4, 204n32, 243–5, 269
  *The Archaeology of Knowledge*, 146, 162, 241, 244, 247
  *Discipline and Punish*, 42n9, 197
  *The Government of Self and Others*, 145, 168–70, 174–5, 188, 247
  Groupe d'Information sur les Prisons, 177, 188–97, 202n25, 277
  *The Hermeneutics of the Subject*, 66–7n7, 169
  *The History of Madness*, 19–20, 143–56, 161, 163–8, 171, 189, 239n21
  *The History of Sexuality*, vol. 3, 139n4
  *Introduction to Kant's Anthropology*, 145, 156–62, 166–8, 169, 172n5, 172n6
  "Nietzsche, Genealogy, History", 241–2
  *The Order of Things*, 11n7, 173n8, 182–5, 204n38
  "What is Enlightenment?", 169
freedom, x, 6, 7, 11n8, 56, 72, 81, 145, 148, 149–50, 153–6, 158–9, 162, 166–7, 169–71, 172n5, 178, 190–1, 246, 248, 252–3, 257, 259, 267, 271–3, 288–9
Freud, 4, 82, 282–3
friendship, 3, 10, 16, 22, 35, 38–9, 111n14, 207–37, 252, 254–9, 269, 288–9
future, 20–1, 24, 40, 184

*Gelassenheit*, 46, 64, 65, 71, 83, 187, 290
generalization, xi, 6, 8, 100–2, 107, 109, 177–8, 195, 205n41, 228, 271
globalization, 1–2, 16, 37, 64, 115, 118, 135, 278
*glossolalia*, 7

Hägglund, 85–6n5
hearing-oneself-speak, 47–51, 55, 74, 115–16, 135–6, 282
Hegel, 68, 77, 111n11
Heidegger, 23, 32, 46, 52–3, 63–4, 69, 72, 104, 172n5, 176, 178–81, 182–5, 187–8, 197–8, 200n4, 201n15, 240n29, 282
  *Kant and the Problem of Metaphysics*, 68, 85n1, 206–7, 222, 234, 282
hiatus, 28, 279, 290
Hofmannsthal, 131, 140–1n12
hope, 85, 158
hospitality, 19, 28, 40, 84, 107
the human, 25, 115, 135, 175, 178, 182–5, 187, 196, 209

305

# INDEX

Husserl, 23–4, 55–7, 67n7, 71, 87, 96, 104
  *The Crisis of European Sciences*, 55–6
  *Ideas I*, 23–4, 55, 72–4

image of thought, 21
immanence, 5, 20, 22, 44, 47, 69–70, 74, 146, 150, 162, 278, 282
imperatives, 8, 19, 77, 80, 89, 91, 108–9, 133, 162, 212–13, 225, 246, 276n25, 283, 290
the impossible, xii, 21, 91, 273
incorporeal transformation, 260
infinity, 30, 284
the intolerable, 59, 71, 80, 139n8, 175, 188, 191–3, 196, 198, 203–4n31
irony, 147, 252, 275n13
iterability (repeatability), 6, 24–5, 27, 28, 39, 50–1, 96, 100, 102, 136, 220, 242–4, 253

joy, 40, 82, 216, 226
justice, 53, 79, 93, 109, 202n17, 279, 281–3, 287

Kant, ix, 8–9, 11n7, 68–9, 115, 145, 156–60, 206–8, 210–25, 226, 227, 235, 237n1, 238–9n10, 249, 270, 283
Kierkegaard, 42n8

land to come, 20, 66
Lawlor, 9, 12n10, 41n4, 85n1, 85n4, 110n6, 111n16
Leibniz, 16
Levinas, 11n7, 86n5, 87, 117, 276n22
life, xii, 9, 10, 22, 41n4, 90, 93–5, 102, 120–1, 134, 199–200n2, 277, 284–5

limit, 15–17, 21–2, 27, 35, 40n2, 69–70, 101–2, 119
lines, 29–31, 35, 42n7, 122, 129
love, 10, 39, 117, 121–2, 207–16, 220–1, 223–4, 226, 227–33, 256–9, 269–72
Lyotard, 1, 53, 71, 275n18

madness, 91, 143, 146–56, 161, 163–8, 280
Marx, 237n3
means and ends, 1, 8–9, 209, 219, 224, 246, 259, 271, 277, 283, 290
memory, 23–4, 41n5, 96–7, 125, 282
Merleau-Ponty, 1, 47, 57–8, 102, 127, 180
messianic, 20
metaphysics, 3–4, 17, 63–4, 69, 176, 179–80, 201n16
minority, 117, 123, 271
  minor language, 259–65, 276n24
moment (*Augenblick*), 95, 99
multiplicity, 4, 25, 27, 29, 51, 76, 122, 136, 272
murmur, 50, 79–80, 82, 286
Murphy, 110n1, 110n3

naming, 39
negativity, 101–2, 154
Nietzsche, x, 44, 61–2, 69, 71, 89, 93–6, 99, 155, 162, 181, 186, 209, 225, 229–32, 235, 238n6, 242, 257
nihilism, x, xii, 10
non-violence, 89, 105–8, 111n14, 280–1

order-word, 243, 260, 266–7
origin (*arche*), 44, 54–5, 62, 79, 83, 95, 176, 182–5, 198, 220, 240n29

# INDEX

the other, 5–8, 23, 26, 87, 96–7, 106–9, 155, 175, 198, 206, 221–2, 228, 233, 240n29, 250, 252, 256, 279, 281–2, 288
outside, 16, 19–22, 27, 38, 39, 41n4

*parrēsia*, 7, 144–5, 148, 169–71, 175–6, 177, 187, 197, 199n2, 202n21, 244–5, 246–53, 271–2, 275n14
passage, 18–23, 27, 40, 69, 75, 138
peace, 1–2, 9, 37–8, 40, 88, 109, 135
'peace without peace', 2, 16, 38, 40, 286–7
people to come, 20, 65, 118, 133–5, 137–8, 187, 198, 199–200n2
performative, xi, 188, 241–3, 245, 247–9, 254–5, 259, 287, 289
phenomenology, x, 5, 8–9, 15, 23, 47–50, 66–7n7, 69, 71–3, 86n6, 143, 146, 206, 225, 278, 282–3, 288
philanthropy, 216–17, 222, 231
philosophy, 3–4, 7–8, 16, 46, 60, 65, 156–61, 169, 174–7, 198–9, 278
Plato, 47, 51–2, 57, 65, 91–3, 171, 252, 277, 278
Platonism, 3–5, 17, 44–7, 63–6, 69, 281
politeness, 219, 224
post-structuralism, x
potentiality, ix, xii, 6, 28, 42n10, 81–2, 84, 121–2, 134, 182, 186, 220, 223, 236–7, 240n29, 266, 270, 273, 280, 287–8
power, 30–4, 38, 42n7, 42n10, 42–3n13, 60, 64, 143, 171, 174–7, 197, 204n37, 271, 291
powerlessness, 6, 9, 15, 17–18, 21, 30–4, 36, 38, 42n7, 42n13, 60, 64, 79, 82–3, 94, 132, 197–8, 277, 289–91

pragmatics, 242–5, 259–60, 273, 287
prepositions, 117, 126–7, 131–2, 140n11, 186–7
presence, 23–4, 63, 77–8, 97, 115–16, 218, 220, 253–4
prisons, 84, 144, 176–8, 188–96, 198, 202n24, 203n28
promise, 63, 108–10, 176, 184, 188, 201n17, 215, 223, 229
Proust, 120, 130–1, 138n1

refrain, 198, 204n40
remainder, xii, 3, 44, 46, 62–4, 285–6
repetition, 51, 54, 75, 78, 95, 96, 98–9, 101, 117, 157, 161, 171, 177–85, 197, 201n11, 262, 279–80, 290
respect, 208–9, 212–13, 221, 258
responsibility, 8, 80, 187, 263, 276n22, 283–5
reversal, 16, 19, 21, 30, 44, 64, 70–1

Sartre, 5, 180
schematism, 206–8, 210, 218, 223, 234
Schmitt, 240n25
secret, 214–15, 226–7, 231
sexual difference, 29, 32, 211, 220–2, 225, 231–2
shame, 4, 40, 72, 80–4, 117, 124, 133, 137, 175–8, 186–8, 192, 196, 198, 282
signs, 1–2, 40
silence, 49, 261, 277, 283
sovereignty, 7, 33, 42n9
speaking in tongues, 7, 244–6, 259, 261–6, 268–70, 281, 287
speaking out, 7, 10, 88, 196, 198, 199n2, 245, 273, 277, 287–90
Spinoza, 72, 82
Spivak, 205n41

307

statements, 170, 195, 202n21, 235, 241–4, 247
struggle, 10, 46, 53, 55, 59, 73
suffering, x, 26, 59, 71, 80, 123–4, 175, 186–7, 192, 196, 198
suicide, 17, 29, 35–7, 70, 82, 118, 120, 285
sympathy, 26–7

*teleiopoesis*, 7, 235–6, 245, 253–9, 272
*telos*, 46, 54–5, 62–3, 79, 83, 95, 124, 160–1, 186, 208, 220, 235–6
tensor, 244, 262–4, 266, 270, 275n18
totalitarianism, 30–4, 37, 42n7
trait, 28, 50–1, 60, 101, 127–8, 136
transcendence, 22, 44, 69, 146, 150, 155, 167, 170, 197
transcendental reduction, 48
truth, 145–9, 151, 154, 155–6, 158–9, 161–2, 165, 172n5, 199n2, 219–20, 248, 269, 289

undecidable, 27, 81, 83, 128, 256, 272
utopia, 122, 199n2, 273

variation, 28, 243–4, 264–6, 268, 276n24
vigilance, 89–90, 103–4
violence
    fundamental violence, xi, 15, 29, 45, 53, 61, 76, 80–1, 83, 97, 101, 109, 246, 279
    the least violence, 3, 64, 70–1, 84, 277, 285, 287–9
    transcendental violence, x–xii, 3, 6, 29, 40, 87–91, 103, 105–6, 281, 287
    the worst violence, x–xii, 2, 4–5, 15–22, 28–9, 38, 40, 42n8, 46, 63–4, 70–1, 76, 82, 84, 170, 272, 277, 280–1, 285–6, 290–1

war, 16, 27, 36–8, 93, 94, 97, 286–7
ways of speaking, 3, 7, 237, 245–6, 269, 271
weak force, 55
will, 2, 4, 6, 71, 83, 105–6, 280
will to nothingness, 10, 36
will to power, 94
work (*oeuvre*), 117
writing, 117, 129–30, 132–4, 137, 193–4, 261, 265, 270, 278–9